I Dream of Dinner
(so you don't have to)

I Dream of Dinner

(so you don't have to)

Low-Effort, High-Reward Recipes

Ali Slagle

Photographs by Mark Weinberg

Clarkson Potter/Publishers

New York

Contents

Recipes

Eggs

Beans

Pasta

Grains

Vegetables

Chicken

Beef, Pork & Lamb

Sea Creatures

Skillet Broccoli Spaghetti **PAGE 154**

Introduction

Some count sheep—I dream up dinner.

My favorite cooks are people who "make food." Their skills and taste buds are honed by real life, by making do with what they have, and by sticking their fingers into lots of hot pots. They cook quickly but thoughtfully, feed extremely hungry people night after night—and then do the dishes whether they want to or not.

That includes my mom and nonna, and not just because I love them so much. Their cooking is soulful, scrappy, confident, and completely delicious. They make dinner with ten ingredients and in 45 minutes, probably, but who's counting? They don't have patience for time-sucks and finicky recipes, but they also won't sacrifice an ounce of joy or flavor along the way.

Take my mom's chili, which is made from cans, jars, and ketchup. It's not real-deal chili but it's so good, people joke it'll be celebrated on her gravestone (it's the Shortcut Chicken Chili on page 286). And when you ask my nonna for her biscotti recipe, what you get is on the next page—good luck! She cooks outside the lines, clearly.

I thankfully inherited their resourcefulness and love for cooking. When I go on walks or zone out on the train, I'm playing Dinner Tetris in my head. I'm imagining the moves I'll make to efficiently, enjoyably use the ingredients I have to make what I want. The results of these daydreams (and actual dreams) become meals for me and recipes for you—I dream of dinner so you don't have to! The 150 recipes in this book meet you wherever you are: hungry, hurried, happy. In need of calm and comfort or fire and fun. On yet another Wednesday. At 6 p.m., realizing *oh right, dinner.*

My promise is that the effort-to-reward ratio is engineered in your favor. The recipes won't use more than 45 minutes, ten ingredients (though usually just five to eight), and your indispensables (meet them on page 16). They approach pantry lurkers and produce on its last leg as enthusiastically as farmers' market celebrities, and are flexible enough to modify wildly. No need to go to the store for one ingredient unless you also need ice cream.

Instead of hiding work in an ingredient list—did you know "½ cup toasted, chopped, skin-off hazelnuts" takes half an hour?—there's a grocery list to scan. When you're ready to cook, bring the ingredients to the counter and follow along: All the prep happens in the recipe itself. You can cling to the recipes for dear life or you may never follow any precisely—cooking is a wild thing that really can't (and shouldn't) be contained within precise steps and amounts.

This book provides just enough structure to get you to excellent meals, in your kitchen, your way. The recipes are organized by the basic processes that turn their main ingredient into dinner. Seeing recipes as templates creates routine, which is practical but rarely boring because it provides avenues for improvisation (a fact of life). Each section starts with quick tricks for each process so that you can off-road and recover if there's a screw-up (another fact of life).

This fast and loose way of cooking will make the mediocre days better and the good days great. It will maximize your time, minimize your waste, spark inspiration, and nourish with food that feels good to make and eat. Just remember: Do more with less. Don't overthink it. And also: It's only dinner.

My nonna's biscotti recipe, a reminder
to cook outside the lines.

Generalmente make 30 Biscotti!! or more

Biscotti
(cranberg. Pistacchio)

$12\frac{1}{2}$ y $3\frac{1}{2}$
Take 6 out of...
make 36? cut 1" o so...

chop 10 finer before

To pour on more
3 to 4
at 375 Minute

Oven 350

1C PISTACCHIO twisted at 375 Minute

1 ⓛ 1C DRY cranberries   Soak 1C Minuti in Hot Water . DRAIN

$2\frac{1}{2}$c flour (NOT whole wheat) King Arthur C. K.)

2/3 c SUGAR   1/3 + 1/3   (Sift in beating Beater well)

1/2 ts each . B.Soda . B.Powd . Salt   (or stir w/ fork 100 Times)

2 ⓢ 1 C + 1 T Butter melted   Mix ADD a bit at temp to

3 Eggs Slightly beaten   DRY ingredienti

VANILLA 2b   ⓛ

3) Toasted the Pistacchio if they are not roasted 2.5M (before ground them in little) OSCAR

DRAIN CRANBERRIES and add to 1 of low Speed fast Cranberries the Pistacchio
1 crunch 2 Pistacchio

On floured Surface Mix the dough Divide in 8 parts 8 □□□ arrange them
in a buttered Baking Steel (baking sheet) BAKE 350 25 MINUTES Cool 15
or more Cut w/ Serate Knife and rebake 7 to 10 M. Cool well CUT
arrange RED

REBAKE in 2 . 16 X 16 Quindi no necessary buttom Cool both together but 1/2 way
Change positions

Choco topping melt 2C Heather in micro 4 to 6 Minuti? baceth 1 set of Biscotti
REWARMED 4.56 on juiced
(it may need to Rewarmed the choco 4 way through if needed)
con Bush (choc) on top use 1C (scarso) cho chips 8M. Nuts Brush lengwell
TRY (dip) biscotti in choco melted (perfore questo need wort choco to . . . . .

Os cranberry make suggestions ok!   (Michaela like cookies 7 M.)

if make smaller Biscotti than $1\frac{1}{2}$ inch Bake meno di 25M.

3 perso
Make about 68 20 each 12 each 16 each 65.4 = 16 each
65.4
Do . NOT USE whole wheat flower

Before We Cook

Indispensables Keep **olive oil, neutral oil, butter, sugar, red pepper flakes, water,** and **S&P (salt and pepper)** close—you'll be using them often. These ingredients won't be listed in the shopping lists because my hope is you'll always have them (if a recipe calls for more than 4 tablespoons of butter, though, that is called out). Unless otherwise specified, olive oil is extra-virgin, neutral oil is canola or grapeseed, butter is unsalted, sugar is granulated, water is whatever you drink, salt is kosher, and pepper is freshly ground black peppercorns.

Salt These recipes were developed with Diamond Crystal kosher salt, the most forgiving of the salts. Its light crystals dissolve quickly, so you can taste the saltiness of your food almost immediately and avoid surprise oversalting. If you use any other kind of salt, use less than is listed and adjust as you go ("season to taste" is not a step to skip). If you switch over to Diamond Crystal, it will take some adjusting—you'll think you're using *so much salt*—but give it time. Transfer some salt into a vessel that easily fits your whole hand. Then, salt food by grabbing the salt with your fingers instead of a spoon so you develop a feel for the right amount of salt for your taste buds.

Serving sizes How hungry are you? Are you feeding kids' stomachs or bigger stomachs? I have no idea! Serving sizes are the biggest gamble in recipe writing. While most recipes in the book "serve four" according to my best judgment, listen to your gut more than the yield. The recipes can be halved easily, but instead consider making the full batch and look forward to leftovers. Some of the recipes are lighter, in which case you may also want a salad, green veg, bread, or rice.

Seasonality What's in season tastes good, but what you want to eat tastes better. No matter the time of year, I still crave the same things (lemon pasta, arugula salad, fried egg on toast). So, the recipes are written with produce that's generally readily available all year. If you find a vegetable you adore or need to use up, swap it in.

Substitutions To make safe swaps, you'll want to zoom out on your ingredients and consider their general category and cook time. Proteins (meat, seafood, but also beans and tofu) can swap well with some adjustment to cook time. Melting cheeses can generally be used interchangeably, as can hard grating cheeses and spoonable dairies (ricotta, crème fraîche, sour cream, yogurt). Vegetables with similar cook times can usually swap too, but if you want to use, say, carrots when a recipe calls for snap peas, add them earlier in the recipe. How an ingredient is cut will also affect cook time (p. 230).

　　When it comes to flavoring your dish, consider what an ingredient is contributing to the dish, then swap within that category: Fat for fat, sweet for sweet—there's so much more about this on page 384. If you're ever not sure if a swap will work, Google it. Someone else has probably also wondered the same thing.

Fixer-uppers Tasting early and often provides more room for adjusting seasoning so that you don't end up with a dish that needs futzing and tweaking. That said, it happens. If your food doesn't taste very good and you don't know why, spoon a little out into a bowl. This is your experimentation station. Start by adjusting the salt and acid, which seem to always improve things. Add a little more salt, taste, and if it's moving in a good direction, add more until you think one more pinch will make it too salty. Now add a squeeze of lemon or lime. Did that make things better? If so, keep going. If your food is too spicy or salty, add sweetness; if it's too acidic or sour, add fat—and vice versa—then doctor your main batch accordingly. If you still don't know, drown it in hot sauce. There's always tomorrow.

EGGS

Beat

Pour a bowlful of beaten eggs into a warm (not hot!) pan and they can fluff and puff into any number of dinners. There's the classic scramble, which can be so much more than a hasty default, but also a frittata, an omelet, and ribbons of scrambled eggs swimming through soup.

A cup for more than measuring.

Bowls are useful; bowls with spouts? Extremely useful. That's exactly what your liquid measuring cup can be to you. Any time you need to pour something, like whisked eggs or a sauce or batter, mix it together in a measuring cup for cleaner pouring. (Also, when it's not holding eggs, put your phone in to amplify your podcast.)

If you can scramble eggs, you can make frittatas and omelets.

Think of a frittata as a cake of scrambled eggs and an omelet as a folded pancake of scrambled eggs. If you know how to scramble eggs, you can make a frittata to serve more people, make a great sandwich middle, and use up lots of leftovers. See Stovetop Frittata Any Way (p. 29) for a hands-off process that doesn't use the oven. If you can scramble eggs, you can make a big, floppy, diner-style omelet whose residual heat barely warms its overstuffed middle, which could be leftovers, cheese, veg, and more (p. 27).

Beat in flavor.

Yes, you can stud eggs with vegetables or cheese or meat, but also consider what you can beat into the eggs themselves. Look to pantry and fridge staples to stir in, like harissa, tomato paste, soy sauce, fish sauce, pesto, hot sauce, and finely chopped herbs. Add water or milk for fluffiness; add cream or yogurt for richness. And always add salt— about ¼ teaspoon for two eggs, depending on if other salty additions like Parmesan or soy sauce are also going in.

Pretend your pan is a hula hoop.

To evenly cook a large quantity of eggs, like in a frittata or an omelet, it's helpful to cover the eggs with a lid, baking sheet, or foil to circulate heat and to give all the eggs a chance to get direct contact with the heat of the pan. Once you see the egg start to set around the edges, run your spatula across the bottom and sides of the pan to pull the eggs from the edges to the center. Then tilt, swirl, and swivel the pan (like the pan is a hula hoop) so the uncooked egg runs into empty spaces and around the edges of the pan.

The emergency scramble. If you're making a frittata or an omelet and things go off the rails or you get impatient, break the egg up with the spatula and you've made scrambled eggs, always there in case of emergency.

Partner with friend or foe. Somehow there's an episode of *Curb Your Enthusiasm* with an entire plotline about Larry insisting that scrambled eggs require toast. Respectfully—nope. It's nice to foil scrambled eggs with crispy-crunchy textures, but it's also nice to give in to their softness. Drown them in cream (p. 23), sour cream, crème fraîche, or melted cheese; top them with avocado; wrap them in a warm tortilla; or leave them alone. If you're with Larry, for contrasting texture, consider toast, sure, but also chips (pita, tortilla, potato), breadcrumbs, nuts, or a green salad. Or offset the rich egg with the sharp tang of something acidic: a squeeze of lemon or lime, salsa or hot sauce, a salad, pickles.

Ribbon eggs into any soup. Some of the world's most beloved soups have tendrils of scrambled eggs floating through them: egg drop soup (adorably also known as egg flower soup), hot and sour soup, sopa de ajo, stracciatella. Feathery bites of soft eggs can be added to any thin soup or broth. Slowly stir the soup with one hand while you just-as-slowly pour the scrambled eggs in with the other. In a few seconds, you'll see strands of egg appear—the faster you stir, the thinner the strands.

Creamed Leeks & Eggs

To soothe babies and large adult children.

LEEKS
LEMON
CRUSTY BREAD
HEAVY CREAM
EGGS
BUTTER
PARMESAN

FOR 4

1. Remove the two outer layers of **2 large leeks.** Thinly slice the white and pale green parts. If they're gritty, rinse them (no need to dry). Using a vegetable peeler, peel large strips of rind from **1 lemon.** Cut **4 thick slices crusty bread.**

2. In a medium saucepan, combine **1⅓ cups heavy cream, ½ cup water,** the leeks, and **1 teaspoon salt.** Twist the lemon rinds over the pot to wake up their oils, then drop them in. Bring to a simmer over medium. Cook, reducing the heat as needed to maintain a gentle simmer, until the leeks are very soft, 7 to 10 minutes.

3. Meanwhile, keeping an eye on the cream so it doesn't bubble over, in a small bowl or the measuring cup you used for the cream, whisk **8 eggs.** Season with salt.

4. In a large nonstick skillet, melt **2 tablespoons butter** over medium. Add 2 slices of bread and cook until golden on one side, 2 to 3 minutes. Transfer to plates, toasted side up, and repeat with more bread and, if needed, more butter. Hold on to the skillet.

5. When the leeks are done, turn off the heat. Whisk a couple tablespoons of the lemony cream into the eggs. Melt **2 more tablespoons butter** in the skillet over medium-low (skip if there's still butter left from before). Add the eggs and cook undisturbed until the eggs around the edges of the pan are set, then use a spatula to fold and scrape across the pan to form big, fluffy curds, 1 to 2 minutes.

6. Spoon plenty of leeks and cream onto the bread, then top with egg and a little more of the cream. Season with pepper and freshly grated **Parmesan.**

Gentle friends for scrambled eggs

· **Creamed other veg:** Swap out leeks for hearty greens, mushrooms, scallions, or tomatoes (p. 225).

· **Soft like Ship's Biscuit:** Add ricotta to your toast before adding the eggs, like the Ship's Biscuit sandwich at the now shuttered Saltie in Brooklyn that smushed ricotta and scrambled eggs between focaccia. You barely had to chew.

· **Pockets of tang:** Add dollops of spoonable dairy (yogurt, sour cream, crème fraîche) into the almost-ready skillet of eggs. Stir just once to melt slightly, then as you eat, you'll find the dollops warm and cozy in their hiding spots.

Harissa Eggs with Pita & Dates

Crispy gone soggy like matzo brei, migas, and fatoot samneh.

DATES

EGGS

HARISSA

BUTTER

PITA CHIPS

LEMON

FOR 4

1. Remove pits from **6 dates** and cut into 4 pieces each (outsides up so the sticky middles don't gunk up your knife). In a small bowl, whisk together **8 eggs** and **¼ cup harissa.** Season with S&P.

2. In a large nonstick skillet, melt **4 tablespoons butter** (½ stick) over medium. Add the dates and **2 cups pita chips,** crushing them in your hands as you add them. Stir with a spatula to coat in the butter, then cook, stirring occasionally, until the butter browns and the dates have softened, 2 to 3 minutes.

3. Reduce the heat to low and pour in the eggs. Use a spatula to slowly scrape across the pan to form big, fluffy curds, 1 to 2 minutes. Eat with a squeeze from **1 lemon.**

· Harissa varies greatly by brand, so try yours on a pita chip before deciding how much to add to your eggs.

· This is inspired by fatoot samneh, a Yemenite-Jewish dish that crisps stale pita in clarified butter before adding beaten eggs. It's eaten both savory and sweet, with honey.

Bok Choy–Gochujang Omelet

An envelope with confetti inside.

EGGS

LIME

GOCHUJANG

SESAME
SEEDS

SESAME OIL

BABY BOK
CHOY

FOR 2

1. In a measuring cup, whisk together **5 eggs** and the zest of **1 lime.** Season with S&P.

2. In a medium bowl, stir together **1 teaspoon sugar, 2 teaspoons gochujang, 1 teaspoon toasted sesame seeds, ½ teaspoon toasted sesame oil,** and the juice from half the lime (about a tablespoon). Thinly slice **8 ounces baby bok choy** (about 2 large) crosswise. Stir into the gochujang mixture and season with S&P.

3. Warm **2 teaspoons toasted sesame oil** in a medium nonstick skillet over medium. Add the eggs and cook undisturbed until the eggs around the edges of the pan are set, 1 to 2 minutes. Use a spatula to lift up a side of the eggs, then tilt the pan so the uncooked egg runs to the open spot on the skillet. Repeat on all sides until the egg is just barely set. Reduce the heat to medium-low, add the bok choy mixture to half the egg, cover, and cook until the egg is set, another minute or two. Shake to loosen the omelet from the pan, then fold the naked half over the bok choy. Halve crosswise and eat with more toasted sesame seeds and a squeeze of the lime.

More filling ideas

· **Leftovers:** Grain salad, fried rice, Indian takeout, fried chicken, kale or radicchio salad.

· **Bite-size vegetables:** Like shaved brussels sprouts (maybe with black pepper and Parm), grated zucchini (with kimchi and Cheddar), or grated sweet potato (with goat cheese and rosemary).

· **Stewy vegetables:** Creamed leeks (p. 23), tomato soup (p. 247), or harissa cauliflower (p. 225).

· **Soft or melting cheese:** Or a creamy dip, like pimento cheese or spinach artichoke.

· **Cured meats:** Crisp the meat in the skillet, remove, then make the omelet in the drippings. Add the meat to the middle.

Green Eggs & Ham Quesadilla

A bacon, egg, and cheese for Dr. Seuss.

CHEDDAR

HAM

GREEN HOT SAUCE

EGG

FLOUR TORTILLA

MAKES 1, though easily repeatable

1. Grate **2 ounces sharp Cheddar cheese** on the large holes of a box grater (about ½ cup). Coarsely chop **a few pieces ham (Canadian bacon, deli ham).** In a small bowl, whisk together **1½ tablespoons green hot sauce** and **1 egg.** Season with S&P.

2. Melt **1 tablespoon butter** in a medium nonstick skillet over medium. Add the ham and cook until it starts to brown, just a minute. Using a spatula, move all the ham to the center of the skillet. Pour the egg over and swirl the pan so the egg spreads out. Once the top of the egg is nearly cooked, just a minute, evenly sprinkle over half of the Cheddar, then nudge the ham so they're all adhered to egg. Top the mixture with **an 8-inch flour tortilla.**

3. Put your hand in the middle of the tortilla. Hold your breath and flip the skillet so the tortilla is now on your hand. Return the skillet to the burner and put the tortilla in the skillet. Sprinkle the rest of the cheese over the egg and cook until the tortilla is golden brown underneath and the cheese is melted, just a minute. Fold the tortilla in half and cut into wedges. Cook as many as you want.

· Instead of hot sauce, your "green" could be chopped cilantro, salsa verde, or finely chopped jalapeño.

· Eat on its own, with more hot sauce, or maybe with guac . . .

Guacamole: For a guacamole with bright punch in every bite, follow Roberto Santibañez's technique: Smash some white onion (though I've used shallot, scallions, chives), jalapeño (or red pepper flakes or hot sauce), cilantro (though I've used parsley or nothing), and salt together into a coarse paste (he recommends a mortar, but a knife works too). Using a spoon or fork, stir the paste into cubed avocado until creamy but still chunky. Add more cilantro and season with lime juice and salt.

Stovetop Frittata Any Way

How to kindly frittata your eggs.

1. Use a large nonstick pan if you're loading the frittata up with lots of vegetables, or a medium nonstick if you're keeping it simple with just cheese and herbs. Opt for nonstick instead of cast iron because there's no risk of stickage—and a cast iron holds so much heat, the outside can brown before the inside is cooked through (cue: rubbery eggs).

2. Next, cook **add-ins** you wouldn't eat raw. Not only will they not cook further when the eggs show up, but you also want the vegetables to release any liquid before mucking up your frittata. For meat, croutons, or hearty vegetables, like potatoes or broccoli, sauté them in the pan you'll cook your eggs in.

3. Meanwhile, whisk the **eggs.** My favorite number is 8 eggs, which, sure, won't result in a sky-high frittata but means each bite is nicely cooked and studded with stuff. Crack the eggs into a measuring cup and season with salt, about a teaspoon for 8 eggs. If you have some sort of dairy around—milk, sour cream, yogurt—add some too, which, along with salt, helps keep the eggs tender. Add **flavorings** if you want: hot sauce, Parmesan, and so on. Whisk. Add any mix-ins that didn't require cooking, like leftover rice, farro, or pasta.

4. If you cooked your add-ins in the frittata skillet, let it cool a bit (keep the add-ins in there). Add grease (olive oil or butter) if necessary, then pour in the eggs. Stir to combine the fillings with the eggs.

5. SIDE STEP: Dollop the eggs with ricotta, pesto, tapenade, or another dippable, spoonable ingredient if you want.

6. Cover your skillet tightly with a lid, baking sheet, or foil. Heat to medium-low. Steaming the frittata keeps it soft and fluffy. Baking or broiling your frittata just seems cruel: How can eggs stay soft under such intense heat? If you hear the eggs sizzling, they're too hot—reduce the heat. This is a slow but hands-off process that only requires checking in from time to time and rotating the pan if some areas are cooking faster than others. This process will take 15 to 25 minutes, depending on everything. When your frittata is done, it could be time to eat—or balance with friend or foe (p. 21).

P.S. A frittata has a whole new life the next day. It's an optimal sandwich middle, but I also like to add cubes of frittata to green and grain salads.

Bacon-Chile Frittata

If hangovers teach us anything, it's that eggs + salt: good.

BACON

SCALLIONS

FRESH CHILE

EGGS

SOY SAUCE

SESAME OIL

FOR 4

1. Using scissors, cut **6 thick-cut bacon slices** over a medium nonstick skillet. Spread them out, then set the pan over medium-high and cook, stirring sometimes, until golden brown, 5 to 7 minutes. Turn off the heat and transfer the bacon to a paper towel–lined plate, leaving the fat in the skillet.

2. Meanwhile, cut **3 scallions** crosswise into 3-inch lengths. Thinly slice lengthwise, then transfer to a small bowl with cold water so their burn mellows (and they curl!). Thinly slice **half to a whole fresh chile (red Fresno, Thai).**

3. In a medium bowl or measuring cup, whisk together **8 eggs** and **1½ teaspoons low-sodium soy sauce.**

4. Pour off all but a tablespoon of the bacon fat. Pour the eggs into the skillet and scatter the bacon and chiles on top. Cover the pan with a lid, baking sheet, or foil and heat over medium-low until the eggs are just barely set, 8 to 12 minutes. Peek from time to time and tilt the pan so the raw egg reaches the warm sides of the pan.

5. Drain the scallions and toss with **1 teaspoon toasted sesame oil.** Eat the frittata with scallions on top.

· In step 1, cook shrimp or corn kernels in the bacon fat before proceeding.

· In step 4, add cooked grains.

· With or instead of scallions, add a crunchy veg, like thinly sliced radish or cabbage.

Ricotta Frittata with Lemon Crumbs

Cheese puddles!

LEMON

THYME

RICOTTA

PARMESAN

EGGS

PANKO

FOR 4

1. In a medium bowl, zest **1 lemon.** Add **1 teaspoon thyme leaves** and set aside. Stir the juice from half the lemon (about 1½ tablespoons) into ½ **cup whole-milk ricotta.** Season with S&P.

2. In another medium bowl, finely grate ¼ **cup Parmesan** (½ ounce). Add **8 eggs,** season with S&P, and whisk to combine.

3. Heat **1 tablespoon olive oil** in a medium nonstick skillet over medium. Add ½ **cup panko or fresh breadcrumbs** and cook, stirring often, until golden brown, 2 to 4 minutes. Scoop into the bowl with the zest and thyme, season with S&P, and pinch until you smell lemon. Wipe out the skillet.

4. Off the heat, add **another tablespoon olive oil** to the skillet. Pour in the eggs, then add big dollops of the seasoned ricotta. Cover the pan with a lid, baking sheet, or foil and cook over medium-low until the eggs are just barely set, 8 to 12 minutes. Rotate the pan every few minutes so the eggs cook evenly. If you hear the eggs sizzling, reduce the heat—you want them to steam, not fry. Eat with a drizzle of olive oil, the breadcrumbs, more Parm, and the remaining lemon juice.

More frittata fillings

· Blanched broccoli rabe + green olives + yogurt

· Caramelized onions (p. 103) + Parm

· Crispy pepperoni + sun-dried tomato + mozz

· Creamed greens

· Sweet potato cooked in brown butter + sage

· Blistered Peppers with Mozzarella & Croutons (p. 233)

· Broccoli Bits with Cheddar & Dates (p. 221)

· Crispy Grains with Kielbasa & Cabbage (p. 197)

Coconut Curry with Swirled Eggs

For steaming faces, warming hands, and slurping fast.

WHITE RICE

GINGER

GARLIC

GREEN CURRY
PASTE

LIME

COCONUT MILK

EGGS

SPINACH

FOR 4

1. Cook **1 cup long-grain white rice** for serving (p. 170 if you need a method).

2. Meanwhile, finely grate **2 inches ginger** and **3 garlic cloves**. Heat **2 tablespoons neutral or coconut oil** in a medium saucepan over medium. Add the garlic, ginger, and **4 ounces green curry paste** (about ⅓ cup). Cook, stirring occasionally, until the paste is fragrant and a shade darker, 3 to 5 minutes. If it's sputtering annoyingly, cover the saucepan.

3. Finely grate the zest of **1 lime** into the pot, then add **1 (14-ounce) can full-fat coconut milk** and **2 cups water**. Season with S&P and gently simmer until the flavors come together, 5 to 7 minutes.

4. Meanwhile, in a liquid measuring cup, whisk **4 eggs** together and season with salt. Off the heat, stir the soup with one hand while you slowly pour the eggs into the soup. In a few seconds, you'll see strands of egg appear—the faster you stir, the thinner the strands. Stir in **2 packed cups baby spinach** (half a 5-ounce box) and the juice of the lime (about 2 tablespoons). Season to taste with S&P and eat over the rice.

· In step 3, swirl the water in the coconut milk can to get every last bit.

· Instead of eggs, poach salmon or shrimp in the broth. Or brown chicken pieces in the saucepan before step 2, remove, then add back with the coconut milk to cook through.

· Add a denser vegetable (carrots, sweet potato) in step 3.

More eggs + rice

· Chicken broth + rice + streamed beaten eggs + lemon

· Chopped 7-minute eggs stirred into hot rice + edamame + furikake

· Smashed 9-minute eggs + cold rice + peperoncini + mortadella + celery

· Kimchi Rice & Runny Eggs (p. 176)

Soft boil

Boiling a dozen eggs for your future self sounds more practical than joyful (which is maybe partly true), but a bowlful of cooked eggs in the fridge can quickly lead to very good dinners.

Count to 7 or 9. If you swear by a certain method for boiling eggs, do that. If you're on the hunt for a new one, here's mine: Start eggs in boiling water. For a yolk that runs slowly, like hot fudge, boil for 7 minutes. For a yolk that's jammy but mostly keeps its shape—like a soft hard boil—go for 9 minutes. Fewer than 7 minutes risks runny whites and more than 9 minutes risks chalky yolks. Transfer to an ice bath to stop the cooking.

Fridge eggs for now and later. Unpeeled boiled eggs will keep in the fridge for 3 to 5 days (I usually put the eggs in their ice bath right into the fridge). Rewarm by simmering in water, peeled or unpeeled, for a few minutes.

Peel underwater. Make it easy on yourself and peel eggs under running water or in the ice-bath water. The water pressure helps the shell dislodge from the egg.

Mayo is eggs plus oil. Mayo is made by emulsifying oil with egg yolk and perhaps some lemon, vinegar, or mustard, so you could think about a soft-boiled egg as the start of a sort-of mayo. If you stir chopped, soft-boiled eggs into a salad dressing so forcefully that the yolk folds into the dressing, you end up with a mayo-like mixture. That's the idea behind the Godmother's Egg Salad (p. 38), where the eggs do double duty both as the substance and to emulsify the dressing.

Into the splash zone: soups and stews.

When peeled soft-boiled eggs are simmered whole in stew, they become a substantial part of the meal instead of a floating afterthought. As they warm in the stew, they soak up the flavors without the yolk cooking further. You'll see whole eggs in tomato-based curries in South India, with pork in fish sauce caramel in Vietnam, and in chicken stew in Ethiopia, but consider adding them to any thick stew where you might usually add tofu or beans: Eggs have a similar texture, with bonus yolky richness.

Into the splash zone: brines and vinaigrettes.

As peeled soft-boiled eggs hang out in a pickling brine, vinaigrette, or acid-based marinade, their outsides absorb the liquid and their yolks get creamy. For example, pickled eggs sit in a solution of vinegar, whole spices, salt, and sometimes beets for color. Tea eggs, a mainstay of Chinese street vendors, night markets, and 7-Elevens, are built on black tea and soy sauce—with their shells cracked but still on for very pretty marbled outsides. Soy sauce eggs, sometimes called ramen eggs because you often find them in bowls of ramen, sit in a mix of soy sauce, sugar (or mirin), and maybe rice vinegar and whole spices.

The longer the eggs sit, the more marinade they'll take in. To prevent rubbery whites, soak them for at most a few hours, then store them without the brine just in case (reuse or eat the brine—see p. 194). Such a delightfully flavorful egg can carry a meal, so you can default to the usual suspects to accompany: grains, greens, rice, toast.

Godmother's Egg Salad

Egg salad meets the Godmother, the mother of all Italian subs from Bay Cities Deli in Santa Monica, California.

EGGS

RED ONION

DRIED OREGANO

RED WINE VINEGAR

PICKLED PEPPERS

CURED ITALIAN MEAT

DIJON MUSTARD

FOR 4

1. Bring a medium saucepan of water to a boil. Add **10 eggs** and boil for 9 minutes. Transfer to an ice bath to cool.

2. Meanwhile, coarsely chop **half a small red onion.** Transfer to a medium bowl. Add **1½ tablespoons dried oregano** and **1 tablespoon red wine vinegar,** season with S&P, and stir to combine. Thinly slice **4 to 8 pickled peppers (peperoncini, Peppadews),** depending on heat tolerance. Cut **4 ounces cured Italian meat (salami, mortadella, ham)** into ½-inch pieces.

3. Peel the eggs, then rip them into 8 to 10 pieces each and drop them into the bowl. Season with S&P. Add **¼ cup olive oil, 2 more tablespoons red wine vinegar, 1 tablespoon pickled pepper brine,** and **1 teaspoon Dijon mustard.** Stir vigorously until the yolks start to emulsify with the dressing (egg yolk + oil = mayo!). Stir in the sliced peppers and meat. Season to taste with S&P.

· Follow the lead of the Godmother sandwich and add provolone, tomato, roasted red peppers, both kinds of pickled peppers, and all, instead of just one, of the meats.

· Eat on toast, with boiled potatoes, or over a heap of shredded iceberg lettuce or radicchio.

· P.S. If you swap the eggs in any egg salad for canned tuna, pasta, or chicken, you'll make . . . tuna, pasta, or chicken salad.

Snappy Veg with Broken Caesar

Kinda like a potato salad, kinda like a sauce gribiche, but with my mom's Caesar dressing. Which is not a Caesar at all. Got it?

POTATOES

GARLIC

CAPERS

LEMONS

PARMESAN

BOILING
VEGETABLES

EGGS

FOR 4

1. In a large pot, cover **1 pound little potatoes (baby Yukon Gold, fingerling)** with 1 inch of water. Salt the water well, then bring to a simmer over medium-high. Cook until tender when pierced with a fork, anywhere from 5 to 15 minutes. Use a slotted spoon to transfer them to a colander, then run under cold water. Keep the pot of water at a simmer.

2. While the potatoes are cooking, make the dressing: On a cutting board, smash and coarsely chop **2 garlic cloves.** Add **10 grinds of black pepper** and **2 teaspoons capers.** Chop and press down on the mixture with the side of your knife until a coarse paste forms. Transfer the paste to a medium bowl, then stir in the zest and juice from **2 lemons** (about 6 tablespoons juice). Finely grate ⅔ **cup Parmesan** (1⅓ ounces) into the bowl, then stir in another **2 teaspoons capers.** Slowly add ½ **cup olive oil,** stirring until emulsified.

3. Trim **1 pound tender boiling vegetables (broccolini, cauliflower, snap peas, green beans).** Use one or a mix.

4. When the potatoes are out, add **4 eggs** to the water and boil for 9 minutes. Use a slotted spoon to transfer the eggs to an ice bath to cool. Next add the vegetables. They'll only take a few minutes. Taste one to see if they're crisp-tender. Transfer to the ice bath to cool (or drain and run under cold water).

5. Peel and quarter or tear the eggs. Add to the dressing and stir to combine. Taste and adjust as needed with acid (lemon), fat (olive oil), and salt (capers and cheese). Smash the potatoes or tear them in two, then combine on plates or a platter with the vegetables and top with the egg mess. Season with S&P and more Parm, too, if you want. Good warm or at room temp. (Keeps in the fridge for 2 or 3 days.)

For something different

- **Broken Caesar on anything:** The vegetables here are boiled because you already have water boiling. Instead, you could sauté or roast them, or fetch leftovers from the fridge—or skip the veg and eat the broken Caesar on toast, with canned fish, or alongside cold cuts or grilled seafood.

- **Mom's Famous "Caesar" Dressing:** For a light dressing with the creaminess and brine of a Caesar, just make step 2. Mom said to chop 36 capers with the garlic, but that's up to you.

- **Egg Salad:** Use 8 to 10 eggs, skip the potatoes and vegetables, and you have a Caesary egg salad. (Or skip the eggs and vegetables and up the potatoes for potato salad.)

Flatbreads with Beet Yogurt & Jammy Eggs

Stubborn beets grate into fluffy shreds you don't even have to cook.

EGGS

BEETS

GREEK
YOGURT

GROUND
CORIANDER

LIMES

FRESH CHILE

FLATBREAD

SOFT HERBS

FOR 4

1. Bring a medium saucepan of water to a boil. Add **4 eggs** and boil for 9 minutes. Transfer to an ice bath to cool.

2. Meanwhile, on the large holes of a box grater, grate **1 pound beets** (about 2 large) into a medium bowl (about 2 cups). Add **2 cups full-fat Greek yogurt**, **¼ cup olive oil**, and **1 teaspoon ground coriander**. Season to taste with S&P and stir to combine. Zest **2 limes** into the bowl, then juice the limes (about ¼ cup) into the bowl and stir to combine. Finely grate **1 fresh chile (jalapeño, red Fresno)** into the bowl to taste.

3. Toast **4 flatbreads, naans, or pitas** in a dry pan over medium-high until very well toasted; you want them crunchy, not sagging like leftover pizza. Peel and coarsely chop the eggs, then add to the beet mixture and fold gently to combine.

4. Top the flatbreads with the egg mixture, then snip some **soft herbs (dill, chives, mint)** over top. Season with more S&P.

· In step 3, fold in feta, goat cheese, or chopped toasted walnuts or pistachios.

· Try with grated carrots or raw butternut squash. Or even grated zukes or cukes (like tzatziki); salt and drain before adding to remove excess moisture. You could also mix cooked vegetables with the yogurt in the style of borani, an Iranian dish named after a queen who loved cold yogurt dishes *that* much.

Egg & Charred Pepper Stew

Boiled eggs taking a swim in the Mediterranean.

BELL PEPPERS

GARLIC

RED ONION

LEMON

TOMATO PASTE

SMOKED PAPRIKA

TOMATO PUREE

EGGS

FOR 4

1. Cut the sides off **2 red, orange, or yellow bell peppers,** remove the seeds, and cut into ½-inch pieces. Thinly slice **4 garlic cloves.** Coarsely chop **1 large red onion** and put ¼ cup in a little bowl. Squeeze half of **1 lemon** over the onion (about 1½ tablespoons) and season with a big pinch of salt. Stir with your fingers until the onion's wet.

2. Bring a medium saucepan of water to a boil. In a large Dutch oven, heat **2 tablespoons olive oil** over medium-high. Add the bell peppers and remaining red onion, season with S&P, and cook, stirring just once or twice, until crisp-tender and charred in spots, 5 to 7 minutes.

3. Add the garlic, **¼ cup tomato paste, ½ teaspoon red pepper flakes,** and **¼ teaspoon smoked paprika,** season with S&P, and cook, stirring, until you smell paprika, a minute or two. Add **24 to 28 ounces tomato puree** and **2 cups water,** season with S&P, and bring to a simmer. Cook until stewy and flavorful, 7 to 10 minutes.

4. Meanwhile, add **8 eggs** to the boiling water and cook for 8 minutes. Transfer to an ice bath to cool. Peel the eggs.

5. Add the eggs to the stew. Cook until the eggs are warm, just a couple minutes. Eat with the macerated onion, a squeeze of juice from the remaining lemon half, and more red pepper flakes.

· Eggs can be made ahead since they'll warm in the soup.

· Really good with something briny added in step 5, like capers, preserved lemon, or olives.

Fry hot

This section is not about the fried eggs that slump like a Salvador Dalí clock on toast. We're here for eggs with lacy outsides, sturdy undersides, and still-runny yolks. Making them is fast and furious, which sometimes is the speed we need.

My forever fried egg. Generously coat a cast-iron or nonstick skillet with olive oil over medium-high. Crack the eggs into the pan and stand back because there will be sputtering (the eggs *will* run together no matter how strategic your placement; if this bothers you, play short-order cook and fry one serving at a time). Leave them to fry for a couple minutes until the edges are rippled and golden brown. Now tilt the pan toward you, spoon up some of the oil, and drizzle it over the whites and the edge of the yolks. By basting, you cook the whites and keep the yolk molten—and you don't have to flip, which is risky business.

Once the whites are bubbly and set, season with S&P and you're done. Will your stove be splattered in oil? Will you maybe burn the roof of your mouth on your first bite? Yes, but it's worth it.

Switch up the fat. Instead of or in addition to olive oil, first fry sausage or cured meat (bacon, pepperoni, chorizo) in the skillet. Remove the meat with tongs or a slotted spoon, then fry the egg in the drippings. Or use chicken or another rendered fat.

If you really want a crispy, buttery fried egg, fry the egg in olive oil, then add a knob of butter after the first couple minutes to use for basting.

Fry it on or in something. Instead of just fat, crack an egg on top of grated potato that's simultaneously sizzling into hash browns, on grated cheese browning into frico, or both (p. 54). Or fry it on top of sizzling breadcrumbs, herbs, scallions, or bacon (the list goes on).

Whatever you fry the eggs on (or in), it's got to be hot. One way to make sure the eggs are in contact with a hot surface is to make divots so that they still reach the pan. So you could crisp rice, make holes for the eggs, then fry (p. 176). Or fry the egg in a bread hole (p. 53), or a bagel hole! I love eggs.

Flavor the oil, then sauce the egg.

A generous amount of oil makes frying and basting the egg easier, and also presents an opportunity to sauce the egg. Steak gets basted with butter and aromatics—why not eggs?

Sliced garlic or ginger, ground or whole and crushed spices, curry paste, hard-stem herbs, capers, anchovies, fresh or dried chile—anything that you bloom in hot oil can meld into a sauce right where your eggs are frying. Follow the method on page 49: When the egg is just about ready, add the ingredients and spoon over the egg until cooked through and fragrant.

The things to keep in mind are: 1. You'll need more oil than if you were just frying the eggs. 2. If the addition risks burning, once the egg is nearly cooked, turn off the heat before adding. And 3. Like in any pan sauce, a hit of acid simmered in the oil or butter will balance the richness.

Egg Sliders

Sometimes dinner just has to be an egg on bread—gladly.

BURGER BUNS

KETCHUP

EGGS

HOT SAUCE

FOR 2 or 4, depending on your day and your appetite.

1. Heat **2 teaspoons olive oil** in a large nonstick skillet over medium-high. Add **4 burger buns,** cut side down, and toast until lightly browned, 1 to 2 minutes. Transfer to plates. Squirt some **ketchup** on the bottom buns.

2. Add **3 tablespoons olive oil** to the skillet. Crack **4 eggs** into the skillet and cook, untouched, until the edges are lacy and golden brown, about 2 minutes. Now tilt the pan toward you, spoon up some of the oil, and drizzle it over the whites and where the white meets the yolk (avoid the yolk). Continue until the whites are set but the yolk is still runny, another minute or two. Transfer to the buns, season with S&P, and douse with **hot sauce.**

Other emergency fried egg sandwiches

· Sauerkraut + bacon + mustard

· Griddled red onions + chile crisp

· Mexican chorizo patty (p. 311) + kale

· Romaine wilted with apple cider vinegar

· Anchovy + butter

· Scallion mayo + potato chips

· Pickled cherry peppers + mozzarella

· Wilted spinach + pickled ginger

Eggs with Smoky Scallion Oil

Zhuzhing this egg starts in the skillet.

SCALLIONS

ASPARAGUS

EGGS

SMOKED PAPRIKA

GREEK YOGURT

FOR 2 or 4

1. Thinly slice **2 scallions**. Trim **1 pound asparagus**. If they're especially thick, cut them crosswise on the diagonal into 1-inch-thick pieces. Heat **2 tablespoons olive oil** in a large nonstick skillet over medium-high. Add the asparagus and cook, tossing occasionally, until tender and blistered in spots, 5 to 7 minutes. Season with salt and transfer to plates.

2. Still over medium-high, heat **6 table-spoons olive oil** in the skillet. Crack **4 eggs** into the skillet, season with S&P, and cook, untouched, until the edges are lacy and golden brown, about 2 minutes. Turn off the heat and tilt the skillet toward you. Add the scallions and **½ teaspoon smoked paprika** to the pooling oil. Spoon up some of the oil and drizzle over the whites and where the white meets the yolk (avoid the yolk). Repeat until the whites are set but the yolk is still runny, another minute or two.

3. Swoosh some **full-fat Greek yogurt** onto the plates (about ¼ cup each). Season with S&P. Spoon the eggs onto the plates, then drizzle the scallions and oil over everything.

For something different

· **More smoky scallion oil:** Use oil with frizzled scallions and bloomed smoked paprika as a marinade for feta, a dipper for bread, a sauce for chicken or shrimp, or with lemon as a salad dressing.

· **More eggs and yogurt:** This combo has lots of room for personal flair. The most classic rendition is çılbır, a Turkish dish in which garlic or dill yogurt is topped with poached eggs and chile-flecked butter, sometimes with toasted walnuts or pine nuts.

Garlic Bread Egg in a Hole with Mushrooms

All-at-once mushroom toast, egg in a hole, and garlic bread.

BUTTER

MUSHROOMS

GARLIC

SOURDOUGH

PARSLEY

EGGS

FOR 4

1. Cut **4 tablespoons butter** (½ stick) into small pieces and set out in a small bowl by the stove to soften. Trim **1 pound mushrooms (cremini, shiitake, maitake)** and rip the caps into bite-size pieces.

2. In a large nonstick skillet, heat **3 tablespoons olive oil** over medium. Add the mushrooms, season with S&P, and cook, stirring occasionally, until all the liquid is released and the mushrooms are browned, 10 to 15 minutes.

3. Meanwhile, grate **2 garlic cloves** into the butter, season with S&P, and smash with a fork to combine. Slice **4 (½-inch-thick) slices sourdough or crusty bread,** then schmear the butter wall to wall on one side of each slice. Using a glass, cut out a circle in the middle of each slice, leaving at least ½ inch of bread on all sides. Finely chop **¼ cup parsley leaves and tender stems.**

4. Transfer the mushrooms to plates, then lower the heat to medium-low. Add the bread slices and circles, buttered sides up (do two at a time if they don't all fit, and add more olive oil between batches). Crack an **egg** in each hole, season with S&P, and cook until the underside of the bread is crispy, 2 to 3 minutes (use the circles as a test). Use a spatula to flip the bread and continue cooking until the egg white is cooked through but the yolk is still runny, 2 to 4 minutes. Eat the eggs in holes with the mushrooms and a parsley shower.

More eggs in holes

· **Spicy turmeric:** Warm ground turmeric and cayenne in olive oil. Add egg to the hole and cook.

· **Chorizo:** Crisp coins of cured chorizo in pan. Remove. Fry egg in the hole in the chorizo drippings. Top with chorizo and squeeze of lemon.

· **Frico:** Melt grated cheese in the skillet. Add egg to the hole. As the egg cooks, the cheese will crisp.

Crispy Potato, Egg & Cheese Tacos

So crisp, you could even skip the tortilla.

CHEDDAR

POTATO

TORTILLAS

EGGS

HOT SAUCE

LIME

MAKES 2

1. On the large holes of a box grater, grate ¼ **cup sharp Cheddar cheese** (1 ounce) and ½ **cup of 1 russet potato.**

2. Warm **2 small corn or flour tortillas** over your flame or in a large nonstick skillet. Transfer to a plate. Read and re-hearse what's happening next. It comes together quickly.

3. Heat **1 tablespoon butter** in a large nonstick skillet over medium. Sprinkle the potato into two piles in the pan, then use a spatula or fork to spread out each pile to about the size of your tortilla. You want the strands touching but not clumped, like a snowflake. The more space between the potato, the crispier the final result. Salt the potato, then evenly sprinkle the cheese over the potato. It's okay if some cheese comes into contact with the pan—it'll taste like the crispy edges of a grilled cheese.

4. Make a little indent in the center of each pile and crack an **egg** right there. S&P the eggs, then cover the skillet and cook until the cheese and potatoes are golden and the egg white is cooked through, 3 to 4 minutes.

5. Use a spatula to wiggle the potato and cheese loose from the skillet, then slide them onto your tortillas. Eat with **hot sauce** and **lime wedges** or what-ever toppings you like (keeping in mind that the yolk is a built-in sauce). Eat and repeat.

· If you have chili powder or another warm spice, add a dash to the grated potato in step 1.

Fried Egg Salad

Spicy, sizzling, cool—and what to do with busted fried eggs.

CARROTS

FRESH CHILE

SHALLOT

LIMES

CILANTRO

CRISP LETTUCE

EGGS

FOR 4

1. Add these things to a large bowl as you cut them: Peel and thinly slice **3 medium carrots.** Thinly slice **½ fresh chile (jalapeño, serrano).** Coarsely chop **1 shallot.** Add the juice of **2 limes** (about ¼ cup), season generously with S&P, stir to combine, and set aside while you do some other things.

2. Pluck **2 cups cilantro leaves.** Finely chop the thick stems and add the stems to the large bowl. Rip **12 to 16 ounces crisp lettuce (Little Gem, romaine)** into bite-size pieces.

3. Heat **¼ cup neutral oil** in a large cast-iron skillet over medium-high. Once it starts to smoke, crack **8 eggs** into the oil. Stand back and get ready to rumble. Once they're super crispy and brown around the edges, just 30 to 45 seconds, flip the eggs away from you and cook until the yolks are almost set but still loose, another 30 to 45 seconds (poke them and see that they still bounce). Transfer to a cutting board and season with S&P.

4. To the bowl with the carrots, stir in **2 tablespoons neutral oil.** Quarter the eggs, then add to the bowl along with the lettuce and cilantro. Toss to combine.

· The mix of vegetables here is inspired by Mexican escabeche, but you could swap in radishes, cucumbers, or green beans.

· Some Cotija, feta, or avocado wouldn't be out of place.

More salads for crispy eggs

· Romaine + Olive Oil–Braised Chickpeas (p. 104)

· Watercress + smoked trout + chives + Parmesan

· Frisée + bacon + mustard-shallot vinaigrette (p. 306), like salade Lyonnaise in France

· Carrots + onion + cilantro + Chinese celery + nước chấm (p. 346), like yam khai dao in Thailand

Croque Monday

Translates to "crunch" or "bite" Monday, which is how to feel about Monday.

SOURDOUGH

EGG

DIJON
MUSTARD

HAM

GRUYÈRE

MAKES 1 rich,
buttery toast

1. In a medium skillet, melt **1 tablespoon butter** over medium. Add **1 slice sourdough or country bread** and toast until golden, 2 to 3 minutes. Transfer to a plate toasted side up.

2. Melt **another tablespoon butter.** Crack **1 egg** into the skillet, season with S&P, and cook until the white is cooked through, 2 to 3 minutes. Use a spoon to baste the white and the edge of the yolk to help it evenly cook. Turn off the heat.

3. Schmear **1 or 2 teaspoons Dijon or whole-grain mustard** on the toasted side of the bread, then top with **2 thin slices ham** (2 to 3 ounces). Top with the egg, followed by a shower of finely grated **Gruyère**— ¼ cup to ½ cup, enough to cover the egg and allow some to melt and some to stay curly.

BEANS

Add crunchies

Sometimes I think about beans in their dark cans. How are they doing in there? Stiff with claustrophobia? Broken down from the pressure? Glistening from being cooped up with their best buds? No matter if you find your beans firm, mealy, perfect, or total stress cases, one approach that works for any state of bean is to not futz with their texture too much. Instead, make them taste great by handling them as little as possible, then find texture elsewhere, specifically CRUNCH that counters their starchy denseness.

To make a bean taste better, dress it up . . . You can eat beans, drained and rinsed, right from the can, but adding fat and salt brings out their best attributes while kicking off any tin-can flavor. After you drain, rinse, and shake your beans dry in the colander, treat them like a salad by coating them with oil, acid, and S&P. Stir them through salad dressing, or mix vinegar and olive oil with the beans to taste. Add shallots or onions, which will lightly pickle in the vinegar; chile (fresh or dried, hot sauce, chile paste or oil); or grated garlic or ginger for a kick. Taste a bean and adjust salt, fat, and acid.

. . . or give it a warm welcome. Even just a few minutes in a greased pan will also give beans their groove back. In a skillet over medium, heat oil or butter (or chicken or bacon fat . . .). Add spices, garlic, onions, or anything else you want to infuse the oil and flavor the beans. Then add the beans, season with S&P, and stir to coat. Cook until warmed, just a few minutes.

To make a warm vinaigrette, add vinegar or lemon or lime juice at the end. For example, cook bacon, remove bacon, warm pinto beans and chili powder in the bacon fat, then add apple cider vinegar and the crispy bacon. Or warm chickpeas in olive oil, then add butter, coriander seeds, and lemon juice and cook until the butter is browned and the lemon-spiced brown butter coats the chickpeas.

Make them ahead.	Unless your beans are so soft you should probably just blend them into soup, both treatments on your left will allow the beans to improve over time, soaking up flavor and the good life outside of a dark can.
	The marinated beans can sit at room temp for a few hours or in the fridge for a few days. Bring them to room temp before eating so the oil liquefies. The warmed beans will keep in the fridge for a few days, too: Eat them at room temp or reheat with a little water. In any case, reseason as needed. Flavors change as time goes by.
Pile on crisp and crunch.	Here's hardly an encyclopedic list of crispy, crunchy ingredients to eat with beans. As you chomp, beans go soft while the additions snap, crackle, crush. Add crunch right before eating so they don't sog.

· **Seeds:** Whole spices, sesame, sunflower, pepitas, poppy, nigella, flax, chia, or quinoa (see p. 191 for how to toast quinoa). Also sprouted seeds.

· **Nuts:** To avoid toasting, purchase roasted or smoked nuts, typically pistachios, almonds, or peanuts.

· **Raw fruits and vegetables:** apple, pear, tomatillo, cucumber, corn, snap peas, radish, celery, carrots, jicama, bok choy, fennel, sprouts. Cut into one- or two-bite pieces.

· **Carbs:** Toast, crackers, chips, corn nuts, breadcrumbs, rice cakes, pretzels, a crisped tortilla, toasted rice powder.

Marinated Beans with Crunchy Vegetables

A tangy, oily bath wakes even the sleepiest of beans.

SHALLOT

FRESH CHILE

RED WINE
VINEGAR

BEANS

CRUNCHY
VEGETABLES

FOR 4

1. Finely chop **1 shallot** and **1 fresh chile (serrano, red Fresno).** Add to a large bowl with **3 tablespoons red or white wine or Sherry vinegar.** Season generously with S&P.

2. Drain and rinse **2 (15-ounce) cans any beans (white, black-eyed peas, chickpeas)**—use a mix if you like. Add to the bowl with ¼ **cup olive oil** and stir to combine.

3. When you're ready to eat, slice up **2 cups crunchy vegetables** into bite-size pieces. For instance: asparagus, bok choy, celery, cucumbers, Savoy cabbage, fennel, Little Gem, radicchio, turnips, snap peas. Taste the beans and reseason with S&P. Add the veg to the beans and toss to coat. (This mix minus the veg will keep for 3 days in the fridge. Add vegetables right before eating.)

· Also good with anything you like in a salad: olives, salami, mortadella, tangerine wedges, canned tuna, shrimps, leftover chicken, fresh thyme or oregano, salad greens, preserved lemon, Parm, or feta.

Pan Con Tomate plus White Beans **PAGE 68**

Pan Con Tomate plus White Beans

For those summer nights.

BIG TOMATOES

WHITE BEANS

CIABATTA

GARLIC

RED WINE VINEGAR

FOR 4

1. Halve **3 big, ripe tomatoes** (like beefsteaks) through their bellies. Place a box grater in a large bowl. Using the large holes on the box grater, grate the cut sides of the tomatoes into the bowl. Stop when you reach the skin; discard or compost the skin. Stir ¼ **cup olive oil** into the tomatoes and season with S&P.

2. Drain and rinse **2 (15-ounce) cans white beans (gigante, butter, cannellini).** Stir into the tomato mixture.

3. Cut **1 ciabatta loaf (or another open-crumb bread)** into large slices. Toast however you toast. Peel **1 garlic clove,** then scrape the bread with the garlic. Put the toasts in shallow bowls or plates with lips.

4. Taste the tomato mixture. If it doesn't taste bright and spritzy, add more salt and perhaps some **red wine vinegar or lemon juice** to perk it up. When it tastes great, spoon some beans and the grated tomato onto the toasts. Pause a few beats to allow the bread to soak up the tomato mixture. Drizzle with a little more **olive oil** and eat.

· Additions to step 2, should they move you: fresh or dried chile, basil or mint, halved cherry tomatoes, sliced cucumbers, avocado, mozzarella, feta.

· Also makes a good raw pasta sauce. Stir with butter and pasta water.

More crunch for white beans

· Blanched broccoli rabe + walnuts + chopped Parmesan

· Thin-sliced fennel + tahini dressing (p. 175) + toasted fennel and coriander seeds

· Kimchi + cucumbers

· Romaine + anchovy breadcrumbs (p. 140)

· Bulgur + parsley + pistachios + lemon

Chickpeas, Yogurt & Za'atar Nuts

Enjoys candlelit dinners and being taken to lunch.

NUTS

ZA'ATAR

GREEK
YOGURT

LEMON

GARLIC

CHICKPEAS

SALAD
GREENS

SOFT HERBS

FOR 4

1. Coarsely chop ½ **cup nuts (walnuts, almonds).** In a small skillet over medium-low, heat the nuts and **5 tablespoons olive oil.** Once the nuts start to sizzle, remove from the heat. Stir in **1 tablespoon za'atar** and season with S&P. Set aside.

2. In a large bowl, stir together **1½ cups full-fat Greek yogurt,** juice from half of **1 lemon** (about 1½ tablespoons), and **1 teaspoon each S&P.** Grate **1 small garlic clove** into the mix and stir to combine.

3. Drain and rinse **2 (15-ounce) cans chickpeas.** Add to the yogurt dressing and toss to combine. Add **2 cups salad greens (baby kale, arugula)** onto the pile of chickpeas (rip any large leaves), then do the same with **1 cup soft herb leaves (basil, mint, parsley).** Toss gently, then stir in the nuts and za'atar oil. Season to taste with more S&P, lemon, and oil. Sprinkle with more za'atar if you like. (Without the greens, the salad will keep for 3 days in the fridge.)

More dressings for emergency chickpeas

· Olive oil + balsamic vinegar (my mom's college diet)

· Olive tapenade + tuna + lemon

· Lemon-feta sauce (p. 214)

· Any green sauce (pesto, chimichurri, zhoug, Green Goddess, Ranch)

· Grated Parm + olive oil + lots of black pepper

· Red wine vinegar + shallot

· Frank's hot sauce + melted butter

ADD CRUNCHIES

Cumin Beans with Tomatillo

If seven-layer dip got a makeover in the produce aisle.

TOMATILLOS
RED ONION
LIME
GREEN HOT SAUCE
BLACK BEANS
GROUND CUMIN
SOUR CREAM
TORTILLA CHIPS

FOR 4

1. Remove the husks from **8 ounces tomatillos** (about 5). Halve and cut into thin wedges. Scatter on a serving platter and sprinkle with salt. Halve **1 small red onion** through the root, then thinly slice. On the cutting board, sprinkle with S&P and toss with your hands until the slices start to wilt.

2. In a small bowl, finely grate the zest of **1 lime.** Stir in **¼ cup olive oil,** the juice of the lime (about 2 tablespoons), and **1 teaspoon green hot sauce** (or to taste depending on heat tolerance). Season with S&P. Pour a little dressing over the tomatillos.

3. Drain and rinse **1 (15-ounce) can black beans.** Heat **2 tablespoons olive oil** in a medium skillet over medium. Add the beans and **1½ teaspoons ground cumin** and cook, stirring, until the beans are warm and fragrant, 3 to 4 minutes. Season generously with S&P.

4. Now layer it all like seven-layer dip: Spoon the beans over the tomatillos, followed by teaspoon-size dollops of **sour cream.** Top with some of the red onion, then spoon over more dressing. Crumble **a couple handfuls tortilla chips** on top. Season to taste with S&P and green hot sauce.

· Raw tomatillos are tart like a green apple and juicy like a tomato. In their place, use thinly sliced tomatoes, cucumbers, iceberg lettuce, or cabbage.

· For more layers, add cilantro, scallions, avocado, crumbled bacon, pickled jalapeños, Cotija, or Fritos.

More crisp and crunch for black beans

· Tostada + avocado
· Coconut flakes + toasted quinoa (p. 191) + hot sauce
· Chile crisp + rice + soy sauce
· Roasted sweet potato (p. 241) + peanuts + lime

Oven Quesadillas

Four quesadillas at once and—perhaps the best part—without flipping.

CHEDDAR

BLACK BEANS

DRIED
OREGANO

FLOUR
TORTILLAS

FOR 4

1. Heat the oven to 450°F and stick a sheet pan in there. Coarsely grate **1 cup sharp Cheddar cheese** (about 4 ounces) into a medium bowl. Drain and rinse **1 (15-ounce) can black beans** and add to the bowl. Add **1 teaspoon dried oregano,** season to taste with S&P, and stir to combine.

2. Lightly grease the heated sheet pan with **neutral oil.** Put **4 (6-inch) flour tortillas** on the baking sheet. Spoon a heaping ½ cup of the bean-cheese mix on top of each tortilla, spread it out, then top with another tortilla. Lightly oil the top of each quesadilla. Bake until golden brown and crispy, 8 to 10 minutes. Sprinkle with salt and let sit for a couple minutes to crisp further.

More filling ideas

· Massaged kale + feta + Cheddar

· Raw corn + jalapeño + mozz

· Shredded chicken tossed in hot sauce + pepper Jack

· Broccoli + Cheddar

· The dried oregano could also be ground cumin or coriander, thinly sliced scallions or cilantro, grated jalapeño or garlic, or pickles—something spiced, spicy, or briny to offset the cheese.

· Add cooked vegetables or protein at room temp so they don't steam and sog the tortilla.

· For more cheese, after you've assembled the quesadillas, grate a couple tablespoons on the top tortilla. As it melts, it'll crisp.

· Eat with green hot sauce, sour cream, or guacamole (p. 28).

BLT Stir-Fry

But the T stands for tofu.

SUSHI RICE
TOFU
CORNSTARCH
SOY SAUCE
RICE VINEGAR
MAPLE SYRUP
ROMAINE
BACON

FOR 4

1. Make rice: In a medium saucepan, bring **1 cup sushi rice, 1¼ cups water,** and **½ teaspoon salt** to a boil. Cover, reduce the heat to the lowest setting, and cook until the rice is tender, 12 to 15 minutes. Remove from the heat and keep covered.

2. Cut **1 (14- to 16-ounce) block firm or extra-firm tofu** lengthwise into ½-inch-thick slices, then cut each piece crosswise in three. Wrap in paper towels to dry. Transfer to a medium bowl and toss to coat with **1 tablespoon cornstarch** and **½ teaspoon salt.** In a measuring cup, stir **¼ cup low-sodium soy sauce, 3 tablespoons unseasoned rice vinegar, 3 tablespoons maple syrup,** and a few grinds of black pepper.

3. Slice **2 heads romaine** crosswise into 1-inch pieces. Cut **6 thick-cut bacon slices** into 1-inch pieces (easiest with scissors).

4. In a large nonstick skillet, heat **1 tablespoon neutral oil** and the bacon over medium. Cook, stirring sometimes, until the bacon is golden brown, 5 to 7 minutes. Transfer to a paper towel–lined sheet pan. Hold on to the skillet, leaving the fat behind.

5. Add the tofu to the skillet and cook, without touching, until very crisp and browned, 2 to 3 minutes. Flip the pieces and repeat on the other side. Transfer to the sheet pan. Add the romaine to the skillet, season generously with S&P, and stir until just wilted. Return the tofu and bacon to the skillet, along with the maple-soy mixture, and stir until everything is glazy, 2 to 3 minutes. Fluff the rice with a fork and eat with the stir-fry.

Crisp

Sizzled, frizzled beans have all the qualities of a good snack, plus they count as dinner. (The same goes for tofu and tempeh, what we in the biz call bean derivatives since they're made from soybeans.) They're cheaper than pistachios, more nutritious than fries, and more substantial than popcorn. You can even eat them with your hands if you want to.

Use firm beans. Firm black beans, chickpeas, tempeh, and big beans (butter, gigante) can hold their shape over high heat, while soft beans might split apart. For instance, a roasted white bean will splay like popcorn (p. 82)—that said, no one ever got mad at popcorn.

Oil up to catch rays. Browning a bean requires the same trifecta as crisping everything from steak to eggs: dry, hot, and greased—like your beans want a sun-tan. Drain and rinse your beans, shake them in the colander, then pat them down with towels. Sometimes I put pieces of paper towel in the colander to absorb more liquid. As you're getting the other parts of dinner ready, spread the beans out on a plate or sheet pan at room temp or in the fridge to air-dry.

Then, cook the beans at a medium-high or hotter temp in the oven or on the stove so they crisp outside and don't risk their insides drying out. So that they don't burn, use plenty of oil. Hot + dry = burnt. Hot + oiled = bronzed.

Crisp first, flavor later. Dry spices risk burning and a wet marinade can inhibit browning. Simplify by crisping beans naked, with just oil and S&P, then tossing them in their seasonings, which will stick, toast, and warm from the residual heat. That could be a sauce or glaze, ground spices, or a fun sprinkle like sesame seeds, nutritional yeast, za'atar, or furikake. That said, a plain crispy chickpea is pretty great, too.

Sauce sloppy. What's falafel without tahini sauce, fries without ketchup, or toast without butter and jam? A dry mouth in search of a glass of water. Crispy starch needs something loose for dolloping, dipping, or dragging through. Grab an already-made sauce (salsa, mayo, mustard, yogurt, sour cream) or make a spoonable something like brown butter (p. 115), green sauce (p. 147), or lemon cream (p. 78).

Cornstarch your tofu. It's a comedy that we try to crisp foods that are packaged in water. That we press, pat, and otherwise coddle tofu in hopes that it'll crisp. While a bean's moisture lives just on its exterior, tofu is a water-bloated sponge, making it sauce-resistant, prone to crumbling, and simply not built to crisp. Haha!

To turn that frown upside down, do a cursory pat dry, then toss it in cornstarch and S&P. The starchy powder will give the tofu the texture of a French fry with creamy middles and actually browned, shattery outsides, no matter how impatient you were with your tofu-drying. Or, there's always tempeh . . .

Let's talk tempeh. This Indonesian ingredient is a nutty, versatile, savory, almost mush-roomy protein. And it crisps in ways tofu only wishes it could. Its advantages come from how it's made: Whole, partially cooked soy-beans are fermented and form a cake that's good at soaking up glazes (p. 93), heady spices (p. 89), and vinaigrettes (p. 88).

If you're making tempeh for the first time, treat it as you would ground meat. Crumble it into large pieces, then brown it in a hot pan with olive oil. Add whatever flavorings sound good and see how you like it. While crumbles give a great mix of textures, you can also cut it into slim triangles, chubby cubes, or rectangles. Markets carry smoked or marinated tempeh, but go for the more versatile original— or mixed, which also includes millet, barley, and brown rice.

Big Beans with Breadcrumbs

Beans dolled up in a shearling coat of breadcrumbs. Glamorous!

BEANS

LEMON

SALAD GREENS

PANKO

SPOONABLE DAIRY

FOR 4

1. Drain and rinse **2 (15-ounce) cans big beans (gigante, butter).** Shake very dry in the colander (or lay them out on a paper towel–lined sheet pan to air-dry). Finely chop half of **1 lemon,** skin, pith, fruit, and all—pluck out the seeds. Transfer the chopped lemon and any juices to a small bowl and mix with a big pinch of salt. Hold on to the other half of the lemon. Tear **4 cups salad greens** into bite-size pieces. It could be something bitter (escarole, radicchio), delicate (Little Gem, mâche), or hearty (kale, raw Swiss chard). Transfer the greens to a big bowl.

2. Heat **3 tablespoons olive oil** in a large skillet over medium-high. Add the beans in a single layer and cook, without touching, until golden brown on one side, 2 to 3 minutes. Add another **2 tablespoons olive oil,** flip the beans, and cook until golden on the other side, 2 to 3 minutes. Season with S&P.

3. Reduce the heat to medium-low and add **2 tablespoons butter.** Swirl it around and once it's foamy, add **½ cup panko breadcrumbs.** Cook, stirring constantly, until the panko is golden and clinging to the beans, 2 to 4 minutes. Remove from the heat.

4. Add **½ cup spoonable dairy (yogurt, crème fraîche, heavy or sour cream)** to the salted lemon. Season to taste with S&P and thin with water as needed so it's the consistency of sour cream. Season the greens with S&P, then squeeze over the reserved lemon (about 1½ tablespoons). Toss with your hands while you drizzle in enough **olive oil** to coat (about 2 tablespoons). Taste and adjust S&P, lemon, and oil to your liking. Eat the beans with the greens and a spoonful of puckery cream (almost rhymed!).

Chickpea-Cabbage Tabbouleh

An any-season tabbouleh that swaps fickle herbs for loyal cabbage.

BULGUR

CHICKPEAS

CABBAGE

SCALLIONS

LEMONS

WARM SPICE

FOR 4

1. Heat the oven to 400°F. Put **½ cup bulgur** in a measuring cup and cover with an inch of boiling water. Let sit until tender and the water is mostly absorbed, about 40 minutes.

2. Drain and rinse **2 (15-ounce) cans chickpeas,** then shake very, very dry in the colander. Transfer the chickpeas to a sheet pan and drizzle with **3 tablespoons olive oil.** Season with S&P and toss to combine. Roast the chickpeas, shaking a few times, until dry and bronzed, 25 to 30 minutes. Season with S&P, then turn the oven off and leave the chickpeas in there to keep crisping.

3. Core and thinly slice **1 medium green or Savoy cabbage** (about 2 pounds or 9 cups sliced). Thinly slice **3 scallions.** Transfer to a large bowl, season with S&P, and squeeze to wilt—as my friend Caroline says, lovingly but firmly like you're massaging shoulders. Add the juice from **2 lemons** (about 6 tablespoons), **¼ cup olive oil,** and **¾ teaspoon warm, ground spice (coriander, allspice, cinnamon).** Toss to combine.

4. When everything's ready, toss the bulgur with the cabbage. Season to taste with S&P and top with chickpeas. (Without the chickpeas, the salad will keep for up to 3 days in the fridge.)

Other crispy chickpeas

· **Spiced:** Sprinkle spices onto the cooked chickpeas and shake the pan to coat. The residual heat will lightly toast the spices.

· **Seeded:** Sprinkle furikake or za'atar onto the cooked beans. Shake the pan to help the seeds adhere.

· **Cheesy:** Halfway through roasting, blanket the beans with finely grated Parmesan or Cheddar.

· **Stove-topped:** Crisp chickpeas on the stovetop in a glut of olive oil in just 10 to 15 minutes. When they start to pop like popcorn, they're ready.

Smoky White Beans & Cauliflower

Paprika-stained and aïoli-swaddled like patatas bravas.

WHITE BEANS

TOMATO PASTE

SMOKED PAPRIKA

CAULIFLOWER

GARLIC

MAYO

SHERRY VINEGAR

SOFT HERBS

FOR 4

1. Heat the oven to 425°F. Drain and rinse **2 (15-ounce) cans white beans (cannellini, Great Northern, butter)**, then shake very, very dry in the colander. Lay out on a paper towel–lined sheet pan to dry further. In a large bowl, stir together **5 tablespoons olive oil, 3 tablespoons tomato paste, 2 teaspoons smoked paprika,** and **1 teaspoon red pepper flakes.** Season generously with S&P.

2. Cut **1 large cauliflower** (2½ to 3 pounds) into small florets, adding them to the bowl as you go. Add the beans and toss to coat. Spread across 2 sheet pans (discard the paper towels; hold on to the bowl). Roast, flipping the pans halfway through, until the cauliflower is tender and browned in spots, 25 to 30 minutes. Season with S&P.

3. In a small bowl, finely grate **2 small garlic cloves.** Stir in **½ cup mayo** and **2 teaspoons Sherry vinegar.** Season with S&P. In the reserved bowl, pluck **1½ cups soft herbs (parsley, cilantro).** Finely chop the thick stems and add to the bowl.

4. When the beans and cauliflower are done, dress the herbs with about **1 tablespoon Sherry vinegar** and **1 tablespoon olive oil.** Season with S&P and toss with your hands to coat. To eat, drizzle the beans and cauliflower with garlic mayo and parsley.

· Also good with polenta (p. 203), a puddle of tomato sauce, and/or nuts.

Spicy Seared Tofu & Broccoli

Finger food, like Buffalo wings and Ranch.

TOFU

BROCCOLI

GREEK YOGURT

LEMON

HARISSA

GINGER

FOR 4

1. Rip **1 (14- to 16-ounce) block firm or extra-firm tofu** into 1-inch pieces. Pat dry and set aside on paper towels to air-dry. Slice the stems of **1 pound broccoli** (about 1 large head) ½ inch thick. Cut the florets into bite-size florets. In a small bowl, combine **2 cups full-fat Greek yogurt** with the zest from **1 lemon;** season with salt. Squeeze the lemon into a large bowl (about 3 tablespoons juice), then stir in **5 to 6 tablespoons harissa** (depending on brand and heat tolerance) and **¼ cup olive oil.** Finely grate **2 inches ginger** into the harissa and stir to combine. Season with salt.

2. Heat **3 tablespoons olive oil** in a large cast-iron skillet over medium-high. Add the broccoli, cut sides down, season with salt, and cook, without touching, until the undersides are dark brown, 3 to 5 minutes. Stir and cook until the stems give a little when poked with a fork, another 3 to 5 minutes. Add more oil if the pan looks dry. Transfer to the harissa mixture and stir to coat.

3. Add **2 more tablespoons olive oil** to the skillet, still over medium-high. Add the tofu, season with S&P, and cook, turning occasionally, until deeply golden, about 2 minutes per side. Stir the tofu into the harissa to coat. Eat the broccoli and tofu dipped into the yogurt.

· To tame the heat, eat with warm pita, pita chips, or grains.

· To the harissa mix, add grated garlic, chopped shallots, and/or olives.

Kimchi Tempeh Salad **PAGE 88**

Kimchi Tempeh Salad

Where kimchi is all-at-once spicy dressing, vegetable, and pickle.

TEMPEH

KIMCHI

RICE VINEGAR

SESAME OIL

SOY SAUCE

CELERY

GINGER

FOR 4

1. Heat **2 tablespoons neutral oil** in a large nonstick skillet over medium-high. Crumble **1 (8-ounce) block tempeh** into the skillet, seeking pieces of all sizes but no bigger than a walnut. Season with salt and cook, undisturbed, until deeply golden, 1 to 2 minutes. Cook, stirring occasionally, until browned all over, another 3 to 5 minutes. Turn off the heat.

2. Dump **1 (16-ounce) jar cabbage kimchi,** including its juices, into a medium bowl. Using scissors, cut the kimchi into bite-size pieces. Add **2 tablespoons unseasoned rice vinegar, 1 tablespoon toasted sesame oil,** and **2 teaspoons low-sodium soy sauce.** Thinly slice **6 celery stalks** and add to the bowl. Peel and slice **2 inches ginger** into thin matchsticks and add to the bowl.

3. Add the tempeh to the bowl and stir until the tempeh is coated red. Because each batch of kimchi is different, it's wise to taste and adjust. For more salt, add soy sauce. For more tang, add rice vinegar. If it's too intense, add more oil or even mayo. If you want it spicier, add red pepper flakes or sambal oelek. (The salad keeps for 3 days in the fridge.)

· Instead of tempeh, use another firm protein: edamame, soft-boiled eggs, leftover chicken, thinly sliced steak, ground pork, salmon, or canned tuna.

· Good on its own, with sesame seeds or furikake, or with something starchy: rice, boiled potatoes, noodles, or a burger bun.

Ginger straight up: When buying ginger, resist the squiggly branches and instead opt for the boring-looking rods, which are easier to peel and chop.

Pastrami-Spiced Tempeh on Rye

Inspired by the Delaney sandwich at Tommy's in Cleveland Heights, Ohio, where vegetarian food (thankfully) isn't health food.

CHARD

PEPERONCINI

TEMPEH

BROWN
SUGAR

GROUND
CORIANDER

SMOKED
PAPRIKA

DIJON
MUSTARD

RYE BREAD

FOR 4

1. Thinly slice the stems and leaves from **1 bunch chard** and transfer to a bowl. Thinly slice **8 peperoncini (hold on to the jar)** and add to the bowl. Cut **1 (8-ounce) block tempeh** crosswise into 4 pieces, then slice lengthwise through the middle so you end up with 8 thin rectangles. In a measuring cup, combine **½ cup water, 2½ teaspoons dark brown sugar, 1½ teaspoons black pepper, 1½ teaspoons ground coriander, 1 teaspoon smoked paprika, 1 teaspoon Dijon mustard,** and **1 teaspoon salt.**

2. Heat **2 tablespoons olive oil** in a medium skillet over medium-high. Add the tempeh and cook, without touching, until golden underneath, 3 to 5 minutes. Flip, add another tablespoon of oil if the pan looks dry, and repeat on the other side. Reduce the heat to medium-low, pour in the spice mixture, and simmer, flipping the pieces halfway through, until the spices are fragrant and glazed onto the tempeh, 2 to 3 minutes. Turn off the heat.

3. Toast **4 or 8 slices rye bread,** depending on whether you want open-faced or closed sandwiches. Schmear the bread with **Dijon mustard.** Season the chard and peperoncini with S&P. Toss with **3 tablespoons olive oil** and **3 tablespoons peperoncini brine.** Season to taste with S&P. Eat the tempeh on the toast with a heap of chard salad on top and alongside.

· Instead of peperoncini, you could use dill pickles, cornichons, or sauerkraut.

· For a hit of umami, add nutritional yeast or grated Parmesan or Gouda to the salad.

· To make this a griddled sandwich, add mayo to the outsides of the bread, then add the tempeh, chard, and a layer of sliced Cheddar or Swiss. Cook over medium until golden brown, 3 to 4 minutes per side.

Chipotle Mushroom-Tempeh Tacos

Really about the spicy, garlicky peanuts.

GARLIC

PEANUTS

CHIPOTLES
IN ADOBO

CUMIN SEEDS

MUSHROOMS

TEMPEH

TORTILLAS

LIME

FOR 4

1. Heat the oven to 425°F. Thinly slice **6 garlic cloves.** Coarsely chop **½ cup roasted peanuts** and **1 to 2 canned chipotles in adobo** (depending on heat tolerance). Transfer the garlic, peanuts, and chipotle to a medium saucepan, along with **6 tablespoons neutral oil** and **1 teaspoon cumin seeds.**

2. Place a fine-mesh sieve over a medium, heat-proof bowl next to the stove. Bring the peanut mixture to a sizzle over medium-high. Reduce the heat and cook, swirling the pot occasionally, until the garlic is golden around the edges and the oil is terra-cotta orange, 4 to 6 minutes. Drain through the sieve, catching the oil in the bowl below. Season the peanut mixture with S&P.

3. Cut **1 pound mixed mushrooms (cremini, oyster, maitake)** into 1-inch pieces. Crumble **8 ounces tempeh** into pieces smaller than a cherry tomato. Toss the tempeh and mushrooms in the chile oil and season with S&P. Spread out on a sheet pan (hold on to the bowl) and roast, shaking the pan halfway through, until golden brown, 15 to 20 minutes.

4. When the mushrooms and tempeh are done, toast **8 corn or flour tortillas** directly on an oven rack or over your flame, 1 to 2 minutes per side. Transfer the peanuts to the reserved bowl and stir in the juice from half of **1 lime** (about 1 tablespoon). Spoon the mushroom filling into tortillas, then top with the peanuts and another squeeze of lime.

· You could also pan-sear chicken thighs, white fish, or skirt steak in the seasoned oil.

· Another good mushroom taco is Heidi Swanson's chanterelle tacos in *Super Natural Every Day,* even with other mushrooms. They're topped with finely grated Parmesan, an untraditional move that would be good here.

Turmeric Black Pepper Tempeh

In the words of an eleven-year-old, this glaze "tastes like when the sun comes up on the first day of summer vacation."

SHALLOTS

WHITE RICE

TEMPEH

RICE VINEGAR

MAPLE SYRUP

TURMERIC

SOFT HERBS

LIME

FOR 4

1. Coarsely chop **2 shallots.** Heat **2 tablespoons neutral or coconut oil** and the shallots in a medium saucepan over medium-high. Cook until the shallots start to brown, 3 to 5 minutes. Add **1 cup long-grain white rice** and stir to combine. Add **1¾ cups water** and **1 teaspoon salt** and bring to a boil. Cover, reduce the heat to low, and cook for 17 minutes. Remove from the heat and keep covered.

2. Cut **1 (8-ounce) block tempeh** crosswise into four pieces, then into squares. Cut each square through the middle so they are half as thick. Cut each square into triangles (you'll have 32 but who's counting). In a measuring cup, stir together **¼ cup unseasoned rice vinegar, 3 tablespoons maple syrup, 2 teaspoons ground turmeric,** and **2 teaspoons black pepper.** Season with salt. Pluck the leaves and tender stems of **1 to 2 cups soft herbs (dill, cilantro, basil)**—whatever needs using up. Transfer the herbs to a medium bowl.

3. Heat **2 tablespoons neutral or coconut oil** in a large skillet over medium-high. Add the tempeh, season with salt, and cook, without touching, until golden underneath, 2 to 3 minutes. Flip the pieces and repeat on the other side, adding more oil if needed. Reduce the heat to medium-low, pour in the turmeric mixture, and stir until the mixture is glazy, 1 to 2 minutes.

4. Season the herbs with S&P, then toss with enough juice from **1 lime** to lightly coat. Fluff the rice with a fork. Eat the tempeh on top of the rice with a jungle of herbs and another squeeze from the lime (I like to put the herbs under the tempeh so they wilt just slightly).

· Instead of rice, eat with farro, rice noodles, or tucked into lettuce cups or pita.

· This glaze is also good on ground chicken, cubed chicken thighs, or tofu.

· For crunch, consider fried shallots or garlic, sprouts, peanuts, or cashews.

Stew

The '90s gave us many important cookbooks, such as Nigella Lawson's *How to Eat,* Deborah Madison's *Vegetarian Cooking for Everyone,* Sri Owen's *The Rice Book*—and *Romancing the Bean* by Joanne Saltzman. Writing from the point of view of a bean (really), Saltzman declares: "We do not judge. We receive, with open heart, flavors of the world." Beans are especially inviting when simmered into a soup, stew, or otherwise brothy mixture. Like pennies glistening in a fountain, they'll catch your eye and draw you in. "Eat me," they'll whisper when you get close.

Look around the world for your starting point.

The whole entire world eats beans. That is so cool. Let geography guide how to flavor your beans. Think about where, say, chickpeas are eaten, and embellish your batch accordingly, whether Italian (p. 99), Spanish and Portuguese (p. 233), Lebanese (p. 81), Mexican (p. 338), and so on. Or kidney beans could go Indian (heavy cream, ginger, green chile), Iranian (soft herbs, turmeric, lamb), or Cajun (Andouille sausage, onion, bell pepper). That said, if you're making chili and only have gigante beans or want pozole and only have cannellini, they'll probably slip right in.

Bean liquid, bean liquid, it's good for your soup.

Canned beans include a combination of water, salt, and the bean's starch. Use that liquid as you would pasta water, as a thickener rather than a source of flavor. When the contents of your pot have a lot going on and can overpower the sometimes tinny or salty bean liquid, add the bean liquid to give it body. When the stew contents are quite neutral (like there's only water and some garlic), drain the bean liquid away and let the mixture thicken with time on the stove.

(FYI: 1 pound of dried beans cooked equals 3 or 4 cans of beans.)

Start with a pow.

An ingredient full of spice, salt, fat, or umami is the fast pass to turning water and beans into stewy beans. Heavy hitters like harissa, red curry paste, coconut milk, dashi, heavy cream, fire-roasted tomatoes, and anchovies will quickly unleash their full potential. White beans, milk, garlic, and rosemary need just 10 or 15 minutes to coalesce into a creamy spoonful (p. 99). Same with pinto beans, jalapeño, scallions, and coriander (p. 96). Even with these confident ingredients, if you can give the ingredients more time to simmer, do it: They'll only get better.

Remember crunchies (p. 62). Crispy toppings can contrast soft, spoonable beans, which you may or may not want (chewing is overrated sometimes). Good toppings include toasted nuts or seeds, crunchy vegetables, a piece of toast, or chips. Somehow there are two recipes with Fritos in this section.

Casserole your beans. Humble beans turn into a joyous, gather-round kind of food when casseroled—meaning baked with a topping of gooey melted cheese or something crispy-crunchy, like breadcrumbs or nuts.

Cook them in a skillet as opposed to a Dutch oven so the topping is exposed to heat and not shielded by the sides of the pot. For a cheesy topping, once your beans are flavorful, grate cheese on top. On the stovetop, cover the skillet and cook until melted. Or broil uncovered for bubbling, burnished cheese. For a crispy topping of breadcrumbs or nuts, scatter over the beans and broil or bake at a high heat until toasted.

Kinda Refried Beans

A mosh pit of creamy, gooey beans. Chip-diving encouraged.

FRESH CHILE

SCALLIONS

CHEDDAR

PEPITAS

PINTO BEANS

WARM SPICE

FOR 4

1. Finely chop ½ **to 1 fresh chile (jalapeño, serrano).** Thinly slice **3 scallions.** Grate 1½ **cups sharp Cheddar cheese** (about 6 ounces) on the large holes of a box grater.

2. In a medium skillet over medium, toast ¼ **cup pepitas** until golden and starting to pop, 2 to 3 minutes. Transfer to a small bowl, season with S&P, and keep the skillet where it is.

3. To the skillet still over medium, add **2 (15-ounce) cans pinto beans** with their liquid, **1 teaspoon ground warm spice (coriander, cumin, smoked paprika),** and half the scallions and chile. Stir to combine, then season with S&P (go easy because some bean liquids are

well salted—you can always salt more at the end). Simmer until the beans are thickened but not dry, mashing with a spoon or potato masher every so often, 10 to 12 minutes. Add water as needed to adjust the consistency.

4. When the beans are just about done, add the remaining chile and scallions to the pepitas. When the beans are ready, turn off the heat and stir in **2 tablespoons butter.** Taste the beans and adjust seasonings as needed. Sprinkle the cheese over the beans. Cover and cook over low heat just until melted, a minute or two. Top the beans with the pepitas and dig in.

Two hot chile tips

· Fresh chiles keep for up to a year in the freezer, so whenever you find in-season or trickier-to-find varieties, buy a bunch and freeze them. Grate or chop from frozen and they'll thaw then and there. (Other treats to freeze: fresh bay and curry leaves, Parmesan rinds, sliced good bread, peanut butter cups.)

· Instead of chopping the stem off your chile, use it as a handle to hold the chile in place. Slice the chile lengthwise, rotate, cut again, and continue until the chile is sliced as thin as you want (this could mean just halved for a Thai chile or quartered for a serrano). Now slice crosswise for finely chopped chile without burning eyeballs.

Creamy Beans & Greens

Warm milk, rosemary oil, beans, greens.

BITTER
WINTER
GREENS

GARLIC

WHITE
BEANS

ROSEMARY

MILK

CRUSTY
BREAD

FOR 4

1. Trim and cut **1 head or bunch bitter winter greens (escarole, kale, broccoli rabe)** into 1-inch-thick strips. Smash and peel **6 garlic cloves.** Drain and rinse **2 (15-ounce) cans white beans (cannellini, Great Northern) or chickpeas.** Use a mix if you're feeling it. Pat **3 rosemary sprigs** dry.

2. In a large Dutch oven, heat **¼ cup olive oil** over medium-low. Add the rosemary sprigs and fry until the leaves are crisp and sizzling subsides, 3 to 4 minutes. Transfer to a paper towel, season with S&P, and keep the pot where it is.

3. Add the garlic and cook until freckled gold, just a minute or two. Add the greens, season with S&P, and toss until wilted, a minute or two. Add **1½ cups whole milk,** the beans, and **½ teaspoon red pepper flakes.** Season with S&P and bring to a gentle simmer (avoid a full boil). Reduce the heat to maintain the simmer, then partially cover and cook until the mixture has thickened slightly and tastes great, 10 to 15 minutes. Season to taste with S&P.

4. Remove the rosemary leaves from the sprigs by pinching the top of the sprig and swiping downward. Crumble them between your fingers and add them to the beans. Eat the beans and greens on top of or alongside **crusty bread,** with a drizzle of olive oil on top. (Keeps for 3 days in the fridge.)

· If you have a Parmesan rind, add it in with the milk in step 3.

Black Bean Soup with Lots of Fritos

Like getting dressed for a Zoom happy hour, party on top, sweatpants on the bottom.

ONION

GARLIC

CHIPOTLE IN ADOBO

TOMATO PASTE

BLACK BEANS

COCOA POWDER

APPLE CIDER VINEGAR

FRITOS

FOR 4

1. Coarsely chop **1 large white onion.** Thinly slice **4 garlic cloves.** Finely chop **1 canned chipotle in adobo** (hold on to the can).

2. In a large Dutch oven or pot, melt **2 tablespoons butter** over medium-high. Reserve ¼ cup of the onion, then add the rest to the pot, season with S&P, and cook, stirring occasionally, until softened, 3 to 5 minutes. Add the garlic and stir to combine. Cook until fragrant, about 1 minute. Add ¼ **cup tomato paste,** the chopped chipotle, and **1 teaspoon adobo sauce** from the can. Cook, stirring occasionally, until the tomato paste is a shade darker, about 2 minutes.

3. Stir in **2 (15-ounce) cans black beans** with their liquid and **2 tablespoons unsweetened cocoa powder.** Fill one can with water and add that, too. Bring to a boil, then reduce the heat to medium-low and simmer, stirring occasionally and smashing some beans on the side of the pot, until thickened and flavorful, 20 to 25 minutes. Stir in **1 teaspoon apple cider vinegar,** then season to taste with S&P. (Keeps for 3 days in the fridge and freezes well.) Eat topped with the remaining onions and **Fritos.**

French Onion White Bean Bake

Hibernation fare.

ONIONS

GRUYÈRE

WHITE BEANS

THYME

APPLE CIDER VINEGAR

CHICKEN STOCK

A rich dish for 4

1. Heat the oven to 475°F. Halve and thinly slice **1 pound yellow onions.** Coarsely grate **½ cup Gruyère cheese** (about 4 ounces)—or a mix of Gruyère and Parm. Drain and rinse **2 (15-ounce) cans white beans (cannellini, Great Northern).**

2. In a medium, ovenproof skillet, melt **2 tablespoons butter** over medium-high. Add the onions and season with S&P. Cover and cook, stirring once or twice, until the onions are softened, 3 to 5 minutes. Uncover, strip the leaves from **3 thyme sprigs** into the pot, and cook until the onions are jammy and deep golden brown, 10 to 15 minutes. As browned bits appear, add a tablespoon or so of water and stir to combine. Once evaporated, add another tablespoon and repeat; this prevents burning and speeds the process up. If you can caramelize the onions even longer, go for it: the darker their color, the sweeter their flavor.

3. Add **1 tablespoon apple cider or white wine vinegar** and stir until evaporated, about 1 minute. Remove from the heat, then add the beans and **½ cup chicken stock.** Season with S&P and bring to a boil. Sprinkle the cheese evenly over top, especially around the edges for crispy bits. Bake until the cheese has melted and browned in spots, 5 to 10 minutes. If the top is not as toasted as you'd like, broil for a minute or two.

Olive Oil–Braised Chickpeas

Always good to have around.

GARLIC

ANCHOVY

CHICKPEAS

LEMON

FOR 4

1. Heat the oven to 375°F. Thinly slice **8 garlic cloves.** Drain **1 (2-ounce) can anchovy fillets** (about 12). Drain and rinse **2 (15-ounce) cans chickpeas.**

2. In a large ovenproof skillet or Dutch oven over medium, combine **1 cup olive oil,** the garlic, anchovies, and **½ teaspoon red pepper flakes.** Cook, mashing up the anchovies, until fragrant but the garlic is not brown, 3 to 4 minutes. Stir in the chickpeas and season with pepper.

3. Cover with a lid or foil and bake for about 40 minutes, until the chickpeas are soft and crisp in parts. Let cool slightly, then taste—soft and savory, right? Balance with some juice from **1 lemon.** Eat with plenty of the oil. (Keeps for 4 days in the fridge.)

- You can also braise a vegetable with the chickpeas, like broccoli rabe, mini peppers, or cauliflower.

- Eat bagna cauda–style with thinly sliced crunchy vegetables and bread. Tumble over pasta, grains, yogurt, feta, or mozzarella. Toss through hearty greens or canned tuna.

More olive oil braises

- Carrots + harissa + black olives

- Cherry tomatoes + thyme + lemon slices

- Whole shallots + vinegar

- Broccoli rabe + capers + rosemary

- Cauliflower + turmeric + red pepper flakes

- Salmon + chile (p. 379)

- Green beans + smoked paprika + feta

Harissa Chickpeas with Feta

A one-pan bear hug.

GARLIC

FETA

TOMATO
PASTE

HARISSA

GROUND
CUMIN

CHICKPEAS

CAPERS

FOR 4

1. Heat the oven to 450°F. Smash and peel **8 garlic cloves.** Slice **4 ounces feta** into ¼-inch slices.

2. In a medium, ovenproof skillet, heat **3 tablespoons olive oil** over medium. Add the garlic and cook, smashing and stirring with your spoon, until golden and sticking to the pan, 3 to 4 minutes. Add **¼ cup double-concentrate tomato paste, 2 teaspoons harissa,** and **1 teaspoon ground cumin** and cook until a shade darker, 2 to 3 minutes.

3. Add **2 (15-ounce) cans chickpeas** with their liquid and **2 tablespoons capers.** Taste and adjust S&P and harissa. Bring to a gentle boil. Break up the feta into bite-size pieces and add to the top of the skillet. Drizzle with **olive oil,** then bake until the cheese is soft and the tomato sauce has thickened, 15 to 20 minutes. Broil if you want crispy cheese in spots. Let sit for a few minutes before going in.

- For something close to garides saganaki, trade the chickpeas for shrimp and ditch the harissa.

- For a soup, skip the oven and feta, add water with the chickpeas, and smash some chickpeas to thicken.

- To tame the heat, eat with honey, yogurt, pita—or pita chips under the chickpeas like fattet hummus.

Lentil Soup on Spring Break

When your brain knows it's spring, but your heart still says "soup."

SCALLIONS

SPRING VEG

LEMON

GREEN LENTILS

FENNEL SEEDS

FOR 4 wannabe
spring breakers

1. Thinly slice **7 scallions,** keeping white and green parts separate. Trim the stem ends from **1 pound spring veg (any mix of snap peas, snow peas, green beans),** then cut into ½-inch lengths crosswise. Using a vegetable peeler, peel **4** wide strips of rind off **1 lemon.**

2. In a large Dutch oven, heat **¼ cup olive oil** over medium-high. Add the scallion whites and cook until softened, 3 to 5 minutes. Add the vegetables and lemon peel. Season with S&P and cook until bright green, 3 to 5 minutes. Add **1½ cups green lentils, 1 teaspoon fennel seeds,** and **½ teaspoon red pepper flakes** and stir to coat. Add **6 cups water,** partially cover, and bring to a simmer. Uncover, reduce the heat to medium-low, and cook until the lentils and vegetables are tender, 20 to 25 minutes. Don't be alarmed: You want the vegetables brown and soft (and therefore sweet), and the lentils cradled by just a little liquid.

3. While you wait, perhaps fry some bread, specifically a turmeric-fried bread (see right), which doubles down on the soup's warmth and earthiness.

4. Remove the lentils from the heat. Add the scallion greens, then season to taste with S&P and lemon juice (it'll need all these things). Eat as is or over toast, with a drizzle of olive oil.

Fried toasts!

- **Classic:** Heat ¼ cup oil over medium, add four ½-inch-thick slices of crusty or sourdough bread, and fry until crispy on both sides, 1 to 2 minutes. Season with S&P. Look: A giant crouton!

- **Spiced:** Mix a teaspoon of ground spices (turmeric, smoked paprika, coriander) into the oil and swirl the pan to combine. Add the bread and fry over medium until golden on both sides.

- **Cinnamon toast:** After flipping the bread, sprinkle cinnamon sugar on the toasted side. When the bottom is toasted, flip again and cook until the sugar sizzles and melts, just 30 seconds to 1 minute. Sprinkle with more cinnamon sugar.

- **Egg in a hole:** See page 53.

Sloppy Lennys

No ordinary Joes.

ONION

PICKLED
PEPPERS

CHILI
POWDER

RED LENTILS

KETCHUP

DIJON
MUSTARD

BROWN
SUGAR

SOY SAUCE

BURGER
BUNS

FOR 4

1. Coarsely chop **1 large yellow onion** and **3 pickled peppers (cherry, Peppadew),** flicking away any seeds (hold on to the jar).

2. In a large Dutch oven, heat **¼ cup olive oil** over medium. Add the onion and peppers, season with salt, and cook until softened and starting to brown, 5 to 7 minutes. Add **1 tablespoon chili powder** and cook until fragrant, 1 minute. Add **1 tablespoon pickled pepper brine** and stir, scraping up browned bits, until nearly evaporated, 1 to 2 minutes.

3. Add all this stuff: **4 cups water, 1 cup red lentils, ½ cup ketchup, 2 tablespoons Dijon mustard, 1 tablespoon dark brown sugar, 1 tablespoon low-sodium soy sauce,** and **1 teaspoon ground black pepper.** Season liberally with salt.

4. Bring to a simmer, then reduce the heat to medium-low and cook, stirring to unstick any lentils, until the lentils are tender and start to fall apart, 20 to 25 minutes. If you want less slop, keep simmering until it's as thick as you want. If the mixture looks dry and the lentils aren't done yet, add more water. (Keeps for up to 4 days in the fridge. Rewarm with water to loosen.)

5. Eat the sloppy lentils—excuse me, Lennys—on toasted **burger buns** with more sliced pickled peppers.

· For crunch, top with Fritos or fried onions.

· For hacked baked beans, swap the lentils for 2 undrained cans of pink, pinto, or navy beans.

· Skip the bun and it's a great stew all on its own.

PASTA

Butter (verb)

A noodle sauced with nothing more than butter and cheese is kind of the best sometimes (see Bad Day at Work Pasta on page 122). But there are many, many ways to butter noodles.

Think outside the dried pasta box.

Delicate and glossy butter sauces are good with curly and ridged noodles, on which sauce can nestle, as well as with long noodles like fettuccine that can be dragged through pools of sauce. But also consider pan-crisped gnocchi (below) for textural contrast to the creamy sauce. Ravioli or another stuffed pasta only need a glaze of butter because they're already thumping with flavor. And this is your chance for fresh pasta: More tender than dried, it won't be trampled by a butter sauce.

Shelf-stable gnocchi, where pasta meets Gummi Bear.

Shelf-stable gnocchi are not like homemade ones: They're chewy like mochi, and, when crisped in a pan, develop a golden-brown crust. Because they don't need to be boiled, they're fast alternatives to pasta or potatoes (Nigella Lawson calls them eight-minute roasted potatoes). To pan-fry store-bought gnocchi (both the vacuum-sealed one in the pasta aisle and the refrigerated gnocchi near the fresh pasta), heat a little olive oil in a large skillet over medium-high. Break up any stuck-together gnocchi, add to the skillet in an even layer, cover, and cook, undisturbed, until golden brown, 2 to 4 minutes. Cook, stirring, until crisp on both sides, another 2 to 3 minutes. Choose a light sauce that won't thwart the crispy outsides. Butter, perhaps?

Multitask with two pots.

If the sauce is just butter and pasta water—without any bloomed aromatics or browned veg—it comes together so quickly that you can make it in the pot after the pasta's drained (p. 119). But generally, drained pasta doesn't like to sit and wait for sauce. It clumps in anger. Instead, get the sauce ready in a second pot while the pasta boils. If the sauce is ready but the pasta isn't, remove the sauce from the burner so it doesn't burn. If it looks like it's going from browned to black, add a little water, vinegar, or lemon juice to really make it stop. When the pasta's ready, add it and some pasta water to the sauce over moderate heat, stirring to warm and combine.

Sauce, starch—and something else? Your pasta pot and sauce pot are both opportunities to add a vegetable or protein. Add boiling vegetables, like kale, broccoli, or peas, or a quick-cooking protein, like shrimp, to the pasta pot during the last few minutes of the pasta cooking, timing the additions so they're ready with the pasta. In the sauce pot, sauté vegetables, like mushrooms, zucchini, or sweet potatoes, or ground meat, sausage, or cured meat in olive oil before adding butter to make sauce.

Infuse the butter. Melted butter carries the flavor of whatever's cooked in it. When you add butter to the pot, you can also add anything that has oils to release: nuts, olives, anchovies, lemon peel, 'nduja, garlic, dried chiles, or spices.

Brown the butter. For campfire feelings in a pot, brown the butter: Cook it over medium-high for a few minutes, until you start to see brown speckles and it smells toasty and nutty. (The visual cues will be most evident in a light-colored vessel.) Once the butter's browned, remove it from the heat and add a little water, vinegar, or lemon juice to stop the cooking—or time it just right so you can add the pasta and pasta water straight away.

Skip fishing for pasta water. Ever try to scoop up pasta water from the pot and end up with a measuring cup full of noodles? Avoid that minor annoyance by putting a measuring cup in your colander. When the pasta's ready to be drained, slowly pour the pot into the measuring cup: If you pour slowly enough, you'll just get water. If you miss, your noodles will be caught in the colander. Remove the cup and continue to drain the pasta into the colander.

Drop acid. Whether it's vinegar, white wine, tomatoes, or citrus, an acidic ingredient will help buttery pastas from tasting one-note (that note being: rich). Vinegar and white wine need to be cooked some to mellow. You can also cook tomatoes down with butter to turn them jammy (p. 143). Add bright notes with lemon zest and juice at the very end. For a softer effect, warm the lemon juice in the sauce.

DIY pre-grated cheese. The second most convenient way to always have grated cheese is to arm eager helpers with a big hunk of cheese and a Microplane. Have them grate the whole block into a container, which you can keep in the fridge for two to three weeks (freeze the Parm rind for soup). This cheese will beat the store-bought pre-grated stuff on taste and meltability, if not on speed.

More butter? You've melted butter, maybe added some flavorings to the butter, added the pasta and pasta water to the butter sauce, tossed and tossed, maybe added something acidic—and yet the sauce isn't as bouncy and luscious as you'd like. A little more butter at the end can fix that: Adding cold butter a bit at a time to warm liquid results in a creamy, emulsified sauce. Cut the butter into small pieces and add to the sides of the pan for even, quick melting. If your sauce breaks, add drops of hot water and toss until it comes back together.

Welcome to heaven: cured chorizo + butter.

50/50 Buttered Noodles & Greens

A cream sauce that forgets all about heavy cream.

BUTTER

BROCCOLI RABE

PARMESAN

LONG NOODLES

FOR 4

1. Bring a large pot halfway filled with salted water to a boil. Cut **8 tablespoons butter** (1 stick) into 8 pieces and stick it back in the fridge. Thinly slice **1 large bunch broccoli rabe** (about a pound), leaving the blossoms whole. Finely grate **1 cup Parmesan** (2 ounces).

2. Add **1 pound long noodles (fettuccine, linguine)** to the boiling water and cook until al dente. It may seem like a snug fit and that's okay—you want extra-starchy pasta water. Two minutes before the pasta's done, add the broccoli rabe. When the rabe and pasta are al dente, reserve **1 cup pasta water** and then drain.

3. Return the pot to the stove over medium-high and add the butter. Cook, swirling occasionally, until the foam subsides, the milk solids turn golden brown, and it smells nutty and toasty, 3 to 4 minutes. Add the pasta and the Parmesan and toss until the cheese has melted. Add pasta water a little at a time until the noodles are coated in sauce, 2 to 3 minutes (you won't need all the pasta water). Season to taste with pepper and more Parm. (P.S. You just made Alfredo, which never used to have heavy cream.)

More classic buttered noodles

- Butter + heavy cream + Cheddar (mac and cheese)
- Butter + crushed peppercorns + Parm + pecorino (cacio e pepe)
- Butter + garlic + red pepper flakes + white wine + parsley + lemon (Scampi, p. 350)
- Whole peeled tomatoes + butter + onion (Marcella Hazan's tomato sauce)
- Butter + garlic + shallot + capers + lemon + parsley (Piccata, p. 289)
- Shallots + white wine + white wine vinegar + butter + lemon juice (beurre blanc)

Salumi Butter Rigatoni

Like a light-on-its-feet ragù, it's got all the umami of meat without much of it.

RIDGED PASTA

SALUMI

BUTTER

PARSLEY

LEMON

GARLIC

FOR 4

1. Bring a large pot of salted water to a boil. Add **1 pound ridged pasta (mezzi rigatoni, elbows)** and cook until al dente. Meanwhile, cut **4 ounces salumi (soppressata, salami, cured chorizo, 'nduja, prosciutto, pancetta).** If the salumi is thinly sliced, like pepperoni or soppressata, rip into bite-size pieces. If it's a log, chop into small cubes. Melt **6 tablespoons butter** in a large Dutch oven over medium-high. Add the salumi and cook until it starts to crisp, 1 to 5 minutes. Turn off the heat and season with lots of black pepper. Use a slotted spoon to transfer the salumi to a plate.

2. Finely chop **1 cup parsley leaves and stems.** Finely grate the zest from **1 lemon** and **1 small garlic clove** over the parsley, then chop it all together. Season with S&P.

3. Reserve **1½ cups pasta water,** then drain the pasta. Add the pasta and ½ cup pasta water to the salumi butter. Cook over medium-high, stirring vigorously and adding more pasta water as needed, until the pasta is well coated. Add the salumi back, along with the juice of half the lemon (about 1½ tablespoons), and stir until the pasta is glossy. Eat with the parsley on top.

Forager's Pasta

Herbs, spices, mushrooms, nature!

MUSHROOMS

CHICKPEAS

LEMON

BUTTER

CHEF'S CHOICE HERBS & SPICES

SHORT PASTA

FOR 4

1. Bring a large pot of salted water to a boil. Trim and tear the caps of **1 pound mushrooms (cremini, shiitake, maitake)** into bite-size pieces. Drain and rinse **1 (15-ounce) can chickpeas.** Peel 2 wide strips of zest from **1 lemon.** Cut **8 tablespoons butter** (1 stick) into 8 pieces and stick it back in the fridge.

2. In a large skillet or Dutch oven (preferably one with a light-colored bottom), heat **3 tablespoons olive oil** over medium-high. Add the mushrooms and chickpeas, season with S&P, and cook, shaking the pan occasionally, until browned, 10 to 15 minutes.

3. Now forage for your **herbs and spices.** Pick up to four of these ingredients: Coarsely smash or grind 1 teaspoon black peppercorns or fennel seeds. Break 1 cinnamon stick in half, or ready a whole nutmeg for dusting. Gather 8 sage leaves, 4 bay leaves, 3 thyme sprigs, or 2 rosemary sprigs.

4. When the mushrooms and chickpeas are just about done, add **12 ounces short, ridged or curly pasta (mezzi rigatoni, gemelli, cavatelli)** to the boiling water and cook until al dente. Reserve **1 cup pasta water,** then drain.

5. When the mushrooms and chickpeas are ready, add the butter around the edges of the pan, then add the herbs, spices, and lemon peel. Season with S&P and cook, stirring, until the butter is golden and foaming, 1 or 2 minutes. Remove from the heat and stir in the juice from the lemon (about 3 tablespoons).

6. Add the pasta to the skillet and return to medium-high. Cook, stirring and adding dribbles of pasta water, until the noodles are coated in sauce. Season to taste with S&P. Pluck out the branches, peels, and sticks as you come across them.

Bad day at work pasta: Some recipes use 12 ounces of pasta so you get the ideal ratio of sauce to pasta. Consider those straggling 4 ounces in the box a gift because you can make yourself pasta with butter and cheese for one of those days. In a medium saucepan, melt a tablespoon of butter over medium-high until it turns brown. Add 2 cups of water and the 4 ounces of pasta—any that cooks in fewer than 10 minutes. Season with a big pinch of salt and cook, stirring, until the pasta is al dente, 8 to 10 minutes. Grate over Parmesan, about ¼ cup but who's watching, and stir to form a glossy sauce. Season with S&P and eat from the pot.

Tortellini with Mortadella & Peas

Ham and peas but make it mortadella.

BUTTER
PISTACHIOS
MORTADELLA
PARMESAN
LEMON
TORTELLINI
CHICKEN STOCK
FROZEN PEAS

FOR 4

1. Cut **4 tablespoons butter** (½ stick) into small pieces and stick it back in the fridge. Coarsely chop **½ cup roasted, unsalted pistachios.** Cut **4 ounces sliced mortadella** into ½-inch pieces. Finely grate **½ cup Parmesan** (1 ounce).

2. In a large nonstick skillet, toast the pistachios in **1 tablespoon olive oil** over medium, stirring occasionally, until golden, 3 to 4 minutes. Transfer to a small bowl. Zest **1 lemon** over the nuts and season with S&P.

3. Heat **another tablespoon olive oil** in the same skillet over medium. Add **16 to 20 ounces fresh cheese tortellini** in a single layer and cook, untouched, until golden brown underneath, 2 to 4 minutes.

4. Add **1½ cups chicken stock, 2 cups frozen peas** (10 ounces), and the mortadella. Stir and season with S&P. Cover and cook until the peas and pasta are tender, 3 to 5 minutes. Add the butter along the edges of the pan and stir until melted, about a minute. Add the Parmesan, stirring until melted. Off the heat, stir in the juice of half the lemon (about 1½ tablespoons). Season to taste with S&P, then top with the pistachios and more Parm.

Other one-pan tortellinis

· **Green olive:** Smash a bunch of green olives and mix with pistachios, lemon zest and juice, Parm, and olive oil.

· **Dipped:** Crisp tortellini and dip in a bowl of tomato sauce like St. Louis's famous toasted ravioli.

· **Creamed shallots:** Simmer heavy cream and chopped shallots together in step 4.

· **In broth:** Warm a very flavorful beef or chicken stock. Drop in the tortellini, maybe peas or greens too, and cook until tender. Grate over lots of Parm.

Olive oil (also a verb)

If pastas competed in an obstacle course, olive oil–sauced pastas would win. They're so speedy, they'd be done before the pasta's cooked. So indestructible, they wouldn't burn like butter. So nimble, they'd support everything from vegetables and proteins to spices, herbs, and nuts. Also, just imagine bucatini on a rope swing, penne tiptoeing across the balance beam, bowties doing the crab walk. Anyway—noodles, on your mark, get set, go.

Utilize all of olive oil's good sides. Olive oil cooks ingredients, carries flavor, and, all on its own, is a sauce with a silky feel and fruity flavor, so anything that you cook in olive oil can potentially become a pasta sauce, as long as it sounds good to you. Warm some olive oil in a large Dutch oven (easier than a skillet for tossing with pasta), then cook and brown the bulky ingredients: vegetables, meat, beans. Add the flavorings—whole or ground spices, hard-stem herbs, chile, garlic, or onions—to the pot to toast and infuse the oil. Remove from the heat until the pasta's ready. Add pasta water and the pasta and that oily mix poofs into pasta sauce.

Breeze into a no-cook sauce. For a sauce that's bright and perky, don't cook it at all. Instead, stir it together in a bowl as you would salad dressing. When you add the hot noodles and pasta water, the components will slacken only a little: Vegetables mostly stay tender, garlic loses a bit of its sting, cheese melts. This approach is especially good for ingredients that swelter instead of bloom in heat, like soft herbs or tender greens. Pesto (p. 153) is a perfect example: While the Parm melts, the basil stays green and the nuts crunchy.

Choose dairy for undoubtedly sauced pastas. To avoid a final bowl that tastes dry or unsauced, toss your pasta vigorously with pasta water and maybe also dairy. Add the drained pasta to the sauce over moderate heat and dribble in pasta water, tossing everything together until the sauce clings to the noodles. Add grated cheese like Parm, a crumbly cheese, like feta, or a spoonable dairy (crème fraîche, yogurt, heavy cream) to give the sauce a second source of richness.

Spaghetti Aglio e Olio

So good at satisfying sudden pasta cravings, it's also known as Midnight Pasta.

GARLIC

PARSLEY

LONG
NOODLES

FOR 4

1. Bring a large pot of salted water to a boil. Thinly slice **8 garlic cloves.** Pluck **1 cup parsley leaves** and finely chop.

2. When the water's boiling, add **1 pound spaghetti or other long noodle** and cook until al dente. Reserve **1 cup pasta water,** then drain.

3. Meanwhile, make the sauce: In a large Dutch oven or skillet, heat ⅓ **cup olive oil** and the garlic over medium. When you start to see the very first signs of browning, 2 to 3 minutes, turn off the heat. Add ½ **teaspoon red pepper flakes** and lots of S&P and stir to combine.

4. When the pasta's drained, return the oil to medium-high. Add the pasta, ½ cup pasta water, and the parsley. Simmer, tossing and adding more pasta water as needed, until the pasta is glossed with sauce. Eat with more red pepper flakes and black pepper.

For something different

· **Crunch:** Top with crispy fried eggs (p. 46) and/or breadcrumbs.

· **Heat:** Stir in chopped Calabrian chile or pickled peppers in step 3.

· **Bulk:** Brown mushrooms, chickpeas, or sausage before adding the garlic in step 3. Boil vegetables (cauliflower, broccoli rabe) with the pasta. Sauté grated butternut squash or zucchini in the garlic oil.

· **Salty brine:** Add anchovies, capers, olives, or fish sauce in step 3.

Lemon Black Pepper Shells

Every Friday growing up, I got to pick the pasta. It was only ever this or Rao's marinara.

SHELLS

PARMESAN

LEMONS

FOR 4

1. Bring a large pot of salted water to a boil. Add **1 pound medium shells** (not jumbo) or another ridged pasta and cook until al dente. Meanwhile, finely grate **1 cup Parmesan** (about 2 ounces) and zest 1 teaspoon lemon zest. Halve **2 lemons.** Coarsely grind **1 teaspoon black pepper.**

2. Drain the pasta (no need for pasta water). In the same pot, make the sauce: Squeeze 3 lemon halves (about ¼ cup lemon juice) into the pot. Add the Parmesan, **⅔ cup olive oil,** and the black pepper and stir vigorously (it may never be fully homogeneous, and that's okay). Add the pasta and stir to combine. Season to taste with salt and lemon juice, then top with the lemon zest and more Parm and black pepper. (Also makes a good pasta salad.)

More no-cook, yes-cheese pasta sauces

· Swap out the oil above for ricotta, crème fraîche, or Greek yogurt. Use pasta water to thin.

· Cubed salami + grated garlic + olive oil + pecorino

· Pistachios + mint + harissa + yogurt

· Lemon + goat cheese + anchovy breadcrumbs (p. 140)

· Hazelnuts + chives + soft blue cheese

· Grated corn + ricotta + smoked paprika

Pasta with Rosemary-Fried Walnuts

Pleasantly, sneakily bitter from asparagus, walnuts, and rosemary.

NUTS

ASPARAGUS

SHORT PASTA

ROSEMARY

FETA

FOR 4

1. Bring a large pot of salted water to a boil. Chop **2 cups walnuts (or pistachios or blanched hazelnuts)** into pieces the size of a lentil. Trim **1 bunch asparagus** (about 1 pound) and slice crosswise ¼ inch thick.

2. When the water's boiling, add **1 pound short pasta (orecchiette, cavatelli)** and cook until al dente. Reserve **1 cup pasta water,** then drain.

3. While the pasta's cooking, in a large Dutch oven, combine **½ cup olive oil, 1 rosemary sprig,** and the walnuts over medium. Season generously with S&P and cook, stirring often, until fragrant and golden brown, 3 to 5 minutes. Add the asparagus, season with S&P, and cook, stirring, until the asparagus is crisp-tender, 1 to 2 minutes. Remove from the heat and pluck out the rosemary. Crumble in **4 ounces feta,** stirring to combine until mostly melted.

4. Add the pasta to the walnuts and asparagus and cook over medium-low, stirring and adding dribbles of pasta water as needed, until the pasta is well coated. Season to taste with S&P.

· Instead of asparagus, use thinly sliced cauliflower, cabbage, or leeks.

· The rosemary could be thyme or sage. Or add fennel seeds, smoked paprika, or red pepper flakes. Instead of feta, use goat cheese or ricotta.

OLIVE OIL (ALSO A VERB)

133

Chile Shrimp Pasta

Hot shrimp, cool cream.

SHRIMP

GARLIC

LEMON

LONG
NOODLES

CRÈME
FRAÎCHE

SAMBAL OELEK

FOR 4

1. Bring a large pot of salted water to a boil. Meanwhile, peel and devein **1 pound large shrimp.** Pat dry and season with S&P. Thinly slice **6 garlic cloves.** Zest and halve **1 lemon.**

2. When the water's boiling, add **1 pound long noodles (spaghetti, linguine)** and cook until al dente. In the last 2 minutes of cooking, add the lemon halves. Reserve **1 cup pasta water,** then drain. Reserve the lemon halves.

3. While the pasta's cooking, in a large Dutch oven, heat **6 tablespoons olive oil** and the garlic over medium-high. When the garlic starts to sizzle furiously, 1 to 2 minutes, add the shrimp. Cook, stirring, until the shrimp are just pink but not yet cooked through, 2 to 3 minutes. Cover and remove from the heat until the pasta's ready.

4. To the pot with the shrimp, add **½ cup crème fraîche, 2 tablespoons sambal oelek,** the lemon zest, the juice from the boiled lemon halves, and the pasta. Toss to coat. If necessary, add dribbles of pasta water so the sauce glosses the noodles. Season to taste with S&P.

· For greenery, stir in some baby arugula, basil, or pea greens at the end.

Tomato

Pasta with tomato sauce is the ultimate fast food: jar of sauce, box of pasta, Parm. Or: chopped ripe tomatoes, salt, olive oil, basil. It's also the ultimate slow food: a big pot of tomatoes bubbling all day long. For something in between, follow along.

Ditch fresh tomatoes. Fresh tomatoes are too unpredictable for making sauce. You never know if they'll be watery, mealy, rock-hard, or just okay. If you were suckered into pretty tomatoes that aren't working for you, don't give up on them: Make Good Sauce of So-So Tomatoes (p. 139) and get canned tomatoes for your next batch of sauce. (If you have great tomatoes, they don't need cooking—chop, salt, mix with olive oil, marinate. Toss with pasta, pasta water, maybe Parm, maybe basil.)

Crack open canned options. Tomatoes are canned at their peak, full of sweetness, acidity, and umami. For sauce, pick canned crushed tomatoes, tomato passata, or tomato puree before whole, peeled tomatoes because their texture is already closer to sauce. Crushed tomatoes have a rustic texture, while tomato passata and puree will be closer to a blended tomato sauce. Fire-roasted tomatoes add a whiff of smoke because they were charred over a real flame. Allegedly. Avoid diced tomatoes, which struggle to break down because they get treated with calcium chloride to preserve firmness (dicey!).

Don't overlook the wee tube of tomato paste. In a tiny tube, can, or jar of tomato paste, nary a drop of water, seed, or peel dilutes the tomato's tomato-ness. Made by cooking down tomatoes for hours, straining, then reducing further to concentrate (so you don't have to!), it can add a savory backbone to many a tomato sauce, chili, soup, pizza, or stewy bean. The tube is doubly concentrated and tastes more like sun-dried tomato than the canned or jarred paste, which is sweeter.

To use tomato paste, fry a few tablespoons in olive oil until it turns a shade darker and sticks to the bottom of the pan (those are the sugars caramelizing). Deglaze with aromatics and water for an oily, thin sauce (p. 140) or follow it with canned tomatoes (p. 144).

Garlic! How you treat your garlic offers an opportunity for self-expression. If you want sweet and gentle garlic, coarsely chop it and let it soften but not color. If you want it deeply toasted, thinly slice cloves and fry until the edges are golden. If you want to taste its full range of flavors, from friendly and golden to spicy and a little bitter, smash garlic cloves and fry until sticky and caramelized. If you like the kick of fresh garlic, grate a clove into the finished sauce.

Make sauce in the oven. When you let sauce ingredients concentrate in the oven, not only do you prevent murder-scene splatters on your stove, but the tomatoes get jammy and so sweet without any attention from you (p. 143). Choose the stove when you need speed or want to pay closer attention to the sauce, like you're simultaneously cooking meatballs in it (p. 333). Partially cover the pot to (partially) avoid splatters.

Bring on fat and salt. Balance tomatoes' sweetness and acid with fat and salt. Fat could be from butter, olive oil, ground meat, sausage, cured meat like pancetta or chorizo, heavy cream, ricotta, or mozzarella. Salt could be from anchovies, olives, capers, cured meat, soy or fish sauce, Parmesan or other hard salty cheeses, and plain old salt. Salt at every stage of cooking the sauce. Taste, salt, repeat.

Don't make sauce at all. A jar of Rao's marinara is pricey but the gold standard of tomato sauce: pure, fresh, well-seasoned tomato in sauce form. Stir it through some pasta, or speaking from experience, eat it like tomato soup (with a fried egg).

Good Sauce of So-So Tomatoes

Roasting with olive oil, salt, and sugar brings out the tomato
in even the duds.

TOMATOES

GARLIC

MAKES 4 CUPS
(for 2 pounds
of pasta)

1. Heat the oven to 400°F. Cut **3 pounds tomatoes**—any size, color, and quality. If they're the size of cherries or grapes, leave them whole. If they're bigger than your fist, quarter them. If they're somewhere in between, halve them.

2. Transfer the tomatoes to an ovenproof dish or pan where they can fit in one layer. Smash but don't peel **6 garlic cloves** and add to the dish. Add **1 cup olive oil, 1 teaspoon red pepper flakes, 1 teaspoon sugar,** and **1 teaspoon salt.** If you have any herbs or fennel or coriander seeds, add those too. Toss to coat in the olive oil and arrange the tomatoes skin side up.

3. Roast until the tomato skins start to lift off and are browned in spots, 30 to 40 minutes. If you can give it more time, the flavors will concentrate further. Let the tomatoes cool until you can touch them, then remove anything you don't want to eat: garlic peels, tomato skins, rosemary sprigs. For small or stubborn tomatoes, don't bother peeling; it's a rustic sauce no matter what.

4. To use right away, transfer to a pot, or if you're making ahead, transfer to a container. Then mash with a fork or potato masher. (For a smooth sauce, puree in a blender.) Season with S&P. (Keeps for 4 days in the fridge or a month in the freezer.) To eat with pasta, simmer with pasta water until the sauce coats the noodles.

One-Pot Puttanesca

With optional but recommended anchovy breadcrumbs.

GARLIC

OLIVES

ANCHOVIES

TOMATO PASTE

CAPERS

SMALL PASTA

SPINACH

FOR 4

1. Thinly slice **6 garlic cloves** and coarsely chop **½ cup Kalamata olives.**

2. Heat **⅓ cup olive oil, 2 anchovies,** and the garlic in a medium saucepan or Dutch oven over medium. Cook, smashing the anchovies with your spoon, until the garlic starts to brown around the edges, 3 to 4 minutes.

3. Add the olives, **6 tablespoons double-concentrate tomato paste, 3 tablespoons capers,** and **¼ teaspoon red pepper flakes.** Season with **½ teaspoon salt** and cook, stirring, until the tomato paste turns a shade darker, 3 to 4 minutes. Add **4 cups water** and bring to a boil over high.

4. Once boiling, add **8 ounces small pasta (ditalini, orzo, mini shells, about 1½ cups)** and **5 ounces baby spinach** (about 4½ cups), ripping the leaves into smaller pieces as you plop them in. Stir to combine, then reduce the heat to medium and simmer, stirring often to keep the pasta from sticking, until cooked through, 10 to 12 minutes. While you wait, maybe make some anchovy breadcrumbs (below). Eat with a sprinkle of those, a drizzle of olive oil, more red pepper flakes, and a spoon.

Anchovy breadcrumbs for salty crunch:
In a medium skillet, heat 2 tablespoons olive oil and 2 anchovies over medium. Add ½ cup panko breadcrumbs and a pinch of red pepper flakes and salt and cook, stirring often, until golden brown, 2 to 3 minutes. Transfer to a bowl. Season to taste.

All-Corner-Pieces Baked Pasta

Every bite saucy, gooey, crispy.

CANNED TOMATOES

ONION

BUTTER

MOZZARELLA

PARMESAN

RICOTTA

RIDGED PASTA

FOR 4, with leftovers

1. Heat the oven to 450°F with a rack toward the top. Pour **2 (28-ounce) cans crushed tomatoes** onto a sheet pan. Halve and thinly slice **1 medium yellow onion.** Cut **8 tablespoons butter** (1 stick) into small pieces. Add the onion, butter, and ½ **teaspoon red pepper flakes** to the sheet pan. Season with **1 teaspoon salt** and a few generous grinds of pepper and stir to combine. Roast, stirring a few times, until the mixture is thickened and concentrated, 30 to 40 minutes.

2. Bring a large pot of salted water to a boil. While the sauce is cooking, cut **6 ounces salted fresh or low-moisture mozzarella** into ½-inch pieces. Finely grate ½ **cup Parmesan** (1 ounce). Season ½ **cup whole-milk ricotta** (6 ounces) with S&P. Toward the end of the sauce cooking, add **1 pound ridged pasta (rigatoni, cavatappi)** to the boiling water and cook until al dente. Reserve **1 cup pasta water,** then drain the pasta and add it back to the pot.

3. When the sauce is done, switch the oven to broil. Mash the sauce with a fork or potato masher, then season to taste with S&P. Spoon or pour it over the pasta, add ½ cup pasta water, and stir to combine. If it seems dry, add more pasta water. Pour the pasta back onto the sheet pan and spread into an even layer. Scatter spoonfuls of ricotta over the pasta, then sprinkle with mozzarella and Parmesan. Broil until the cheeses are melted and everything is golden, rotating the pan for even browning, 5 to 7 minutes.

· For a faster version, sub in 4 cups of jarred tomato sauce.

How to turn (most) any pasta into baked pasta:
Heat your oven between 450°F and 500°F. Make pasta and toss with a creamy, tomato, or vegetable-based sauce (avoid olive oil or butter sauces, which won't behave well in the oven). Transfer the sauced pasta to a shallow baking dish or skillet. Add a crispy and/or gooey topping—cheese, panko, nuts, Ritz crackers—and bake until the sauce bubbles, the cheese melts, and the top browns, just 5 to 10 minutes.

TOMATO

Spicy Lamb Ragù

Just as good on rice, on couscous, or between buns.

CARROTS

ONION

GROUND LAMB

TOMATO PASTE

HARISSA

CANNED TOMATOES

LONG NOODLES

RICOTTA

FOR 4

1. Bring a large pot of salted water to a boil. Coarsely chop **2 large carrots** and **1 large yellow onion**. In a large Dutch oven, heat **2 tablespoons olive oil** over medium-high. Add the carrots and onion, season with S&P, and cook until soft and browned in spots, 5 to 8 minutes.

2. Add **1 pound ground lamb**, **3 tablespoons tomato paste**, **2 to 3 tablespoons harissa** (depending on brand and heat tolerance), and **1 teaspoon ground black pepper**. Season generously with salt and cook, undisturbed, until the lamb is browned, about 3 minutes. Break the lamb up into smaller pieces and cook, stirring occasionally, until the tomato paste is a shade darker, another 3 to 5 minutes. Add **1 (28-ounce) can fire-roasted or regular crushed tomatoes**. Fill the can halfway with water and add that to the pot too. Season with S&P, bring to a simmer, and cook until thickened and really flavorful, 20 to 25 minutes. (The sauce keeps for 4 days in the fridge.)

3. When the sauce is just about ready, add **1 pound long noodles (pappardelle, bucatini)** to the boiling water and cook until al dente. Reserve **1 cup pasta water**, then drain. Add the pasta to the ragù and simmer, tossing until the noodles are well coated. Thin with drops of pasta water as needed.

4. To eat, plate a little pasta, then add a few small spoonfuls of **whole-milk ricotta**. Repeat until you have as much pasta as you want (this way, you'll get warm pockets of ricotta as you eat).

For something different

· **Crispy lamb and lentils:** After the lamb is browned, add cooked green lentils and cook until the lentils start to crisp. Eat with yogurt, pita, lemon, and rice.

· **Beef ragù:** Use ground beef instead of lamb, nix the harissa, and add garlic, red wine, and rosemary. Simmer until flavorful.

· **Lamb curry:** Sauté ginger and garlic along with the carrot and onion. Use curry powder, garam masala, and/or turmeric in place of the harissa. Add a cubed bulky starch (sweet potato, parsnip) when you add the tomatoes. Eat with rice, roti, pita, or yogurt.

Vegetables plus pasta

Some vegetables can be like tomatoes: With enough chopping, time, fat, and pasta water, they'll become saucy enough to coat noodles. For sturdy vegetables, like broccoli or onions, they'll need to be cooked to submission. For others, like basil or sweet peas, you needn't cook them at all.

Breaking it down. The smaller the vegetable pieces, the more easily they relinquish into sauce. You can grate juicy vegetables like corn, tomatoes, and summer squash. Leave small things like peas alone since you can smash them in the pot. Blanch and finely chop greens to expedite their softening. Everything else (cauliflower, cabbage, brussels sprouts, leeks, shallots, fennel, mushrooms) can be thinly sliced or coarsely chopped.

Slow-roast for an especially sweet situation. The more immediate version of a cooked vegetable sauce is basically sautéing the veg, maybe with aromatics and definitely with salt, until it resembles sauce. The hands-off version happens in the oven. Roast vegetables and aromatics with a generous amount of olive oil until very soft. The vegetables will caramelize and concentrate while the oil gets intensely delicious with whatever's swimming in it. Mash all of that up with a fork or potato masher, then toss this jammy, oily mess with pasta water and it becomes sauce.

Not-so-secret ingredients: salt and time. We need these vegetables tasting like their best selves, like our pasta depends on it. So season with enough salt to draw out the vegetables' water and help them collapse and distill. The longer the vegetables mingle with salt, fat, and seasonings, the more flavorful the sauce.

Find bright spots for brown food. A long-cooked vegetable is a flavorful vegetable, but it may also need some texture and freshness. You can do this by adding less-cooked versions of the same vegetables, like on page 217. Also consider adding brightening, acidic ingredients: Deglaze with wine or vinegar, or add grated cheese or lemon to servings. This is also a great place for a fresh, soft herb, like mint, parsley, or dill.

Make a bright green sauce, even in winter. Thanks to greenhouses and other farming genius, soft herbs and similar tender greens are reliably delicious and available anytime, even when it's snowing. Use the pesto ratio on page 153 to make a perky green pasta sauce: 2 cups packed greens, 1 cup grated Parm, ½ cup nuts, ½ cup olive oil, and some garlic. The greens could be parsley, basil, mint, dill, arugula, spinach, carrot tops, or beet greens. Use a mix or just one, but know that some (mint, dill) are more flavorful than others (parsley, spinach). The nuts, which add heft and creaminess, could be walnuts, hazelnuts, almonds, pistachios, or pine nuts. The garlic could also be scallions, shallot, or chives. Chop it all together and it'll smell like summer.

Corn & Spicy Sausage Orecchiette

This sauce is basically one-ingredient creamed corn.

CORN

SCALLIONS

ORECCHIETTE

HOT ITALIAN
SAUSAGE

FOR 4

1. Bring a large pot of salted water to a boil. Shuck **6 ears of corn.** Place a box grater in a large bowl. Using the large holes, grate 3 of the ears all the way to the cobs (hold on to the cobs). Thinly slice **3 scallions** and add them to the bowl. Cut the corn kernels off the other three cobs and leave them on the cutting board. Using the back of the knife, scrape the liquid off the cobs into the bowl until they're wrung dry. Add all 6 cobs to the pot of water.

2. Once boiling, add **1 pound orecchiette** to the water and cook until al dente. Scoop out **2 cups pasta water–corn stock,** then drain. Discard the corn cobs.

3. While the pasta's cooking, in a large Dutch oven, heat **2 tablespoons olive oil** over medium-high. Remove the casings from **1 pound hot Italian sausage.** Add to the Dutch oven and cook, breaking pieces up with your spoon, until browned, 5 to 8 minutes. Using a slotted spoon, transfer the sausage to the large bowl, leaving the fat behind.

4. Increase the heat to high and add the corn kernels from the cutting board, season with S&P, and cook, undisturbed, until browned, 3 to 4 minutes. Add everything from the large bowl—grated corn, corn juices, scallions, and sausage—to the Dutch oven and stir to combine. Add the pasta and 1 cup reserved water and cook, stirring vigorously, until the pasta is coated in the sauce. Add more pasta water as needed to help the sauce gloss the pasta. Season to taste with S&P.

More veg sauces

· Cauliflower rice + onion + tomato paste + rosemary

· Fennel + fennel seeds + shallot + white wine + cream

· Grated tomato + grated butter

· Smashed peas + fresh mozz + jarred Calabrian chile

· Grated summer squash + thyme + time

Mushroom Orzotto

Fancy-pants mushroom risotto in a quarter of the time.

DRIED MUSHROOMS

GARLIC

MUSHROOMS

PARMESAN

RED WINE VINEGAR

ORZO

FOR 4

1. In a medium saucepan, bring **5 cups water** and **½ ounce dried porcini mushrooms** to a boil over high. Reduce the heat to medium-low to simmer while you . . .

2. Coarsely chop **4 garlic cloves.** Trim and tear the caps of **8 ounces mixed mushrooms (cremini, shiitake, maitake)** into bite-size pieces. Finely grate **½ cup Parmesan** (1 ounce).

3. In a large Dutch oven or saucepan, heat **3 tablespoons olive oil** over medium. Add the fresh mushrooms, season with S&P, and cook, stirring occasionally, until all the liquid is released and the mushrooms are browned, 10 to 15 minutes. Deglaze the pan with **1 tablespoon red wine or Sherry vinegar.** Keep the heat on under the mushrooms while you tend to the stock momentarily.

4. Turn the heat off from under the stock. Spoon out the dried mushrooms and finely chop. To the Dutch oven, still over medium, add **1 tablespoon butter.** Once it's melted, add **1 cup orzo,** the garlic, the chopped rehydrated mushrooms, and **1 teaspoon each S&P.** Cook, stirring, until the garlic is fragrant and the orzo is toasted, about 2 minutes.

5. Add a ladle of the mushroom stock into the orzo, stirring until it's mostly evaporated. Repeat until the orzo is al dente and suspended in a creamy liquid, 10 to 12 minutes. (You probably won't use all the stock—closer to 3 cups. And if you get tired and only stir occasionally, it will still come together.)

6. Off the heat, stir in **2 tablespoons butter** and the Parm. The mixture will be loose but will tighten as it sits; if it already seems dry, add more stock. Season with S&P and more Parm.

· If you have a Parm rind or thyme, sage, bay leaves, or rosemary, by all means add to the stock in step 1.

Pasta with Chopped Pesto & Peas

A coarse pesto is sauce, herb salad, and nut garnish in one.

WALNUTS

SOFT HERBS

PARMESAN

GARLIC

CURLY PASTA

FROZEN PEAS

FOR 4,
hot or cold

1. Bring a large pot of salted water to a boil. In a small or medium skillet over medium, toast ½ **cup walnuts,** shaking the skillet occasionally until toasted (try one to see), 4 to 6 minutes. Transfer to a cutting board to cool.

2. While the nuts are cooling, pluck **2 packed cups soft herb leaves (basil, parsley).** Into a large bowl, grate **1 cup Parmesan** (about 2 ounces) on the small holes of a box grater (or pulse chunks in a blender).

3. Add **1 garlic clove** and a pinch of salt to the pile of nuts and coarsely chop the nuts and garlic together. Add a handful of herbs and another pinch of salt and coarsely chop. Opt for forceful, purposeful chops as opposed to soft, timid ones. Toss and smash the mixture every few chops. Repeat with the remaining herbs, continually salting at each step, until a wet, coarse paste forms. Stir into the cheese, then stir in ½ **cup olive oil.** Season to taste with S&P.

4. Add **1 pound curly pasta (casarecce, fusilli)** to the boiling water and cook until al dente. In the last 3 minutes of cooking, add **2 cups frozen peas** (10 ounces) to the pasta. Reserve **1 cup pasta water,** then drain. Add the pasta and peas to the pesto and stir to combine. Add pasta water as needed to loosen the sauce. Season to taste with S&P, more oil, and more Parm.

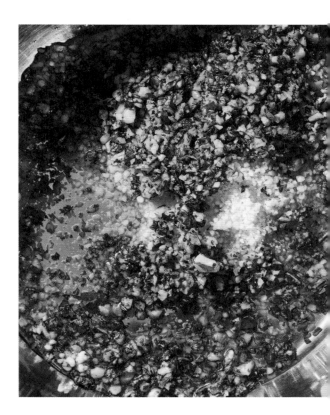

Skillet Broccoli Spaghetti

A watched pot is slow to boil, so skip it.

GARLIC

BROCCOLI

BUTTER

ANCHOVIES

SPAGHETTI

PARMESAN

FOR 4

1. Thinly slice **6 garlic cloves** and transfer to a large skillet with high sides. Cut the florets off **1 to 1½ pounds broccoli,** keeping as much of the branch connected to the trunk as possible. Peel the branch and cut the trunk and branches into ½-inch pieces. Transfer to the skillet. Roughly chop the florets so even the biggest pieces fit on a soup spoon. Leave the florets on the cutting board.

2. To the skillet, add **4 tablespoons butter** (½ stick) and **4 anchovies** and set over medium-high. Cook, smashing the anchovies and stirring the butter around, until the garlic and broccoli are softened, 2 to 3 minutes.

3. Add **12 ounces spaghetti** or any other noodle that cooks in 10 minutes, the florets and any broccoli bits on the board, **2 teaspoons salt,** and **½ teaspoon red pepper flakes.** Pour over **5 cups water.** Increase the heat to high and cook, tossing often with tongs, until the spaghetti is al dente, 8 to 10 minutes. If the pasta is looking dry, add more water. Eat with grated **Parmesan.**

How to make any pasta in a single pan:

In a large skillet or Dutch oven, warm ¼ cup olive oil or butter over medium. Add aromatics and any sauce components that need to be cooked through, like garlic, hearty vegetables, or sausage. Once soft, add 12 ounces of any pasta that cooks in 10 minutes, along with 5 cups water and 2 teaspoons salt. Turn the heat to high and cook, stirring and tossing the pasta constantly, until al dente, 8 to 10 minutes. If it looks dry, add water. Season to taste with S&P.

Chill

Is a pasta salad a pasta ... or a salad? That's a question that probably hasn't crossed your mind, understandably. In this section, pasta salads are made like pasta—there will be noodles and sauce—but they're best cold or at room temp like most salads. Besides that, anything goes.

Dress loud. Flavors mute when they're cold (think about brain-freezing ice cream versus its melty puddle, or salad right from the fridge versus at room temp). To avoid blahness, consider an in-your-face dressing, like pesto (p. 153), puckery lemon cream (p. 78), or tahini-citrus (p. 217). Boost flavor by replacing oil with a big-personality fat, like peanut butter, miso, coconut milk, finely chopped nuts, avocado, egg yolk, or a spoonable dairy.

Go past al dente. It's hard to think of a pasta or noodle that doesn't take to the cold treatment. From little guys, like orzo, Israeli couscous, and ditalini; to big rigatoni or shells; to long soba, udon, or spaghetti; and even stuffed pastas—they all work.

No matter your shape, cook your pasta in salted, boiling water a couple minutes past al dente, until they're soft but not mushy. As they cool, they'll firm to a just-right al dente.

Chill out in the pool of sauce. Drain your pasta, then rinse with cold water just until the steam dies down and you can see the noodles. Toss the noodles in the sauce while they're still warm so they'll soak up the dressing as they cool. Not only will this flavor the noodles, but the fat in the sauce will keep the pasta from clumping.

Add in just at the end. Add fresh and crunchy stuff just when you're ready to eat so they retain their bite. Small bits of raw vegetables and soft herbs are natural additions. You could also add cooked vegetables or proteins, from leftovers to soft-boiled eggs (p. 36), tofu, tinned fish, or beans. Don't forget the treats that keep you going back for another bite. Cube or shave hard cheese. Chop or tear briny, salty ingredients: olives, capers, pickled peppers, pickles, and nori. Contemplate a crunchy sprinkle, too, like chopped nuts, seeds, toasted rice powder, togarashi, furikake, or dukkah.

Fridge if you dare. Despite the kudos pasta salads get for being make-ahead magic, once they're refrigerated, they're never really as good as on Day 1. The flavors need adjusting. The texture can be—interesting. So fridge if you want, but no promises.

Noodles with Juicy Fruits & Peanuts

A tropical vacation.

COCONUT MILK

SAMBAL OELEK

JUICY FRUITS

SALTY PEANUTS

CILANTRO

RICE NOODLES

FOR 4 on a really hot day

1. Bring a large pot of salted water to a boil. Stir **1 (14-ounce) can full-fat coconut milk** with a fork to distribute the cream. Stir in **3½ teaspoons sambal oelek** and **¾ teaspoon salt.**

2. Cut up **2 cups bite-size pieces of juicy fruits (pineapple, mango, oranges, grapefruit, kiwi).** Pick one or some. Coarsely chop **½ cup roasted, salted peanuts** and pick **1 cup cilantro leaves and tender stems.**

3. When the water's boiling, add **20 ounces thin rice vermicelli noodles** and cook according to the package directions. Drain and rinse under cold water until cool to the touch, then shake to get rid of any water. Divide the noodles among bowls, then pour over the coconut dressing. Top with the fruit, peanuts, cilantro, and more sambal oelek.

· You could definitely top these noodles with more than fruit: A number of Southeast Asian dishes combine chewy noodles, a sweet-salty coconut sauce, a fish-saucy sauce, and lots of toppings, including protein (grilled pork, fried tofu, dried or poached shrimp), crunch (toasted coconut, lettuces, sprouts), or zingers (pickled carrot or thinly sliced garlic and ginger).

Couscous & Lentil Greek Salad

Briny, fresh, with twinning Israeli couscous and lentils.

GREEN LENTILS

ISRAELI COUSCOUS

TOMATOES

CUCUMBERS

SHALLOT

RED WINE VINEGAR

OLIVES

BASIL

FETA

FOR 4

1. Bring a large pot of salted water to a boil. Add **½ cup green lentils.** After 10 minutes, add **½ cup Israeli couscous** and stir to combine. Cook until the lentils and couscous are tender, another 10 to 12 minutes.

2. Meanwhile, get everything else ready: Halve **1 pint cherry, grape, or Sungold tomatoes** and chop **4 Persian or mini seedless cucumbers** into bite-size pieces (peel if you like). Transfer the tomatoes and cucumbers to a fine-mesh sieve, toss with **1½ teaspoons salt,** and leave to drain into the sink.

3. Coarsely chop **1 small shallot,** then stir the shallot with **2 tablespoons red wine vinegar** and a pinch of salt in a small bowl. Rip **½ cup pitted Kalamata olives** and **½ cup packed basil leaves** in half (pretty please leave small, cute leaves whole).

4. When the couscous and lentils are just about ready, shake the tomatoes and cucumbers to rid them of any liquid, then transfer to a large bowl. Drain the couscous and lentils into the sieve and add to the tomatoes and cucumbers, along with **¼ cup olive oil.** Use a spoon or your fingers to scoop out the shallot from the vinegar and add to the large bowl. Stir to combine, then add the olives and crumble in **4 ounces feta.** Season to taste with S&P and the shallot vinegar (if your tomatoes are ripe and spritzy, you may not need any vinegar). Stir in the basil.

Tahini-Herb Pasta Salad

Tahini does what dairy can't, like sitting out in the sunshine.

GARLIC

LEMONS

TAHINI

DIJON
MUSTARD

SOFT HERBS

CHICKPEAS

RIDGED PASTA

SESAME SEEDS

FOR 4

1. Bring a large pot of salted water to a boil. Meanwhile, in a large bowl, grate **1 small garlic clove** and the zest of **1 lemon.** Use a fork to vigorously stir in **½ cup tahini** and **1 teaspoon Dijon mustard.** Squeeze in ¼ cup lemon juice (from **1½ lemons**) and stir to combine. Season to taste with S&P. (The mixture will be thick. The dressing will keep in the fridge for a week. Re-season and loosen with S&P and water before using.)

2. Pick **2 cups leaves and tender stems from soft herbs (parsley, dill, mint).** Rip any big leaves in half. Drain and rinse **1 (15-ounce) can chickpeas.**

3. When the water's boiling, add **1 pound ridged or curly pasta (rigatoni, cavatappi)** and the chickpeas and cook until the pasta is just past al dente. Reserve **1 cup pasta water.** Drain and rinse under cold water until cool to the touch, then shake to get rid of any water.

4. Vigorously stir ¼ cup pasta water into the dressing until smooth, then add the pasta and chickpeas and toss until the noodles are well coated. Add more pasta water as needed. Stir in the herbs and **2 tablespoons toasted sesame seeds,** then season to taste with S&P.

More pasta salads

· Giardiniera and its brine + fusilli + salami + chickpeas + provolone

· Chopped green olives + chopped whole lemon (p. 354) + parsley + spaghetti

· Jarred Calabrian chile + crème fraîche + tortellini + mint

· Tzatziki + rigatoni + chopped roasted broccoli rabe

Ginger-Scallion Soba & Shrimp

A zinger with lots of raw, juicy ginger and scallions.

GINGER

SCALLIONS

RICE VINEGAR

SOY SAUCE

SNOW PEAS

SHRIMP

SOBA

FOR 4

1. Bring a large pot of salted water to a boil. Peel and coarsely chop **4 inches ginger.** Coarsely chop **4 scallions.** Make the ginger and scallions into a little pile and top with **2 teaspoons sugar** and **½ teaspoon salt.** Chop and smash together into a coarse paste. Transfer to a large bowl. Stir in ¼ **cup unseasoned rice vinegar, 2 tablespoons low-sodium soy sauce,** and **2 tablespoons neutral oil.**

2. Trim **2 cups snow or snap peas,** then thinly slice on a very sharp diagonal so they're almost shredded. Add to the dressing bowl but don't stir. Peel and devein **1 pound large shrimp.**

3. Add **10 ounces dried soba** to the boiling water and cook according to the package directions. When your soba has 3 minutes remaining, add the shrimp and cook until pink. Drain and rinse under cold water until cool to the touch, then shake to get rid of any water. Add to the bowl of dressing and toss to coat. Taste and add more salt (or soy sauce) as needed.

Other ways to use this dressing

· Spoon over salmon, chicken, tofu, or roasted vegetables (from broccoli to asparagus to squash).

· Stir through rice, udon noodles, scrambled eggs, or soup.

· Dress crisp lettuces, cucumbers, hard-boiled eggs, grains, or slaw.

CHILL . . . .

GRAINS

Fluff

This section is all about the absorption method, which uses a precise amount of water to grains so the water's evaporated when the grains are tender. While it requires more diligence (and luck?) than boiling grains like pasta (p. 184), it has its perks. The main advantage is that the grains are seasoned throughout: Cook the grains with flavorings (even just salt and a pat of butter), and as the liquid is absorbed and the steam is trapped, everything coalesces around the grains. After a short rest and a fluff, you'll have grains exciting enough to be center stage.

Read the back of the package. The cooking method on the back of the package is the most streamlined and reliable: In one of her many trips down black holes, my friend Sarah Jampel found that those instructions were formulated as a one-size-fits-all method for all kitchens and skill levels. When she tested them against methods with more steps and that required more equipment, the package directions didn't always win the side-by-side, but they never failed her.

You can skip the rinse. If you rinse your rice, no one's stopping you. If you have your ideal way of making rice, do that. But you don't *need* to rinse your rice. And before you throw this book away, know that this was focus-grouped and tested endlessly.

In side-by-side tests using a variety of pots, stoves, brands, and both long-grain and sushi rice, rinsed grains were more gummy and mushy than unrinsed grains. I'm not positive why, but here are a few hunches. We are told to rinse rice to remove surface starch, but unless you do a very thorough job of rinsing the rice and shaking it dry, are starches still glommed to the grains? Or because unrinsed rice isn't as agitated, does it hold on to its starch instead of letting it out into the pot? The thinking behind toasting rice is that drier rice absorbs liquid more slowly and better maintains its shape; is unrinsed rice "drier" than rinsed rice?

There is one exception (again, not sure why): When adding other ingredients to the pot that contribute moisture or fat, like coconut milk or vegetables, doing a precursory rinse and shake dry do keep the grains from getting weighed down and gummy.

Bake it. Sometimes I feel like I can only make rice on a certain burner in a certain pot—and more assuredly in the oven. A reliable oven mimics a rice cooker in that it's a controlled, indirect heat source. The even flow of heat from all directions means more even cooking. It's great for rice-cooking novices (and geniuses!) as well as big batches since it can accommodate larger baking dishes than your burner can.

Pilaf it. At its simplest, a pilaf is made by toasting grains in warm fat and perhaps some aromatics, then adding liquid, covering, and cooking until the grains are tender and the liquid's absorbed. The resulting rice is nutty and seasoned to its core, special in few moves.

Beyond classic pilafs like biryani, mujaddara, pulao, plov, and paella, there are options within this structure of fat + flavorings + toasted grain + add-ins + liquid. So many. The fat could be olive or neutral oil, coconut or sesame oil, bacon or chicken fat, or butter or ghee. Bloom aromatics or spices in the warm fat. Then soften bite-size pieces of vegetables. Brown meat. Add fruit or nuts: raisins, currants, almonds. Use one or a mix of grains that cook in the same amount of time. Throw in another starch, like orzo, broken noodles, beans, or lentils. Use stock, coconut milk, or another liquid. Add seasonings like soy or fish sauce, kimchi, citrus peel, harissa, or pesto.

Butter. You can always add butter to cooked grains, but cooking grains *with* butter is like everyday magic. Instead of being coated in a thin slick of butter, the rice is plumped *with* butter, rendering each grain creamy and, um, buttery through and through.

One of my can't-deal-anymore dinners goes like this: Melt a pat of butter in a saucepan. Toast rice, add water and soy sauce, bring to a boil. Cook. Off the heat, top with torn kale, spinach, or other greens. Steam covered. Garnish liberally with any mix of seeds, chile sauce, eggs, and leftovers.

Use your grains as a steamer. As your grains rest off the heat, they firm slightly, making them easier to scoop without squishing. During this waiting period, they can also simultaneously serve as a hot bed where vegetables can steam.

Once your grains are done cooking, off the heat, sprinkle a few handfuls of anything that steams in about 5 minutes over the grains. That could be edamame, fresh or frozen peas, torn kale, spinach, bok choy, or chopped green beans. Season with S&P, cover, and let sit until the veg is tender, about 5 minutes. Fluff and stir with a fork.

My old-faithful white rices. To make white rice on the stove, bring 1¾ cups water to a boil in a covered, medium saucepan. Add 1 cup long-grain white rice and 1 teaspoon salt and stir to combine. Cover, reduce the heat to low, and cook for 17 minutes. Let rest off the heat for 5 minutes, or until the rest of dinner's ready.

To make it in the oven, follow this simplified version of Pierre Franey's method: Heat the oven to 400°F. Combine 1½ cups water, 1 cup long-grain white rice, and ½ teaspoon salt in a medium, oven-proof saucepan or pot. Cover and bake for 17 minutes. Let rest off the heat for 5 minutes, or until the rest of dinner's ready.

Buttered Quinoa with Bok Choy

Raw bok choy's a twofer, with bulbs like celery and leaves like butter lettuce.

QUINOA

FROZEN EDAMAME

BABY BOK CHOY

LIME

FOR 4

1. Melt **2 tablespoons butter** in a medium saucepan over medium until it turns golden and smells nutty, 3 to 5 minutes. Add ¾ **cup quinoa** and ½ **teaspoon salt** and stir to coat in the butter. Add **1¼ cups water** and bring to a boil. Reduce the heat to low, cover, and cook until the water is absorbed and the quinoa is tender, 15 to 17 minutes. Turn off the heat, add ½ **cup frozen, shelled edamame**, season with S&P, cover, and let sit for 5 minutes.

2. Meanwhile, thinly slice **8 ounces baby bok choy** crosswise.

3. When the quinoa is done resting, add the bok choy and the juice from **1 lime** (about 2 tablespoons). Fluff with a fork to combine. Season to taste with S&P. (Leftovers keep for up to 3 days.)

More to steam on hot, cooked grains

· Tofu + basil + ginger
· White beans + marinated artichokes
· Pinto beans + corn + scallions
· Snow peas + preserved lemon
· Thinly sliced kale + fennel + dill
· Shrimp + green beans (p. 366)

Bulgur with Radicchio & a Little Sausage

Takes the bitter with the sweet.

SPICY
SAUSAGE

SESAME
SEEDS

BULGUR

CUCUMBERS

RADICCHIO

LIMES

TAHINI

HONEY

FOR 4

1. Heat **1 tablespoon olive oil** in a medium saucepan over medium-high. Remove **8 ounces spicy sausage (lamb merguez, Mexican chorizo)** from their casings and add to the saucepan. Cook, breaking up with a spoon, until browned and cooked through, 5 to 7 minutes. Using a slotted spoon, transfer the sausage to a plate, leaving the fat behind. Sprinkle the sausage with **2 tablespoons toasted sesame seeds.**

2. To the saucepan, still over medium-high, add **1 cup bulgur** and a pinch of salt and cook, stirring, until it smells toasty, 2 to 3 minutes. Add **1½ cups water** and bring to a simmer, then reduce the heat to low, cover, and cook until tender, 12 to 14 minutes. Let sit off the heat, covered.

3. Thinly slice **2 Persian or mini seedless cucumbers.** Add to a large bowl and season with salt. Rip **2 medium or 4 small heads radicchio** into bite-size pieces. Add to the cukes but don't stir. In a small bowl or measuring cup, zest and juice **1 lime** (about 2 tablespoons juice). Add **¼ cup tahini, ¼ cup water, 1 tablespoon olive oil,** and **2 teaspoons honey.** Season with S&P and stir to combine.

4. When the bulgur's ready, drizzle the radicchio with **2 tablespoons olive oil** and the juice from **another lime** (about 2 tablespoons). Season with S&P and toss with your hands to combine. Fluff the bulgur with a fork, then stir in a tablespoon of the tahini sauce. Add the bulgur to the salad and toss to combine. Put the salad on a platter or plates and top with the sausage, a drizzle of the tahini, and more sesame seeds. (Keeps in the fridge for 3 days and is good warm or at room temp.)

· Make this vegetarian by nixing the sausage and adding soft eggs, roasted winter squash, or crispy chickpeas (p. 81).

· Good with feta, pita chips, nuts, orange slices, and pickled shallots.

Kimchi Rice & Runny Eggs

Two eternal comforts, shakshuka and kimchi fried rice, finally meet.

SCALLIONS

KIMCHI

WHITE RICE

EGGS

SOY SAUCE

FOR 4

1. Thinly slice **4 scallions.** Finely chop **1½ cups cabbage kimchi** (about 8 ounces). Rinse **1 cup long-grain white rice** until the water runs (mostly) clear. Place a large nonstick skillet on a burner, then add **1¾ cups water,** the rice, kimchi, half the scallions, and **1 teaspoon salt.** Bring to a boil over medium-high, then cover with a lid, baking sheet, or foil. Reduce the heat as low as it will go and cook until the rice is tender, 15 to 17 minutes.

2. Uncover the skillet and use your spoon to make 4 large holes in the rice all the way down to the bottom of the pan (this will be where the eggs go). Increase the heat to medium and pour **3 tablespoons neutral oil** down the sides of the pan and into the divots. Cook undisturbed until you see golden rice at the edges, 2 to 3 minutes. If you don't see oil bubbling around the edges or in the holes, drizzle in another tablespoon or two. Adjust the heat as needed to avoid burning.

3. Crack **eggs** into each divot. Season with S&P, then cover and cook until the whites are set and the yolks are still runny, 2 to 3 minutes. Shower with **2 tablespoons low-sodium soy sauce** and the remaining scallions.

· In step 3, before you cover the eggs, you could also grate a cup of Cheddar over the rice. Cheddar and rice: good. Cheddar and eggs: good. Cheddar and kimchi: good!

· For more kick, add some kimchi juice from the jar with the soy sauce.

Do you see Oscar the Grouch too?

Green Rice with Singed Feta

Spring for the golden feta, stay for the herb rice.

SPINACH

DILL

RADISHES WITH GREENS

GARLIC

SCALLIONS

WHITE RICE

LEMON

FETA

FOR 4

1. Coarsely chop **4 cups baby or mature spinach** and **1 cup dill leaves and stems.** Transfer to a big bowl. Remove the greens from **1 bunch radishes** (wash if they're gritty). Coarsely chop the radish greens and add to the bowl. Season with **1½ teaspoons salt** and squeeze with your hands to wilt.

2. Coarsely chop **3 garlic cloves.** Thinly slice **6 scallions,** keeping the white and green parts separate.

3. In a large, oven-proof skillet, heat **¼ cup olive oil** over medium-high. Add the scallion whites, season with S&P, and cook until softened, 3 to 5 minutes. Add **1½ cups long-grain white rice, another tablespoon olive oil,** the garlic, the bowl of greens, and **1 teaspoon salt.** Cook, stirring, until the rice is toasted, 3 to 5 minutes. Add **3 cups water.** Bring to a boil, then cover with a lid, baking sheet, or foil. Reduce the heat as low as it will go and cook until

the rice is tender and you no longer see steam coming from the skillet, 16 to 18 minutes.

4. Meanwhile, heat the broiler with a rack 5 or fewer inches from the heat source. In a medium bowl, stir together the juice of **1 lemon** (about 3 tablespoons) and **2 tablespoons olive oil.** Season with S&P. Thinly slice the radishes. Slice **1 (8-ounce) block feta** into ¼-inch slices, then break each piece in half.

5. Let the rice sit off the heat, still covered, for 5 minutes. Fluff the rice with a fork, then top with feta. Drizzle with **olive oil** and broil until the feta is molten and charred in spots, 6 to 8 minutes. (Depending on your broiler, you may need to rotate the pan for even cooking.) Stir the radishes and scallion greens into the lemon dressing. Eat the rice and feta with the radish-scallion mixture and its dressing.

For something different

· **Spanakorizo:** Diane Kochilas calls spanakorizo "one of the great, classic, simple vegetarian dishes of the Greek table." Instead of mixed greens, just use spinach. Skip the browned feta and top portions with dill, lemon, olive oil, feta, and/or yogurt.

· **Chicken and rice:** Brown both sides of bone-in chicken thighs before softening the aromatics. Continue with the recipe, then add the chicken on top of the rice before you cover it.

Chipotle-Tomato Baked Rice

Slumped tomatoes and their sweet juices, all soaked up by rice.

ONION

CHIPOTLES IN ADOBO

TOMATOES

CINNAMON STICK

WHITE RICE

PEANUTS

LIME

FOR 4

1. Heat the oven to 450°F. Coarsely chop **1 medium yellow onion** and **1 to 2 canned chipotles in adobo,** depending on heat tolerance.

2. In a 9 by 13-inch or other 3-quart baking pan, add **6 tablespoons olive oil, 2 pints cherry or grape tomatoes, 1 cinnamon stick,** and the onion and chipotle. Season with S&P. Roast until the tomatoes are soft, 15 to 20 minutes.

3. Meanwhile, rinse **1½ cups long-grain white rice** until the water runs clear. Coarsely chop **½ cup roasted, salted peanuts.** Add the rice in an even layer on top of the tomatoes, followed by **2½ cups water** and **1 teaspoon salt.** Seal the pan tightly with foil and bake until the rice is tender, 20 to 22 minutes.

4. Remove from the oven and let sit, still covered, for 5 minutes. Stir the rice to mix, and discard the cinnamon stick. Eat with a healthy sprinkle of peanuts and a squeeze of juice from **1 lime.**

· For on top: lime-dressed watercress, a fried egg, melted Cheddar, cilantro, black beans.

FLUFF

One-Pot Rice & Beans

The power couple.

ONION

GARLIC

WHITE RICE

GROUND
CUMIN

BLACK BEANS

FOR 4

1. Coarsely chop **1 yellow onion** and **3 garlic cloves.**

2. In a large saucepan or Dutch oven with a tight-fitting lid, warm **2 tablespoons olive oil** (or butter) over medium. Add the onion and garlic, season with salt, and cook until softened, 3 to 5 minutes. Add **1 cup long-grain white rice, 1 teaspoon salt,** and **½ teaspoon ground cumin** and stir until toasted, 1 to 2 minutes. Add **1 (15-ounce) can black or pinto beans** with the liquid. Fill the can with water or stock and add that too (that's 1¾ cups if you're not using canned beans).

3. Bring to a boil over high, then cover, turn the heat down as low as it will go, and simmer, untouched, for 17 minutes. Let sit off the heat for a few minutes, then mix with a fork. Season to taste with S&P.

More rice and beans

- **Chipotle-style cilantro-lime rice:** Add chopped cilantro and lime juice and zest.

- **Spicy rice and beans:** Replace some water with spicy V8 juice.

- **Coconut-ginger rice and beans:** Add grated ginger with the onion. Replace some of the water with a can of coconut milk (add enough water with the milk to equal 1¾ cups).

- **Turmeric-Dill Rice & Chickpeas** (p. 193)

Simmer like pasta

Some have all their water-to-grain ratios for the absorption method (p. 168) memorized like they did their times tables in the second grade. For the rest of us (delinquents), don't even worry about it. Boil grains like you do noodles, lapping in boiling water until al dente. Drain, shake dry, and you have grains without math—but this method's real benefit is that the grains are distinct and separate. Not glommed to one another, they're ideal for salads, soups, frittatas, and stir-fries.

Stock simply. Farro and a long-grain white rice like jasmine or basmati are my default grains—they're relatively quick to cook and equipped to do most jobs I ask of grains.

For a more expansive grain pantry, stock small quantities of wildcards from bulk bins. Get through them in a meal or two, then pick a new grain du jour. Also consider small, fast-cooking options like quinoa and bulgur, and if you like mush (p. 198), sushi rice or cornmeal.

Multitask with boiling water like you do sheet pans. Save yourself a pot (and some time) by simmering grains with other ingredients. The good news is nearly everything can be cooked in a pot of hot water: eggs, vegetables, beans, lentils, pasta, chicken, fish, and so on. Add ingredients with the same cook time together, or stagger those with different cook times so everything's ready together. Add quick-cooking kale or broccoli in the last few minutes of boiling farro. Simmer wheat berries and brown rice together, or quinoa and white rice together. Even if you just mix different grains, you'll end up with a great jumble of textures.

Don't forget about chickpeas (how could you?). Simmer a can of rinsed chickpeas with grains and you'll be tricked into thinking the chickpeas were cooked from scratch: soft, creamy, without any tinny aftertaste. They can go for up to 30 minutes before they risk falling apart. (Other types of beans may disintegrate more quickly, so simmer those at your own risk.)

Cool them down fast.	To prevent mushy, clumpy grains, you want to cool them down quickly after cooking. When the grains are tender, drain and rinse under cold water to get rid of any sticky starch. Shake them dry. Now you can dress, sauce, or soup them. If you're not using them right away, spread them out on a plate or sheet pan and refrigerate to cool and dry further. Once they're chilly, transfer to a container.
Crisp rice— and more.	The whole world has a name for crisp-bottomed rice, including, but definitely not limited to, nurungji, pegao, socarrat, and tahdig. Spread the cheer to other grains by crisping cooked and cooled grains in a hot, oiled nonstick pan. Spread them out and press them down, even up on the edges of the pan. Poke a few holes to let moisture escape and add more oil if you don't see bubbling. Let the bottom layer brown before stirring and browning some more. For more surface area, which you might need for small grains like quinoa or bulgur, crisp by broiling oiled grains on a sheet pan.

Make-It-Grain Salad

How to, with everything but the kitchen sink.

GRAINS

DRESSING

ADD-INS

1. Choose **grains,** one type or a mix. Simmer them in a pot of boiling water, like pasta. Drain, rinse under cold water until cool to the touch, then shake dry. You could also use leftover cooked grains that aren't stuck together (clumpy grains are better repurposed in soup or porridge). Usually 2 cups of cooked grains is good for 4 servings, or use as many grains as you cooked or need using up and adjust the other components accordingly.

2. Mix up your **dressing.** Earthy grains need acid to perk them up and dissolve any commentary about rabbit food. There are sauces and dressings all over this book that'll do just that, but even a simple red wine vinaigrette or squeeze of lemon will do lots of good.

While your grains are cooking, stir the dressing together in a large bowl. If you're using 2 cups of grains and 2 cups of other stuff (see step 3), shoot for ½ cup dressing. Or eyeball it and compensate with the other stuff once you've tasted everything together and deemed the salad overdressed. More dressing is better than too little, though, because the grains will soak up dressing as they sit.

3. A diversity of **add-ins** makes each bite tumble in your mouth with a riot of flavor and texture, but a pared-down selection is good too: Farro + cucumbers + nước chấm sounds perfect. The categories of add-ins to consider would be: crunch (p. 63), protein (cheese, tempeh, egg, leftover meat and seafood, chopped-up frittata, beans, smoked fish), softness (avocado, soft cheese), exciting gimmes (dried fruit, pickles, corn nuts, seeds), and anything else that needs using up. It's nice to layer raw and cooked additions for a wealth of textures (some ideas are on p. 188).

Cut everything small into one-bite portions so they nicely fit on your fork or spoon. An equal quantity of add-ins to grains is a good starting point, but tipping either way will just create a new (not inferior) salad. The grain can be the lettuce or the crouton, the star or the backup dancer.

4. Eat or pack it for later. If you're making the salad for the future, wait to add anything that risks wilting, browning, sogging, or bleeding (herbs, avocado, panko, ricotta) until just before eating. The salad will keep in the fridge for around 4 days. If you're eating a grain salad from the fridge, let it sit out for a few minutes to warm up. Flavors change with time and the chill of the fridge, and grains guzzle up liquids as they sit, so taste and reseason before eating.

Farro & Lentils with Coriander

Citrusy and bright, spicy and nutty, all from a single plant's seeds, stems, and leaves.

FARRO

GREEN
LENTILS

CORIANDER
SEEDS

CARROTS

CILANTRO

GARLIC

SHERRY
VINEGAR

GOAT
CHEESE

FOR 4

1. Bring a large saucepan of water to a boil. Add **½ cup farro, ½ cup green lentils,** and **1 tablespoon coriander seeds** and simmer until tender but still with some bite, 20 to 25 minutes. Drain, rinse under cold water until cool, shake dry, and salt heavily.

2. Meanwhile, grate **2 large carrots** on the large holes of a box grater into a large bowl. Cut off the roots and any white stem from **1 small bunch cilantro.** Then chop the rest: Start at the leaves and coarsely chop. As you get to the stem, chop finer. You're looking for about ¾ cup.

3. Add the farro and lentils to the bowl. Finely grate **1 small garlic clove** over. Add **2 tablespoons olive oil** and **1 tablespoon Sherry or red wine vinegar.** Stir to combine. Taste and adjust S&P, oil, and vinegar as needed. Add the cilantro and crumble **6 ounces goat cheese** over top. (Keeps for 2 days in the fridge.)

· For some juiciness, add torn Castelvetrano olives or chunks of orange or tangerine.

· The goat cheese could be feta or fresh mozzarella. A drizzle of tahini sauce would also be great.

Whole Grains, Chorizo & Dates

A good-for-you grain salad that doesn't side-eye sausage.

WHOLE GRAINS

WALNUTS

HARD SALAMI

DATES

CELERY

SHERRY VINEGAR

FOR 4 for dinner, or many lunches

1. Bring a medium saucepan of salted water to a boil. Add **1¼ cups whole grains (farro, brown rice)** and cook until al dente. Drain, rinse under cold water until cool, then shake dry.

2. While the grains are cooking, coarsely chop **1 cup walnuts, 6 ounces cured chorizo or other hard salami,** and **4 dates** (remove pits as you find them). Finely chop **6 celery stalks.** Reserve any celery leaves.

3. Return the saucepan to medium to dry, then add the walnuts, chorizo, and **¼ cup olive oil.** Cook, stirring occasionally, until the nuts are toasted and the chorizo is crispy, 3 to 5 minutes. Remove from the heat, season generously with S&P, and add **3 tablespoons Sherry vinegar.** Stir in the farro, celery, and dates (or transfer everything to a big bowl to toss). Season to taste with S&P, vinegar, and more oil so it's lip-smackingly delicious. (Keeps for 3 days in the fridge.)

More grain salads

· Wild rice + mushrooms + Parmesan + furikake

· Brown rice + black beans + chipotle in adobo + dried apricot + lime

· Rye berries + smoked trout + cukes + crème fraîche + everything bagel seasoning

· Farro + beets + pickled red onion + harissa + goat cheese

· Quinoa + roasted winter squash + fresh scallions + kimchi dressing

· Wheat berries + grilled zucchini + smashed raw green beans + tahini-mustard dressing (p. 162)

· Freekeh + raw and roasted fennel + feta-dill dressing (p. 214)

Rice with Lots of Herbs & Seeds

In this stunt, quinoa (a seed!) is cooked with rice and also toasted raw like sesame seeds.

COCONUT
CHIPS

QUINOA

WHITE RICE

SHALLOT

LIME

SOFT HERBS

FISH SAUCE

FOR 4

1. Bring a large saucepan of salted water to a boil. In a medium skillet over medium, toast **1 cup unsweetened dried coconut chips** and **1 tablespoon quinoa** until the coconut turns golden brown and the quinoa starts to pop, 3 to 4 minutes. Transfer to a small bowl.

2. Add **1 cup quinoa** and **1 cup long-grain white rice** to the boiling water and cook until tender and the quinoa grows tails, 10 to 12 minutes. Drain, rinse under cold water until cool to the touch, then shake dry.

3. Meanwhile, finely chop **1 shallot** and transfer to a large bowl. Zest **1 lime** over the shallot. Season with S&P and stir to combine. Chop **2 cups soft herbs— any combination of basil, mint, dill, parsley,** and **cilantro.** If you're using dill, parsley, or cilantro, chop the stems too. Add to the large bowl.

4. Add the cooled grains to the bowl. Season with **2 tablespoons fish sauce** (or soy sauce) and the juice of the lime (about 2 tablespoons). Stir to combine, then season to taste, adjusting salt and umami with fish sauce and acid with lime. Top with the toasted coconut and quinoa.

· Good with something fatty (avocado, browned ground pork, hot-smoked salmon) or more crunch (toasted rice powder, fennel seeds).

· Turn leftovers into fried rice or a frittata (p. 29).

Turmeric-Dill Rice & Chickpeas

A beach of sun-kissed rice with pebbles of chickpeas, waves of tahini, and dill like seagrass.

CHICKPEAS

WHITE RICE

ONION

TURMERIC

GROUND CUMIN

TAHINI

LEMON

DILL

FOR 4

1. Bring a large pot of salted water to a boil. Drain and rinse **1 (15-ounce) can chickpeas.** Add **1½ cups long-grain white rice** and the chickpeas to the boiling water and cook, stirring occasionally, until the rice is al dente, 10 to 12 minutes. Drain, rinse, and shake dry.

2. Meanwhile, coarsely chop **1 large yellow onion.** Heat **3 tablespoons olive oil** in a large nonstick skillet over medium-low. Add the onion, season with S&P, and cook, stirring occasionally, until the rice and chickpeas are ready. The longer the onions cook, the sweeter and softer they'll be.

3. When the rice is done, add **1 teaspoon ground turmeric** and **1 teaspoon ground cumin or coriander** to the onions and cook, stirring, until

fragrant, 2 to 3 minutes. Increase the heat to medium-high, add the rice and chickpeas, and stir to coat. Spread along the bottom and sides of the pan, season with S&P, and cook, without touching, until the rice starts to brown on the bottom, 6 to 8 minutes. Add more oil if you don't see bubbling.

4. Meanwhile, stir together **½ cup tahini,** the juice from **1 lemon** (about 3 tablespoons), and enough water so the sauce is pourable (about ⅓ cup). Season with S&P. Coarsely chop ⅓ **cup dill fronds and stems.** When the rice is ready, scatter the dill on top of the rice. Scoop the rice into bowls, including crispy bits on the bottom, and drizzle with sauce. Season with S&P as needed.

More earthy turmeric + sunny dill

· **Chá cá lã vọng:** Pan-fry turmeric-stained white fish and toss with dill and basil or green onion. Alongside: rice noodles, peanuts, lettuce, chile, nước chấm.

· **Kuku sabzi:** Similar to a frittata (p. 29), bake beaten eggs with lots of soft herbs, alliums, and turmeric or other spices.

· **Big beans and corn:** Sauté like on page 78 with turmeric, black pepper, and dill.

· **Turmeric omelet:** Follow page 27, adding turmeric to the beaten eggs. Fill with dill, feta, and asparagus.

· **Turmeric-soy pork:** Grill and toss with pineapple and dill (like on page 324).

Chilled Brothy Grains with Soy Eggs

Marinating eggs in a soy broth begets custardy yolks, umami-salty whites, and a slurpable broth that's good both warm and cold.

GINGER

EGGS

SOY SAUCE

RICE VINEGAR

BROWN RICE

CABBAGE

CITRUS

FOR 4

1. In a medium saucepan, bring **4 cups water** to a boil. Thinly slice **1 inch ginger.** Smash with the heel of your knife to break up its fibers and add to the water. When it's boiling, add **4 eggs** and cook for 7 minutes. (If the water doesn't cover the eggs, add more to cover.) Using a slotted spoon, transfer the eggs to an ice bath to cool. Transfer the gingery water to a medium bowl or deli container (big enough to hold the eggs), then stir in **¼ cup low-sodium soy sauce, 3 tablespoons unseasoned rice vinegar,** and **½ teaspoon sugar.** Peel the eggs, add to the ginger-soy broth, and refrigerate until everything else is ready (you can also make the eggs a day ahead).

2. Bring a medium saucepan of salted water to a boil. Add **1 cup long-grain brown rice** and cook until al dente, 25 to 30 minutes.

3. Meanwhile, halve and core **½ medium Savoy or green cabbage** (about 1 pound). Cut into 1-inch pieces (about 6 cups). Four minutes before the rice is done, add the cabbage to the water. Drain and rinse until cool to the touch (they can also be refrigerated until you're ready to eat). Transfer the rice and cabbage to bowls. Remove the eggs from the broth, halve them, then top each bowl with an egg. Pour the broth over the eggs and hit with a squeeze of **lemon or lime.**

More with soy sauce eggs

· **Soup:** In Japan, these eggs are sometimes called ramen eggs. Use that as inspiration: After soaking, warm the eggs and broth, then add noodles and maybe a veg. Soup!

· **Egg salad:** Chop the eggs and mix with Kewpie mayo, some of the chilled broth, and scallions.

· **Hand rolls:** Quarter the eggs and wrap them in nori with crunchy vegetables and sushi rice. Dip into the chilled broth.

· **Rice bowls:** Eat the eggs over a grain porridge (p. 206) or plain white rice, with a drizzle of the broth.

· There's more about marinating eggs on page 37.

Crispy Grains with Kielbasa & Cabbage

Scandal: Stew ingredients escape pot, flee for ripple of heat under broiler.

FARRO

SOUR CREAM

HORSERADISH

CABBAGE

KIELBASA

APPLE CIDER VINEGAR

FOR 4

1. Heat the broiler with a rack 5 or fewer inches from the heat source. Bring a medium saucepan of salted water to a boil. Add **1¼ cups farro** and cook until al dente, 20 to 25 minutes.

2. Meanwhile, stir together **½ cup sour cream** and **2 to 3 tablespoons prepared horseradish** in a small bowl. Season to taste with S&P. Thinly slice **1 medium green or purple cabbage** (about 2 pounds, or 9 cups sliced). Coarsely chop **1 pound smoked kielbasa** into ¼-inch pieces. On a sheet pan, toss the cabbage and kielbasa with **1 tablespoon olive oil**. Season with S&P and spread into an even layer. Broil until the sausage and cabbage are browned and singed in spots, 5 to 7 minutes (rotate the pan as needed for even coverage). Transfer to a plate and hold on to the sheet pan.

3. Drain the farro, rinse, shake very dry, and spread onto the reserved sheet pan. Toss with **2 tablespoons olive oil,** then spread into an even layer. Broil, shaking the pan occasionally, until lightly toasted and crackling, 5 to 7 minutes. Add back the cabbage and kielbasa, plus **1 tablespoon apple cider or red wine vinegar,** and stir to combine. Eat with the horseradish sour cream.

· In step 1, you could also cook green lentils or a can of drained chickpeas with the farro.

· Could also use leftover grains (because they're drier, they'll crisp well).

· In step 2, broil sliced red onion or shallots with the cabbage and kielbasa.

· In addition to or instead of the horseradish cream, consider harissa, honey mustard, vinegared shallots, crème fraîche, pickle relish, or lemon.

Make mush

When you want simple comfort and easy joy, cozy up to a warm bowl of mush. With simmering and stirring, dishes like arroz caldo, congee, grits, juk, khichdi, oatmeal, polenta, and risotto turn starchy grains into cushioned, soft porridge. You can stop here, each bite the same, reassuring. Or you can keep going, adding garnishes, seasonings, sprinkles.

Every grain mushes differently. On one end of the spectrum, milled specks like cornmeal or farina will absorb liquid, release their starch, and become creamy with only occasional stirring (think polenta or cream of wheat). At the other end of the spectrum, a whole grain, which still has its outer layers, requires vigorous stirring for it to let go of its starch and become tender.

Somewhere in the middle are the rices. Short-grain rice is very starchy, so it willingly clumps together (like in onigiri). Medium-grain rice gets creamy as it simmers (like arborio rice in risotto). Long-grain rice is low in starch but will turn to mush with time and stirring. Use the endless options to your benefit and simmer multiple types of grains together for a mix of textures (p. 206).

Build like soup. Porridge is basically soup with a greater amount of grain to liquid, so build it the same way. Bloom aromatics. Use chicken stock or another well-seasoned stock. Make it creamy with milk, heavy cream, or coconut milk. Some days, you may want gentle seasonings (p. 293). Other days, something feisty (p. 378), fresh (p. 248), or cheesy (p. 200) might feel better.

Hands off the polenta. Plot twist: Polenta, infamous for requiring constant attention and stirring, can make itself: A recipe from Mary-Frances Heck taught me that if you sit your polenta on the counter and let it absorb hot water, it will swell and soften all on its own (p. 203). Once it's tender, any clumps will go away with a few good whisks.

Tinker and taste for your ideal texture. Think about oatmeal: Depending on time, liquid quantity, and heat, it can be tacky and sturdy or nearly slurpable. There are days for both, so adjust your pot of porridge as you wish. If you simmer your mush so long that it's a tight ball of grains with little liquid, add more liquid and keep simmering until you reach your desired consistency. Alternatively, if you find grains floating in broth, keep simmering.

What else cooks forever? It's hard to overcook mush because you want grains that've fallen apart, slumped with an exhausted "phew." With such a merciful pot simmering, add other similarly forgiving ingredients. Consider ones you often braise, like chicken thighs and cured meats. Frozen spinach, grated corn, and grated or diced winter or summer squash will melt right in. Cauliflower is cool because it will release pectin and thicken the mix. More vegetables that cook forever are on page 244.

Rice & Cheese

Mac and cheese but swap mac for (very comforting, plain old, gluten-free) rice.

MILK

SUSHI RICE

MELTING CHEESE(S)

FOR 4

1. In a medium saucepan, combine **5 cups whole milk, 1 cup sushi rice,** and **2 teaspoons salt** over medium. When the mixture begins to bubble around the edges of the pan, reduce the heat to medium-low and gently simmer, stirring often and scraping the bottom of the pot, until the rice is tender and the milk resembles heavy cream, 20 to 25 minutes. If the mixture looks dry, add more milk.

2. Meanwhile, grate your **cheeses.** For a pseudo mac and cheese, coarsely grate 2 cups aged Cheddar (about 8 ounces). For more of a cacio e pepe, finely grate 1 cup Parmesan or pecorino (about 2 ounces). Using Cheddar or Parm as the base, you can also add other melting cheeses, like Gruyère or Gouda, to taste.

3. Off the heat, stir in the cheese until melted. Taste and adjust the seasonings with S&P—and more cheese!

More rice and cheeses

· Frozen spinach + garlic + Parm + panko (creamed spinach rice and cheese)

· Leftover chicken + carrots + peas + thyme + Gouda (potpie rice and cheese)

· Roasted garlic + Gouda + pecorino (like the Gilroy Mac at Homeroom Restaurant in Oakland, California)

· Leeks + goat cheese

· Broccoli + Cheddar

Fresh Corn Polenta with Lime Butter

(Without stirring more than twice!)

CORN

CORNMEAL

BUTTER

EGGS

PEPITAS

CUMIN
SEEDS

LIME

HONEY

FOR 4

1. Bring **3½ cups water or chicken stock** to a boil in a medium saucepan. Using the large holes on the box grater, grate **4 ears of corn** into a large bowl.

2. Stir **1 cup medium or coarse cornmeal** into the boiling water, then stir in the grated corn. Season with **½ teaspoon each S&P.** Remove from the heat. Cover and let sit until tender, 40 to 45 minutes. There's not much to do now except thank Mary-Frances Heck for this ingenious method.

3. When the polenta's done, set it over medium and stir in **2 tablespoons butter.** Taste and season with S&P (don't be shy on the pepper; it brings out the sweetness of the corn). Off the heat, cover to keep warm.

4. In a large nonstick skillet, heat **¼ cup olive oil** over medium-high. Crack **4 eggs** into the skillet, season with S&P, and cook, untouched, until the edges are lacy and golden brown, about 2 minutes. Spoon up some of the oil and drizzle over the whites and where the white meets the yolk (avoid the yolk). Repeat until the whites are set but the yolk is still runny, another minute or two. Turn off the heat.

5. Spoon the polenta into bowls, then top with the eggs. Return the skillet to medium. Add **2 tablespoons butter, ¼ cup pepitas,** and **1 teaspoon cumin seeds.** Cook until the butter is melted and the seeds are toasted, 1 to 2 minutes. Squeeze half of **1 lime** (about 1 tablespoon) into the skillet and swirl to combine. Spoon the seeds and butter over the bowls and eat with a squeeze from the remaining lime and a drizzle of **honey.**

Alternate butters for step 5

· Soy sauce + ginger + sesame seeds

· Turmeric + smoked almonds + honey

· Fish sauce + lime (eat with watercress)

· Shallot + sambal oelek (replace some of the boiling water in step 2 with coconut milk)

· Walnuts + dried mint (finish with lemon and feta)

MAKE MUSH

Mixed Grain Porridge **PAGE 206**

Mixed Grain Porridge

Heaven for nearly empty and never-ending baggies of grains.

GARLIC

SHALLOTS

GINGER

MIXED GRAINS

SOY SAUCE

SESAME OIL

FOR 4

1. Thinly slice **6 garlic cloves** and **2 large shallots**. Peel **3 inches ginger**, then cut into thin matchsticks.

2. In a large Dutch oven or pot, heat the garlic, shallots, and ginger with **¼ cup neutral oil** and a pinch of salt over high. When the vegetables start to bubble quickly, reduce the heat to medium and cook, stirring occasionally, until light golden, 5 to 7 minutes. Turn off the heat, then use a slotted spoon to transfer about half the mixture to a paper towel. Season with more salt.

3. To the pot, add **6 cups water (or stock)** and **2 cups any mix of grains.** Bring to a boil, then reduce the heat to medium and simmer until all the grains are tender. The quicker-cooking grains will break down, thickening the porridge, while the longer-cooking grains will add a tender bite. Add more water if the mixture looks dry or if you want a soupier porridge. Stir vigorously from time to time to break down the grains.

4. Off the heat, season to taste with salt, **low-sodium soy sauce,** and **toasted sesame oil** (start with 2 teaspoons soy sauce and 1 teaspoon sesame oil). Top each bowl with the fried garlic, shallots, and ginger.

· Ideally you'd have at least one quick-cooking grain (white rice, quinoa, oats) and one longer-cooking grain (brown rice, farro, spelt) for a mix of textures. You can also use leftover, cooked grains.

Farro Carbonara with Brussels Sprouts

Farro risotto meets carbonara, with bacon-roasted brussels just because.

**BRUSSELS
SPROUTS**

SHALLOT

BACON

FARRO

**CHICKEN
STOCK**

EGGS

PARMESAN

FOR 4

1. Heat the oven to 425°F and place a sheet pan inside. Trim and halve **1 pound brussels sprouts.** Coarsely chop **1 large shallot.** Put **4 thick-cut bacon slices** and **1 tablespoon olive oil** in a large Dutch oven over medium-high. Cook until the bacon is golden brown, 2 to 3 minutes per side. Off the heat, transfer the bacon to a paper towel–lined plate.

2. Add the brussels sprouts to the bacon fat in the Dutch oven and stir to coat. Using a slotted spoon, transfer the brussels sprouts to the heated sheet pan. Season with **¼ teaspoon black pepper** and arrange cut sides down. Roast, flipping after 15 minutes, until golden brown and tender, 25 to 30 minutes.

3. Add more **olive oil** to coat the bottom of the Dutch oven. Return to medium-high and add the shallot, **1½ cups farro,** and **½ teaspoon black pepper.** Cook, stirring, until the farro starts to crackle-pop like popcorn, about 2 minutes. Add

3 cups chicken stock and bring to a vigorous simmer over medium-high. Partially cover and cook, stirring often, until the liquid is mostly absorbed, 10 to 15 minutes. (Now's a good time to flip your brussels sprouts.)

4. Add another **cup chicken stock** and **1 cup hot water,** partially cover, and cook, stirring often, until the farro is tender and suspended in a thick liquid, 10 to 15 minutes. When you drag your spoon across the bottom, the risotto should trail behind. Add more water as needed—it'll thicken as it sits.

5. While the farro is cooking, stir together **1 egg, 2 egg yolks,** and **½ teaspoon black pepper** with a fork. Finely grate **6 tablespoons Parmesan** (about 1½ ounces) into the egg mixture. Off the heat, add the egg mixture to the farro and stir until a glossy sauce forms. Eat the farro topped with crumbled bacon, brussels sprouts, and more Parm and black pepper.

Other farro risottos (all finished with Parm)

· Lemon peel + lemon juice

· Peas + Canadian bacon + mint

· Broccoli rabe + furikake

· Grated winter squash + sage + apple cider vinegar

· Mushroom (splice method with page 150)

Coconut-Ginger Rice & Lentils

Cuddly but not snoozy.

ONION

GINGER

TURMERIC

GROUND
CORIANDER

COCONUT
MILK

RED LENTILS

BROWN RICE

LIME

FOR 4

1. Coarsely chop **1 medium yellow onion.** Finely grate **2 inches ginger.** In a large pot, heat **3 tablespoons neutral or coconut oil** over medium. Add the onion, ginger, **1½ teaspoons ground turmeric,** and **1 teaspoon ground coriander.** Season with S&P. Cook, stirring occasionally, until softened and golden brown, 8 to 10 minutes.

2. Add **2 (14-ounce) cans full-fat coconut milk, 1 cup red lentils, 1 cup long-grain brown rice,** and **2 teaspoons salt.** Fill both cans with water and dump into the pot. Bring to a boil, then reduce the heat to medium-low and simmer, stirring occasionally, until the lentils are broken down and the brown rice is tender, 40 to 45 minutes. Add more water if the pot looks dry or if you want a bowl that's more soupy than stewy.

3. Ladle into bowls. Finely grate some zest from **1 lime** and a little **ginger** on top, then stir to combine and season to taste with S&P. Eat with a squeeze from the lime.

For something different

· **Trade the rice and lentils:** Use green lentils with white long-grain rice. The rice will break down while the lentils retain their bite (the reverse of the above).

· **Riff on khichdi:** Use white long-grain rice, mung beans, and water. Bloom cumin or mustard seeds and dried chile in ghee for over top (more on tadka on p. 227).

· **Swap spices:** Use ground cumin or cinnamon, or add ¼ cup red or green curry paste.

VEGETABLES

Cook quicker (or not at all)

If you cut vegetables into bite-size pieces, you're front-loading everything that comes next: The vegetables (even sturdy squashes) will cook quickly—or may not need to be cooked at all. And when it comes to eating, just remember the salad bar days: continuous fork-to-mouth consumption, no knives required (RIP Souplantation and Sweet Tomatoes).

Two-for-one vegetables.
Vegetables get on the frequently purchased list if they can be eaten raw and cook in fewer than ten minutes: They are multipurpose, super fast to cook, and if you undercook them, no big deal. That includes corn, snap and snow peas, asparagus, green beans, kale, fennel, radicchio, radishes, cabbage, bok choy, and romaine.

For a range of textures, use one veg two ways (p. 217), or cook them hot and fast enough that their outsides char but they otherwise stay crisp (this is especially easy under the broiler, like on page 349).

Eat scraps.
Broccoli and cauliflower stems can be sliced thin and roasted or seared—mild and juicy, they're a nice contrast to frilly florets. Fennel stalks not only look like celery stalks but they have a similar texture and are good raw, simmered, or seared. Cilantro, dill, and parsley stems are good until they turn white or you hit roots. Thinly sliced, they're crunchy, concentrated bursts of flavor, and unlike the leaves, they can also be sautéed with aromatics at the start of a recipe.

It's great to grate.
A Microplane is one of the most used tools in this book: In addition to grating citrus zest and cheese, it's a fast way to finely chop ginger, garlic, and little chiles. (Freeze ginger and chiles for cleaner grates.) Graters do dull, so replace yours when it gives you trouble.

The large holes of a box grater (or the grating disk on a food processor) can turn rock-hard vegetables into downy snow, diminishing their cooking time in a few strokes. It can help you make butternut squash pasta sauce (p. 228), beet yogurt (p. 43), carrot salad (p. 187), tomato vinaigrette (p. 68), and cauliflower rice.

Coordinate your cutting board. If your cutting board gets so jammed it needs an air traffic controller, there are a few things to do (besides get a bigger cutting board). Combine ingredients that will be cooked together in a bowl to make room for the next round of chopping. Or, if there's time in the recipe, once the first batch of chopped ingredients is cooking, chop the next batch on the now-empty board. When possible, cut juicy stuff, onions, and raw meat last to avoid messes and tears.

Commit the sear-steam to memory. For a side dish of any vegetable, heat a little olive oil or butter in a skillet over medium-high. Add a single layer of bite-size pieces of the vegetables, such as asparagus, broccoli, brussels sprouts, carrots, cauliflower, Chinese broccoli, fennel, green beans, or kale. Season with salt and cook, without touching, until browned. Now add a tablespoon or two of water (or stock), reduce the heat to medium, and cover. Cook, checking things out and stirring things around, until the vegetables are crisp-tender. (When you uncover, swing the lid vertically so the moisture drips into the pan instead of sputtering on your stove.) If the pan's dry, add more water. Alternatively, the vegetables may be cooked before all the liquid has evaporated, in which case pluck them out with tongs or a slotted spoon. The vegetables will come out browned, crisp-tender, and tasting like their best selves; I know because this is how my mom makes every single vegetable.

Smacked Vegetables with Feta & Dill

Vegetables with so many nooks and crannies, dressing can't not get comfortable.

LEMONS

FETA

DIJON
MUSTARD

CAULIFLOWER

PICKLED
PEPPERS

GREEN BEANS

RADISHES

DILL

FOR 4

1. In a medium bowl, zest **1 lemon** and crumble **4 ounces feta cheese** (about 1 cup). Add **1½ teaspoons Dijon mustard,** season with S&P, then mash with a fork until a paste forms. Stir in the juice of **1½ lemons** (about ¼ cup). Stir in **olive oil** until it tastes rich but still puckery (around ¼ cup).

2. Cut **1 small cauliflower** (about 1 pound) into small florets. Stir into the dressing, along with any bits on your cutting board. Thinly slice **6 peperoncini** and add to the salad.

3. Trim **8 ounces green beans.** Trim and halve **1 small bunch radishes.** Smash the green beans and radishes with a meat pounder, rolling pin, or the side of your knife until the vegetables split. Rip them into bite-size pieces, then stir into the dressing and season with S&P. (Let sit for up to 2 days in the fridge and the vegetables will get even silkier.)

4. When you're ready to eat, finely chop **½ cup dill fronds and stems.** Eat the vegetables with dill and black pepper.

More smashed vegetables

· Cukes + marinated beans (p. 64) + tahini

· Radish + green beans + gochujang + lime + rice

· Roasted beets + green sauce (p. 317)

· Green beans + tuna + yogurt Ranch

· Boiled little potatoes + pickle butter

· Crispy-Skinned Fish with Creamy Cukes (p. 354)

A Springy Noodle Stir-Fry

The bounty of spring veg both raw *and* charred.

ORANGES

TAHINI

SOY SAUCE

GINGER

SPRING VEG

RAMEN
NOODLES

FROZEN
EDAMAME

SESAME
SEEDS

FOR 4

1. Bring a large pot of salted water to a boil. Use a vegetable peeler to peel the rind from an orange. Squeeze 1 cup juice from **2 oranges** into a large bowl. To the OJ, add the rind, **½ cup tahini,** and **¼ cup low-sodium soy sauce.** Finely grate **1 tablespoon ginger** into the bowl, season with S&P, and stir.

2. Trim the stem ends from **2 pounds spring veg (any mix of asparagus, green beans, snap peas, snow peas).** Thinly slice on a diagonal ½ inch thick. Add half—only half—to the bowl, season with S&P, and stir to combine.

3. Add **10 to 12 ounces ramen noodles (preferably fresh)** and **½ cup frozen, shelled edamame** to the boiling water and cook according to the package directions. Drain, rinse, then stir into the sauce.

4. In the same pot, heat **2 tablespoons neutral oil** over medium-high. Add the remaining half of the vegetables. Season with S&P and cook, stirring just once, until browned in spots, 2 to 4 minutes. Add everything in the sauce bowl and cook, tossing until the sauce is warm and glazy, 1 to 2 minutes. Shower with **toasted sesame seeds.**

· Good hot, warm, or room temp.

· Instead of ramen noodles, use soba, dried or fresh udon, or lo mein.

· Brown tofu or ground chicken or pork before adding the vegetables in step 4. Remove, then add back with the sauce.

Buffalo Salad with Blue Cheese Toasts

Turns out the most optional part of Buffalo wings is the wings.

BACON

FRANK'S HOT
SAUCE

GARLIC

CELERY

CRISP LETTUCE

CRUSTY BREAD

BLUE CHEESE

LEMON

FOR 4

1. Heat the oven to 450°F. Put **4 bacon slices** on a foil-lined sheet pan and put in the oven while it heats up. Cook until browned, 10 to 20 minutes. Transfer to a paper towel–lined plate to crisp. Reserve the bacon fat and sheet pan.

2. Meanwhile, in a large bowl, stir together **3 tablespoons olive oil** and **2 tablespoons Frank's hot sauce.** Grate **1 small garlic clove** into the dressing, then season with S&P. Thinly slice **4 celery stalks.** Rip or thinly slice **a couple heads crisp lettuce (romaine, iceberg).**

3. Put **4 slices crusty bread or sourdough** in the bacon fat on the sheet pan. Toast in the oven until lightly toasted, 3 to 5 minutes. Flip the bread, top with **some blue cheese or Cambozola,** and return to the oven until the cheese is just melted, 3 to 5 minutes. Spread the blue cheese on the toasts.

4. Add the romaine and celery to the bowl and season with salt and enough juice from **1 lemon** to coat (a couple teaspoons). Toss to combine. Rip up the bacon and add to the bowl. Season to taste with S&P and lemon juice. Eat with the toasts.

More answers to the timeless question "Will it Buffalo?"

· **Roasted vegetables:** Swap Cholula for Frank's in the butter mixture on page 369, then toss with any roasted veg.

· **Pizza:** Toss pulled chicken with dressing in step 2, then pile onto tomato-sauced pizza dough and bake. Top with blue cheese and/or Ranch.

· **Kale grilled cheese:** Toss sliced kale with dressing in step 2, then pile into grilled cheese with mozzarella.

Broccoli Bits with Cheddar & Dates

Best shoveled into your mouth with a spoon.

CHEDDAR

ALMONDS

BROCCOLI

DATES

SHERRY
VINEGAR

HONEY

FOR 4,
warm or cool

1. Chop **4 ounces (¾ cup) sharp Cheddar cheese** into ¼-inch bits and coarsely chop **½ cup smoked or roasted almonds.** Transfer to a large bowl. Cut the florets off **2 pounds broccoli,** keeping as much of the branch connected to the trunk as possible. Peel the trunk and cut the trunk and branches into ½-inch pieces. Roughly chop the florets into small pieces so even the biggest ones fit on a teaspoon. Pit and coarsely chop **8 dates** (outsides up so the sticky middles don't gunk up your knife).

2. In a large skillet, heat **1 tablespoon olive oil** over medium-high. Add the dates and cook until they're softened and browned in spots, 2 to 3 minutes. Transfer to the bowl and season with S&P.

3. In the same skillet still over medium-high, heat **2 tablespoons olive oil.** Add the broccoli (including the specks on the cutting board) and **1 teaspoon red pepper flakes,** season with S&P, and cook until the broccoli is bright green and browned in spots, 3 to 5 minutes. Transfer to the bowl. Stir in **1 tablespoon Sherry vinegar, 1 tablespoon olive oil,** and **1 teaspoon honey.** Taste and adjust salt, acid (with vinegar), sweetness (with honey), and spice (with red pepper flakes) accordingly.

· Instead of Cheddar, chop up Parmesan or pecorino. Instead of broccoli, try cauliflower.

· Cook cubes of Spanish chorizo or kielbasa—or, you know, bacon—then cook the dates and broccoli in the drippings.

Salad That Never Repeats

Composed salad 101.

LEAVES
VEGETABLES
PROTEIN
FAT
WAKE-UP
CALLS
DRESSING

1. Unbutton your collar: Though Niçoise and Cobb salads are food of stuffy luncheons and country clubs, a composed salad can be greens, dressing, and any random ingredients. To make a salad that's just composed enough, use ingredients that fit the categories here.

2. Leaves: Choose soft leaves that are bitter and/or sweet. Herbs count. Put them on a platter or plates and season with S&P. You can also dress them lightly if you want.

3. Vegetables: Cut ideally more than one vegetable into bite-size pieces. Cook any that need cooking and keep others raw. Variety is ideal. Add them in piles or rows onto the leaves. Season with S&P.

4. Protein: Beans, cured meats, or any simply cooked protein (boiled eggs, poached shrimp, rotisserie chicken) will keep this salad from feeling like a side. Slice or tear into big pieces and add to your plates.

5. Get rich: Add **something fatty,** like boiled eggs, creamy cheese, avocado, or dollops of yogurt or crème fraîche. These treats soften the crunchy bites.

6. Wake-up calls: This is the stuff that, in a normal tossed salad, would sink to the bottom of the bowl, playing hard to get because they know they're the best part. Seek out tangy, punchy, briny, bright, and crunchy bites that keep the salad pulsing: seeds, olives, pickles, dried fruit, preserved lemon, chips, fried bread or shallots. Add any that sound good with your mix.

7. Dressing: Use any dressing that you're craving, though it could be just olive oil and lemon or vinegar because your salad is already full of attention-grabbers. Drizzle over the platter or plates, with a bowl of more at the table.

Harissa-Creamed Cauliflower

Like cream of tomato and cauliflower soups in one.

HEAVY CREAM

HARISSA

CAULIFLOWER

CANNED TOMATOES

CRUSTY BREAD

FOR 4

1. In a large Dutch oven, stir together **1 cup heavy cream** and **¾ teaspoon harissa** (you can always add more at the end). Season with **1 teaspoon each S&P.** Cut **1 large cauliflower** (2½ to 3 pounds) into small florets and coarsely chop the stem. Add the cauliflower, including any bits from the cutting board, to the pot. Add just the tomatoes from **1 (28-ounce) can whole, peeled tomatoes** (use a spoon or drain into a colander; save the liquid for chili or tomato sauce).

2. Bring the mixture to a simmer over medium. Reduce the heat to medium-low, cover, and cook, smashing the tomatoes and cauliflower from time to time, until the cauliflower is very tender, 15 to 18 minutes. Uncover and cook until the cream is slightly thickened, 3 to 5 minutes. Taste and reseason with S&P and more harissa.

3. Toast **4 slices sourdough or crusty bread** and plop them into shallow bowls or on rimmed plates. Spoon the cauliflower, tomatoes, and cream over. Eat with a fork and knife.

More tender veg + heavy cream

· Drained whole tomatoes + cinnamon stick

· Broccoli rabe + lemon peel

· Butternut squash + curry powder

· Peas + basil

· Broccoli + Parmesan rind

Charred Vegetables with Turmeric Peanuts

To keep sweet vegetables from cloying, burn them. A little.

SWEET
POTATOES

FENNEL

RED ONION

PEANUTS

FENNEL SEEDS

TURMERIC

YOGURT

LEMON

FOR 4

1. Cut **2 pounds sweet potatoes** (about 4 small) into ½-inch pieces. Pluck ¼ cup fronds off **2 pounds fennel** (about 2 medium). Thinly slice the stalks. Halve the bulb through the root, then cut into ½-inch pieces. Cut **1 red onion** into ½-inch pieces. Coarsely chop ¼ **cup roasted, salted peanuts.**

2. In a small skillet or saucepan, heat ¼ **cup olive oil** and the peanuts over medium-low. Cook, swirling the pan occasionally, until golden brown, 3 to 4 minutes. Remove from the heat and add **1½ teaspoons fennel seeds, 1 teaspoon ground turmeric,** a pinch of salt, and a lot of black pepper. Swirl to combine and set aside.

3. In a large cast-iron skillet or Dutch oven, toss ¼ **cup olive oil** with the sweet potatoes. Season with S&P, then place over medium. When the sweet potatoes start to sizzle, add ½ **cup water,** cover, and cook until the sweet potatoes are fork tender, 5 to 7 minutes (they won't be fully cooked yet).

4. Raise the heat to medium-high, add the fennel stalks and bulb pieces and the onion, season with S&P, and stir to combine. Spread into an even layer and cook, undisturbed, until the vegetables are charred in spots, 2 to 3 minutes. Stir and repeat until the vegetables are tender, another 4 to 6 minutes. Add more oil if the pan is dry.

5. Eat with a dollop of **full-fat Greek or regular yogurt,** the peanuts and their sunshiny oil, a squeeze of juice from **1 lemon,** and some fennel fronds.

The final flourish: The peanut sprinkle employs an essential Indian technique with many names, including tadka, or chhonk, or vagar. In it, spices and other aromatics are bloomed in hot fat (ghee or oil) until sizzling and fragrant, then poured over a final dish. Use this format and sizzle any number of flavorings (cinnamon sticks, seeds, dried chiles, garlic, rosemary) in hot oil, then pour the sizzled bits and infused oil over whatever needs a pulse racing through: rice, lentils, baked potatoes, soup, or grilled fish and meat.

Squash & Sage Skillet Lasagna

Winter squash and lasagna, profoundly slow-cooking foods, swerve into the fast lane.

BUTTERNUT SQUASH

SAGE

FLOUR

MILK

LASAGNA NOODLES

PARMESAN

RICOTTA

FOR 4 to 6

1. Peel **1 small butternut squash** (about 2 pounds). Using the large holes of a box grater, coarsely grate the squash into a large bowl (you should have about 5 cups; spoon out the seeds and stringy bits when you reach them). Thinly slice **3 tablespoons sage leaves.** The hardest part is behind you!

2. In a large ovenproof skillet that holds at least 3 quarts (12 cups), melt **2 table-spoons butter** with **2 tablespoons olive oil** over medium-high. Add the sage and **1 pinch red pepper flakes** and cook until fragrant, 1 to 2 minutes. Add the squash, season with S&P, and stir to coat. Cook, stirring just a few times, until soft and browned in spots, 5 to 7 minutes. Add **2 tablespoons all-purpose flour** and stir until combined, 1 to 2 minutes.

3. Slowly pour in **5 cups whole milk,** stirring as you go to break up any clumps. Stir in **2 teaspoons salt.** When the milk starts to bubble around the edges, turn off the heat. Snap **9 ounces lasagna noodles** (about 15 noodles, boil or no-boil both work) in half, then use your spoon to submerge them into the sauce. Leave a little squash under and above each noodle so they don't stick together. Return to a gentle simmer over medium-low, then cover with a lid, baking sheet, or foil and cook, without stirring, until the noodles are tender, 10 to 12 minutes. Reduce the heat if you hear rapid bubbling.

4. Finely grate **½ cup Parmesan** (about 1 ounce) evenly over the top, then dot with **½ cup whole-milk ricotta.** Cover and cook until melted, 2 to 4 minutes. For a crisp top, broil uncovered until the cheese is browned, 2 to 4 minutes. Let sit for a few minutes before eating.

· Measure your skillet by filling it with a measured amount of water, then dump the water into your kettle or plants. If you don't have a big enough skillet, use a 3-quart or larger Dutch oven, knowing it'll be trickier to broil.

· For a crunchy topping, toast panko or chopped nuts in browned butter or olive oil—maybe with more thinly sliced sage. Sprinkle over top before eating.

Roast

With nothing more than oil, salt, and pepper, a roasted vegetable reveals a twinkle in its eye. Sweet and golden, it may be just a carrot, but it's not *just* a carrot.

Feeling hot hot hot. Heat the oven somewhere between 425°F and 450°F. Stick an oven thermometer inside your oven, which will give you an accurate temperature (the dial on your oven is probably lying).

One size doesn't fit all. In this book, you'll find sweet potatoes cut into cubes for a stir-fry (p. 226), half-moons for a side (p. 312), wedges for a knife-and-fork salad (p. 242), and halves to headline dinner (p. 241). To decide how to cut your vegetables, ask yourself: How much cutting do you want to do and how much do you want to foist onto eaters? Are you in it for caramelized outsides or buttery middles? How much time do you have?

In general, small pieces will roast more quickly and produce lots of browned, crispy outsides. Bigger pieces are main-event vegetables that eaters can cut up themselves. They will take longer to cook but offer a greater proportion of tender middles to caramelized outsides. Once you pick the shape, seek uniform pieces for even cooking.

More oil means more browning. If your roasted vegetables turn up shriveled or only spotted brown, they probably needed more oil. Generously coat your vegetables and if you go overboard and find pooling oil on your tray of finished vegetables, use it to make a dressing by tossing the vegetables and oil with some lemon, lime, or vinegar.

No touching. Spread the vegetables out on a sheet pan, cut sides down. (Okay, if you really don't want to wash the pan, line it with parchment paper but know it's one count against browning.) If the vegetables are touching one another, steam won't be able to escape and they won't brown, so divide them between two sheets. Then roast them on the rack closest to the heat source (usually the bottom rack): This gets the sheet pan really hot, which in turn gets the cut sides in contact with the pan really hot and browned. Then don't touch.

Repeat: No touching. Forget about flipping roasting vegetables halfway through: At some point I decided I preferred one really crisp side instead of two kinda roasty sides. One side of the vegetable might be a little softer than the other; it's a nice textural contrast, but you might not even notice because, hey, would you just look at that golden-brown side? Plus, depending on the vegetable and oven, even browning can take so long, you risk overcooking.

Finish with freshness and acid. Roasting brings out vegetables' sweetness, so balance with acid and/or freshness, like milky mozz, macerated apricots, pickled onions, yogurt, salsa, or a drizzle of lemon juice or vinegar.

I especially like to dress them in a "pan sauce" of butter and vinegar by tossing the roasted vegetables with a knob of butter and tablespoon of vinegar right on the sheet pan until the butter's melted. It's just a little flair to make them memorable.

Blistered Peppers with Mozzarella & Croutons

Like if Romesco sauce never got blitzed.

MOZZARELLA

CHICKPEAS

GARLIC

SMOKED PAPRIKA

SWEET MINI PEPPERS

NUTS

CRUSTY BREAD

SHERRY VINEGAR

FOR 4

1. Heat the oven to 450°F. Take **8 ounces salted fresh mozzarella** out of the fridge to warm up. Drain and rinse **1 (15-ounce) can chickpeas.** Smash but don't peel **4 garlic cloves.** In a 9 by 13-inch baking dish or large Dutch oven, stir together **½ cup olive oil, 1 teaspoon smoked paprika,** and **1 teaspoon red pepper flakes.** Stir in the garlic, chickpeas, and **1½ pounds sweet mini peppers.** Season with S&P and roast until the peppers are slouched and blistered in spots, 20 to 25 minutes. (The peppers and chickpeas will keep in the fridge for 2 days.)

2. Meanwhile, coarsely chop **½ cup almonds or blanched hazelnuts** and remove any loose skins. Tear **5 to 6 ounces crusty bread** into 1-inch pieces (about 3 cups). Transfer the nuts and bread to a sheet pan, season with S&P, and toss with **2 tablespoons olive oil.** Toast in the oven, shaking occasionally, until golden, 5 to 7 minutes.

3. Remove any loose nut skins, then pour or spoon ¼ cup of the oil from the peppers onto the baking sheet of toasted bread and nuts. Finely grate over **1 small garlic clove,** add **2 tablespoons Sherry vinegar,** and season with S&P. Stir until the bread is shiny. Taste a piece of bread and adjust S&P, vinegar, and oil to taste.

4. Cut or tear the mozzarella into one- or two-bite pieces. On a platter or serving plates, layer half the cheese, peppers, chickpeas, bread, and nuts, then repeat, drizzling the vinaigrette and more seasoned oil from the peppers as you go. Season to taste with S&P, vinegar, and olive oil.

· Make just step 1 as the start of a salad, a side to chicken, or to top a yogurt-schmeared piece of toast.

· Blanched hazelnuts are a luxury: Their skins are already off!

· To easily tear crusty bread, slice 1 inch thick, then into 1-inch-thick logs, then tear from there.

· If the Romesco in your head has tomatoes, use a mix of sweet mini peppers and cherry tomatoes.

Fennel & Radicchio with Macerated Apricots

With just a wink wink of bitter.

DRIED APRICOTS

SHALLOT

RED WINE VINEGAR

WHOLE GRAINS

RADICCHIO

FENNEL

PARMESAN

FOR 4

1. Heat the oven to 425°F. Bring a medium saucepan of salted water to a boil. Coarsely chop **½ cup dried apricots** and thinly slice **1 shallot.** Add both to a large bowl with **¼ cup red wine or balsamic vinegar.** Season with S&P, stir, and set aside.

2. Add **½ cup whole grains (farro, brown rice)** to the boiling water and cook until al dente (20 to 30 minutes for farro and brown rice).

3. Meanwhile, cut **2 radicchio** (about 1 pound) into ½-inch-thick wedges through the root. If you're using Treviso radicchio (the oval one), you may just need to halve lengthwise depending on their size. Transfer to a sheet pan.

4. Cut the stalks and fronds off **2 medium fennel bulbs** (about 2 pounds) and hold on to them. Cut the bulbs in half lengthwise through the root, then slice ½-inch-thick through the root. Add to the sheet pan. Drizzle with **¼ cup olive oil,** season with S&P, and toss to coat. Spread in an even layer, spreading across 2 sheet pans if the sheet's cramped. Roast until the fennel is golden brown on the bottom and crisp-tender when poked with a knife, 15 to 20 minutes (no need to flip).

5. Meanwhile, drain the farro and stir into the apricot-shallot mixture. Thinly slice at most 1 cup of the fennel stalks crosswise. Coarsely chop up to ½ cup of the fronds.

6. Transfer the vegetables to plates and top with the grains, stalks, and fronds. Drizzle with olive oil, season with S&P, and grate or shave **½ cup Parmesan or pecorino** (about 1 ounce) on top. (You can also add the vegetables to the bowl and toss together.) Does it need more kick? Add vinegar and salt. More fat? Add olive oil. More sweetness? Drizzle with honey. Eat hot or at room temp. (Keeps for up to 3 days in the fridge.)

Asparagus, Scallion & Tofu Tangle

Sweet spears of spring come marching in.

TOFU

ASPARAGUS

SCALLIONS

CORNSTARCH

SESAME OIL

PEANUTS

MINT

LIMES

SOBA

FOR 4

1. Heat the oven to 425°F. Bring a large pot of salted water to a boil. Cut **1 (14- to 15-ounce) block firm or extra-firm tofu** in half lengthwise, then into ½-inch-thick slabs crosswise. Cut each slice through its middle crosswise so you end up with bricks about 2 by ½ by ½ inches. Pat very dry.

2. Trim the stem ends from **1 pound asparagus** and **8 scallions,** then cut into 2-inch lengths. Transfer to a sheet pan and toss to coat with **3 tablespoons olive oil** and S&P.

3. In a medium bowl, stir together **2 tablespoons olive oil, 1 tablespoon cornstarch,** and **2 teaspoons toasted sesame oil.** Season with S&P. Add the tofu and stir to coat, then spread out on a second sheet pan. Roast the vegetables and tofu, without flipping, until browned and crispy, 20 to 25 minutes.

4. Meanwhile, coarsely chop **1 cup roasted, salted peanuts** and **1 cup mint leaves.** Zest and juice **3 limes** (a little more than ⅓ cup of juice) into a large bowl, then add **¼ cup olive oil** and **4 teaspoons toasted sesame oil.** Add **10 ounces dried soba** to the boiling water and cook according to the package directions. Drain and rinse under cold water until cool to the touch, then shake dry. Toss with **a little toasted sesame oil** in the colander.

5. Let the vegetables and tofu cool slightly, then add to the bowl, along with the soba, peanuts, and mint. Toss to combine and season to taste with S&P and more lime juice and sesame oil.

· Use any vegetables that roast in 20 to 25 minutes (shishito peppers, green beans, halved brussels sprouts).

· Instead of soba, use grains or salad greens.

· Make this a peanut sauce by swapping the peanuts and olive oil for ½ cup chunky peanut butter and thinning with hot water.

Cheddar Broccoli with Mustard Crumbs

An enchanted broccoli forest.*

BROCCOLI

DIJON
MUSTARD

WHOLE-GRAIN
MUSTARD

PANKO

CHEDDAR

CHIVES

FOR 4

1. Heat the oven to 450°F. Slice the stalks of **2 pounds broccoli** (about 2 large heads) crosswise ½ inch thick. Cut the heads into 4 or 6 wedges, depending on the size of your broccoli.

2. On a sheet pan, toss the broccoli with **¼ cup olive oil** and S&P. Arrange cut sides down. Roast, without flipping, until tender when poked with a knife, 20 to 25 minutes.

3. Meanwhile, in a medium skillet, melt **3 tablespoons butter** over medium-low. Add **2½ teaspoons Dijon mustard** and **1 teaspoon whole-grain mustard** and stir to combine. Add **¾ cup panko or fresh breadcrumbs,** season with S&P, and cook, stirring often, until golden brown, 3 to 4 minutes. Transfer to a small bowl.

4. When the broccoli is tender, flip them so their golden sides are facing up. Finely grate enough **sharp Cheddar cheese** over the broccoli to cover (¾ to 1 cup or 3 to 4 ounces if you want a number). Return to the oven and roast until the cheese is melted, 3 to 4 minutes.

5. Thinly slice **1 small bunch chives** and stir into the breadcrumbs. Eat the broccoli with a whole lot of breadcrumbs (make sure to get any crispy cheese on the sheet pan, too).

· If we're being honest with each other, you could trade the panko for some crushed honey mustard pretzels.

· *Also the glorious name of a cookbook by Mollie Katzen.

More cheese + roasted broccoli

· **Roasted broccoli & Parmesan:** An all-the-time side from Ina Garten, roast broccoli, grate Parmesan over, then roast until melted and crisp. Squeeze with lemon.

· **Chili-lime broccoli & black beans:** Coat broccoli with chili powder and roast with black beans. Shower with grated Cheddar and melt. Eat with rice or tortillas.

· **Broccoli-sauerkraut melts:** Mix chopped, roasted broccoli with sauerkraut. Spoon onto toasts, blanket with Swiss or provolone, and broil.

· **Baked feta:** Roast broccoli with slabs of feta and lots of smashed garlic and olives. Eat over orzo with butter and lemon.

Ideal Sweet Potatoes with Buttered Nuts

A sweet-potato roasting method for always-caramelized cut sides
and creamy middles.

SWEET
POTATOES

NUTS

KALE

BUTTER

GARLIC

LIME

FOR 4

1. Heat the oven to 425°F. Halve **4 small sweet potatoes** (about 2 pounds) lengthwise. On a sheet pan, toss with **2 tablespoons olive oil** and S&P. Arrange cut sides down. Roast, without flipping, until the undersides are browned and the insides are tender, 35 to 40 minutes.

2. Meanwhile, coarsely chop **½ cup any roasted nuts (peanuts, pistachios, almonds)**. De-stem **2 bunches Tuscan kale** and thinly slice crosswise. In a large skillet, melt **4 tablespoons butter** (½ stick) over medium. Add the nuts and **½ teaspoon red pepper flakes**. Once sizzling, add the kale, season with S&P, and cook, stirring, until dark green and wilted, 2 to 3 minutes. Turn off the heat. Finely grate **1 small garlic clove** and the zest of **1 lime** over the kale and stir to combine. Squeeze in lime juice to taste until it's bright but still buttery. Eat the sweet potatoes with the kale.

Other ways with dark leafy greens

· **Marinate:** Massage with salt until slackened, then toss in an assertive dressing.

· **Grill or roast:** Cook whole leaves for sweet, singed, crackling chips.

· **Braise:** Melty-tender and not at all green (p. 253).

· **Cream:** Drown any bitterness in fat, whether heavy cream or coconut milk (p. 250).

· **Confit:** Turn greens bed-sheet soft by cooking low and slow in a large quantity of olive oil (p. 104).

Roasted Roots with Green Salsa

Psst: This salsa perks up just about any protein, veg, grain, or salad.

SWEET POTATOES

CARROTS WITH THEIR TOPS

SCALLIONS

TOMATILLOS

FRESH CHILE

LIMES

CRUMBLY CHEESE

FOR 4

1. Heat the oven to 450°F. Halve **2 medium sweet potatoes** (about 2 pounds) lengthwise, then cut lengthwise into ½-inch-thick wedges. Transfer to a sheet pan. Trim **1 pound small carrots with green tops** of their greens. Transfer the carrots to the sheet pan and coarsely chop ½ cup of the greens (wash if gritty). Transfer the greens to a medium bowl.

2. Add **5 scallions** to the sheet pan. Season the mixture with S&P and toss with enough **olive oil** to coat. Spread the vegetables out in an even layer, dividing between 2 sheet pans if they're cramped. Roast on the bottom rack until browned and tender, 15 to 20 minutes.

3. Meanwhile, make the salsa. Add these things to the carrot greens as you cut them: Remove the husks from **8 ounces tomatillos** (about 5) and coarsely chop. Finely chop **1 or 2 fresh chiles (serrano or jalapeño)**, depending on heat preference. Season generously with S&P, then add the juice from **2 limes** (about ¼ cup) and **1 tablespoon olive oil**. Stir and adjust seasonings to taste (the mixture will loosen as it sits).

4. Snip the charred scallions with scissors into the salsa and stir. Transfer the root vegetables to plates and top with the salsa and lots of **crumbly cheese (Cotija, feta, ricotta salata).**

· If your carrots don't have greens, add cilantro to the salsa.

· Instead of tomatillo, use cucumbers, corn, or zucchini.

· Good with grains, black beans, peanuts, pepitas, avocado, sour cream.

· Everything here is good at room temp; components will keep for 3 days in the fridge.

Let them slouch

Past al dente, past tender—oh, there goes "done"—are slouching vegetables (not a real cooking term). Even bitter and imperfect vegetables will turn sweet and slackened when simmered, confited, or braised with mood-boosting flavorings. The resulting soup, stew, mash, or unidentifiable jumble may not be much in the texture department, but that's not the point.

Layer flavor every step of the way.

Build the ground floor for your vegetables by browning or blooming aromatics and seasonings. In a greased pot or pan, warm aromatics like garlic, onion, ginger, lemongrass, whole or ground spices, hard-stem herbs, or pastes (tomato, curry, chile).

Next, pick the liquid by considering what sauces or soups you like with your chosen vegetables. You could go sweet and spicy with coconut and green curry paste (p. 250), creamy with milk (p. 249), or fermented and sour with gochujang and vinegar (p. 253). Add tang and smokiness with bacon and apple cider vinegar or smoked paprika and Sherry vinegar. Or let the vegetables shine with fruity olive oil (p. 104). Salt all along the way.

Not just for Tough and Fibrous.

It's hard to think of a vegetable that wouldn't benefit from this kind of treatment, but especially mind-tangling (in a good way) are crunchy vegetables, which get so buttery-soft. Try radishes + honey + red pepper flakes. String beans + farro + gochujang (p. 253). Celery + bay leaf + chicken thighs. Lettuces + white beans + lemon.

More of the Seven Dwarfs can come, too.

Wilty, Droopy, and Squishy are welcome because we're not trying to preserve a vegetable's crispness. Avoid mold, though, you know?

Switch up your mashed veg. Mashed potatoes go like this: Boil potatoes in water, drain, return to their pot, mash with cream and butter. But by streamlining and reworking this process, options open up.

Use the cauliflower mash on page 249 as your guide: Fill the pot with bite-size pieces of your veg—sweet potato, squash, broccoli, cauliflower, carrots, parsnips, what have you. Then add enough liquid to reach halfway or three-quarters up your veg. Throw in some aromatics if desired. Like milk + thyme + nutmeg. Coconut milk + sambal oelek + turmeric. Chicken stock + Parm rind + black pepper. Soy sauce + water + ginger + lemon peel.

Bring the mixture to a simmer, cover, and cook until the vegetables are super tender and have released their juices into the pot. Then, instead of draining, mash it all together with a fork, spoon, or potato masher. If the pot is dry at any point, add a little more liquid. If it's soupy, return it to the heat.

Ready when you are. These vegetables have a forgiving timeline where the line between "done" and "overcooked" is a little more wiggly than for, say, a fried egg or steak. Like a soup, your vegetables could be ready, or you could let them go longer for flavors to concentrate further. The worst that could happen is things start to get dry (just add a little water) or burn (unlikely at a low temperature).

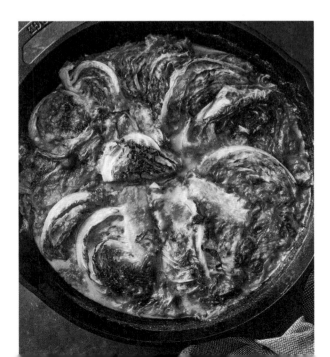

Creamy Tomato Soup (No Cream)

For vegans and grilled cheese lovers alike.

GARLIC

TOMATO PASTE

CANNED TOMATOES

TAHINI

FOR 4

1. In a large Dutch oven, finely grate **4 garlic cloves.** Add **3 tablespoons olive oil, 3 tablespoons tomato paste,** and **1 teaspoon red pepper flakes.** Cook over medium, stirring, until the tomato paste is one shade darker, 3 to 5 minutes.

2. Add **2 (28-ounce) cans fire-roasted or regular crushed tomatoes** and **1½ cups water.** Season generously with S&P. Bring to a boil, then reduce the heat to medium-low and simmer, smashing the tomatoes on the side of the pot, until flavorful and thickened slightly, 8 to 10 minutes. If you want a smoother soup, blend in batches. Off the heat, stir in **3 tablespoons tahini.** Season to taste with S&P.

3. Eat the soup with a drizzle of tahini and olive oil (or any way you like tomato soup).

· In step 2, pour the water into the cans to get every last bit of tomato.

· Good with fried bread (p. 109) sprinkled with za'atar, crumbled pita chips, or a grilled cheese.

Green Soup to the Rescue

Fresh-feeling even when you don't feel the same.

SHALLOTS

FRESH CHILE

COCONUT OIL

COCONUT MILK

FROZEN
SPINACH

RICE NOODLES

PEANUTS

LIME

FOR 4

1. Bring a medium saucepan of water to a boil. Coarsely chop **2 shallots.** Halve **1 fresh chile (jalapeño, serrano)** lengthwise and remove the seeds. In a separate medium pot, warm **1 table-spoon coconut oil** over medium. Add the shallots, season with S&P, and cook until very soft and sweet, 4 to 6 minutes.

2. Add **2 (14-ounce) cans full-fat coco-nut milk, 10 ounces frozen chopped spinach,** and half or all the chile, de-pending on your heat preference. Fill up one coconut-milk can with water and add that to the pot. Season with S&P. Cover, bring to a boil over high, then reduce the heat to medium-low, partially cover, and simmer, breaking up spinach as needed, until the spinach is soft and the soup is slightly thick-ened, 8 to 10 minutes.

3. While the soup's cooking, add **10 ounces rice vermicelli noodles** to the boiling water and cook according to the package directions. Drain, rinse, and transfer to bowls. Taste the soup and adjust with S&P. Coarsely chop **¼ cup roasted, salted peanuts.** Top the noodles with soup and peanuts. Eat with a squeeze of **lime** juice.

· There are a bazillion things you could add. Cook edamame or shrimp with the noodles, brown broccoli or mushrooms before the shallots, simmer tofu or white fish in the coconut broth. To bowls, add leftover sweet potato or chicken, raw shaved carrots, corn kernels, or herbs. Shift the flavor with fish sauce, sambal oelek, or miso.

Cauliflower Mash with Smoked Trout

Kinda sorta colcannon.

CAULIFLOWER
POTATOES
SCALLIONS
GARLIC
BUTTER
MILK
SPICY GREENS
SOUR CREAM
SMOKED TROUT

FOR 4

1. Coarsely chop the stem and head of **1 medium cauliflower** (about 1½ pounds). Cut **1 pound Yukon Gold potatoes** (about 3) into ½-inch pieces (no need to peel unless you want to). Thinly slice **6 scallions,** keeping white and green parts separate. Thinly slice **4 garlic cloves.**

2. In a large Dutch oven, melt **2 tablespoons butter** over medium. Add the scallion whites and garlic and cook until soft, 1 to 2 minutes. Add the cauliflower, potatoes, **2 cups whole milk,** and **1 teaspoon each S&P.** Bring to a simmer over medium, then cover, reduce the heat to low, and simmer, stirring occasionally, until tender, 15 to 20 minutes.

3. Meanwhile, finely chop **3 cups spicy greens (watercress, arugula, mizuna).**

4. Remove the cauliflower and potatoes from the heat and mash with a potato masher until the mixture is smooth(ish). Stir in **another tablespoon of butter** until melted, then **¼ cup sour cream (or yogurt or crème fraîche).** Add more milk if it's dry; if it's soupy, stir over low heat until it resembles mashed potatoes. Season to taste with S&P, then stir in the spicy greens and **5 to 6 ounces hot-smoked trout,** ripping it into bite-size pieces as you add.

5. Top each bowlful with the scallion greens, a pat of butter, and more pepper. (Keeps for 2 days in the fridge.)

More with hot-smoked trout

· **Everything lentils:** Toast everything bagel seasoning and capers in olive oil. Stir into cooked lentils with smoked trout, lemon, and bagel veg (tomatoes, cukes).

· **Coconut chowder:** Simmer leeks, ginger, little potatoes, coconut milk, and fish sauce. When the potatoes are tender, add celery, hot-smoked trout, and lemon juice.

· **Omelet:** Add smoked trout, crème fraîche, and dill into the middle of an omelet (p. 27). Crumble potato chips on top.

· **Rice bowl:** Eat on rice with nori, avocado, chile oil, pickled red onions, and/or straggling vegetables.

· **Potato hash:** Fry cubed potatoes, then add corn kernels, smoked trout, furikake, and lime. Top with a fried egg.

Coconut–Green Curry Cabbage

The singe of a roast plus the melt of a braise.

COCONUT MILK

SOY SAUCE

GREEN CURRY
PASTE

GINGER

CABBAGE

WHITE RICE

QUINOA

FOR 4

1. Heat the oven to 450°F. Bring **2 cups water** to a boil in a medium saucepan. Crack open **2 (14-ounce) cans full-fat coconut milk** and pour one into a measuring cup. Stir in **¼ cup low-sodium soy sauce** and **3 to 4 tablespoons green curry paste** (depending on heat preference). Finely grate in **2 inches ginger** and season with S&P. Halve **1 medium Savoy or green cabbage** (about 2 pounds) through the root. Cut inch-thick wedges through the root.

2. In a large, ovenproof skillet, heat **¼ cup neutral or coconut oil** over medium-high heat. Add one layer of wedges and cook, undisturbed, until golden, 2 to 4 minutes. Transfer to a plate and repeat with the remaining cabbage, adding more oil as needed. Flip the wedges and return all cabbage to the skillet, browned side up. Pour in the coconut milk mixture and the second can of milk (the cabbage won't be covered in liquid). Roast until the cabbage is tender when poked with a fork, 20 to 25 minutes.

3. Add **½ cup long-grain white rice, ½ cup quinoa,** and **1 teaspoon salt** to the boiling water and stir to combine. Cover, reduce the heat to low, and cook for 17 minutes. Remove from the heat and keep covered until the cabbage is ready. Eat the cabbage and sauce on top of the quinoa and rice.

Other braise-roasted cabbages

· Kimchi + sesame oil + water (finish with scallions and sesame seeds)

· Tomato paste + Sherry vinegar + shallots + water (eat with garlic mayo)

· Bacon + pickled peppers + pepper brine + chicken stock (over egg noodles)

· Kielbasa + chicken stock (eat with sour cream and dill)

Green Beans & Grains with Gochujang Butter

Limp in looks but not in flavor.

GREEN BEANS

GOCHUJANG

RICE VINEGAR

GARLIC

GINGER

FARRO

EGGS

SESAME SEEDS

FOR 4

1. Trim the stem ends of **1½ pounds green beans** (line up a handful and trim all the stems off at once). In a measuring cup, stir together **¼ cup gochujang** and **¼ cup unseasoned rice vinegar.** Finely grate in **2 garlic cloves** and **2 inches ginger.**

2. Place a large Dutch oven over medium-high. When it's just smoking, add the green beans and cook, tossing just once or twice, until bright green and charred in spots, 4 to 5 minutes. Add **3½ cups water, 1 cup farro,** and the gochujang mixture. Bring to a boil, then reduce the heat, cover, and cook until the beans are very tender and no longer squeaky, 40 to 45 minutes. Stir the beans from time to time, adding water if the pot's dry.

3. When the beans are just about done, fry some eggs: Heat **3 tablespoons neutral oil** in a large nonstick skillet over medium-high. Crack **4 eggs** into the skillet and cook, untouched, until the edges are lacy and golden brown, about 2 minutes. Now tilt the pan toward you, spoon up some of the oil, and drizzle the oil over the whites and where the white meets the yolk (avoid the yolk). Repeat until the whites are set but the yolk is still runny, another minute or two. Season with S&P.

4. Add **2 tablespoons butter** to the beans. Cook, stirring, until the beans are glazed. Season to taste with S&P. Eat a big bowl of the farro and green beans with a fried egg and **toasted sesame seeds.**

For something different, a game of telephone

· **Harissa braised beans & farro:** The above recipe is inspired by something my editor, Jenn, made one night: She sautéed green beans in oil, fried tomato paste with harissa and ground spices, then added farro and water. She covered and baked until tender. It was inspired by a recipe of mine . . .

· **Baked farro with lentils:** In a 2-quart baking dish, combine 1 cup farro and ½ cup green lentils with 28 ounces warm tomato sauce (p. 333). Bake at 400°F until tender, 40 to 50 minutes. Stir, add slabs of feta and olive oil, then broil (like on page 178).

CHICKEN

Brown, bother, repeat

You know why you came to this section: crackly chicken skin, juicy meat, and a real need to switch up your chicken-cooking routine. Welcome. Keep reading.

Work those thighs.

Chicken thighs, both with and without skin and bones, are difficult to overcook and endlessly versatile. You can cook boneless, skinless thighs at a high heat to get a nice hard sear. Leave them on there a little longer, just to *make sure* they're cooked through, and they'll still shine with juices as you cut in. Eat whole or cube, slice, or shred for soup, salad, stir-fries, or saucy dishes.

While bone-in, skin-on thighs take a little longer to cook, no matter how much or little you embellish them, they consistently yield juicy meat, brittle skin, and generous drippings for cooking your side. Dinner that starts with bone-in thighs can easily be a one-pot or one-pan endeavor, no matter how you spin it.

Really do pat dry.

If you only use paper towels for one thing, choose dabbing raw chicken dry, even though the activity doesn't make you say "yum." That exterior liquid is part of the reason why chicken (and other meat and fish) sputters, sticks to the pan, and doesn't brown.

Salt early when you can.

Sprinkling salt on the surface of chicken 45 minutes to a few days before cooking seasons the meat and helps the skin crisp and the meat stay succulent. If you know bone-in, skin-on chicken's in your future, pat it dry and season it with about ½ teaspoon salt per pound. Refrigerate the salt-sprinkled chicken uncovered for up to a few days. Let the chicken come to room temp before cooking.

Two old-faithful bone-in methods. Roast thighs skin side up in a 425°F to 450°F oven for 30 to 35 minutes (they're cooked through when the internal temp is 165°F in the thickest part). The chicken's juices can be soaked up by vegetables, beans, or anything else that's also cooking on the sheet pan.

For the skillet option, dribble a little olive oil in a big cast-iron skillet. Add the thighs skin side down, then heat over medium. Let them sizzle until golden brown and the skin releases easily from the pan, about 15 minutes. It's okay if they're squeezed in the skillet; as the fat renders, they'll shrink. Press them down with tongs to help them cook evenly, but try not to peek or move them. If your stove is getting splattered, partially cover the skillet with a baking sheet or lid. Flip the thighs over and cook until cooked through (165°F), 10 to 15 minutes.

A skillet can't accommodate much beyond chicken like a sheet pan can, and that's okay: Take the chicken out to rest, then cook a quick side in the warm chicken fat. Springy vegetables (p. 264)? Creamed greens? A sauce of tomatoes and white wine? An even simpler pan sauce of the browned bits scraped up with a little water and lemon juice?

Best of the breast. If you really can't get behind dark meat, *fine,* here are the safest bets for juicy, flavorful breasts. For boneless, skinless chicken breasts, simmer softly (p. 284). For bone-in, skin-on, place a large cast-iron skillet in the oven and heat the oven to 425°F. Pat the chicken dry and season with S&P. When the oven's heated, pat the chicken dry again and rub all over with olive oil. Place the chicken skin side down in the preheated skillet and roast, flipping halfway through, until the internal temperature in the thickest part reaches 150°F, 20 to 25 minutes. Transfer to a cutting board skin side up to rest for at least 5 minutes, then remove the bone and slice against the grain.

Schmaltz often. After cooking skin-on chicken, the floor of the sheet pan or skillet glistens like the ocean. That rendered chicken fat brings oomph to an aimless dinner, resuscitating any old veg or regular-seeming side. Use the chicken fat anywhere you'd use olive oil: to cook vegetables, coat beans, toast bread, or make salad dressing. Chicken and broccoli is fine. Chicken with schmaltz-roasted broccoli gets a kiss from the chef.

Curveball your meatballs. A good first step to combat common problems with chicken (and turkey) meatballs—*so dry, so heavy, no flavor*—is to use a ground chicken that's high in fat. Then add juicy ingredients to the meat. Itty pieces of zucchini (p. 271), tomato, peppers, herbs, or alliums will soften as they cook. Curry paste (p. 290), tomato paste, mayo, miso, and other spoonable pantry items add moisture and personality, as do soft or meltable cheeses like ricotta (p. 333), mozz, and Cheddar.

Next, reconsider the egg and breadcrumbs. They bind everything together but also dilute flavor—and you just don't always need them. Instead, mix meatballs that are pretty soft and wet (use wet or oiled hands to roll). If you're still nervous, refrigerate the meatballs for 10 to 15 minutes to firm up a little before cooking.

Chicken with So Much Garlic

With special guests rosemary toast and roasted garlic dressing.

LOTS OF GARLIC

BONE-IN, SKIN-ON THIGHS

ROSEMARY

SALAD GREENS

CRUSTY BREAD

LEMON

DIJON MUSTARD

GARLIC FOR 4
(7½ cloves per person!)

1. Heat the oven to 425°F. Smash but don't peel **30 fat garlic cloves** (from 3 to 4 heads). Toss on a sheet pan with enough **olive oil** to coat. Pat **2 pounds bone-in, skin-on chicken thighs** dry. Transfer to the sheet pan and season all over with **1 teaspoon each S&P** and enough **olive oil** to coat. Arrange the chicken skin side up around the garlic, then nestle some **rosemary sprigs** under the chicken. Roast, without flipping, until the chicken is cooked through, 30 to 35 minutes. (Remove garlic cloves if they start to burn, which might happen with small ones.)

2. Meanwhile, in a large bowl, combine bite-size pieces of **4 cups full-flavored salad greens (radicchio, frisée, arugula).** Cut **4 thick slices crusty bread.**

3. Remove the chicken, garlic, and rosemary from the sheet pan, leaving the fat behind. Pluck some of the rosemary leaves and add back to the sheet pan. Add the bread and turn to coat in the chicken fat. Arrange the bread so the rosemary is under slices (look at you, making rosemary bread). Roast until the bread is toasted, 5 to 10 minutes.

4. Meanwhile, in a measuring cup, stir together the juice from **1 lemon** (about 3 tablespoons) and **1 tablespoon Dijon mustard.** Squeeze 10 garlic cloves into the lemon dressing. Smash with a fork, then add **½ cup olive oil,** stirring to combine. Try the dressing on a salad leaf and season accordingly with S&P, lemon, and oil. Toss the greens with enough salad dressing to coat.

5. Eat the chicken, toasted bread, and salad with the extra garlic cloves for smushing on the bread.

· In step 3, you could add a veg that roasts in 5 to 10 minutes, like broccolini, torn kale leaves, or string beans.

261

Sesame Chicken Meatballs

Broiling solves nearly all the meatball conundrums: the hockey pucks, paleness, splatters, and all.

WHITE RICE

BROCCOLI

TAHINI

SOY SAUCE

SESAME OIL

SAMBAL OELEK

GINGER

LIME

GROUND CHICKEN

SESAME SEEDS

FOR 4

1. Heat the broiler with a rack 5 or fewer inches from the heat source. Cook **1 cup long-grain white rice** for serving (p. 170 if you need a method).

2. Meanwhile, peel the stalks of **1 pound broccoli** (about 1 large head). Slice the stalks crosswise ¼ inch thick. Cut the florets into 1½- to 2-inch pieces. Toss on a sheet pan with **2 tablespoons olive oil** and season with S&P.

3. In a measuring cup, combine **½ cup tahini, 2 tablespoons low-sodium soy sauce, 2 tablespoons toasted sesame oil,** and **1 tablespoon sambal oelek.** Finely grate **1 tablespoon ginger** and the zest of **1 lime** into the cup and stir with a fork to combine.

4. Put **1 pound ground chicken** and **2 tablespoons toasted sesame seeds** in a medium bowl. Season with S&P. Add ¼ cup of the sesame sauce to the bowl and stir until combined. Using wet hands, shape into 12 meatballs (about 2 tablespoons or 1½ ounces each) and plop them among the broccoli (they will be soft). Broil, flipping the broccoli and rotating the pan as needed for even coverage under the broiler, until the meatballs are golden and cooked through (165°F) and the broccoli is crisp-tender and browned in spots, 8 to 12 minutes.

5. To the remaining sesame sauce, add **¼ cup water,** the juice of the lime (about 2 tablespoons), and **1 teaspoon sugar.** Eat the meatballs and broccoli with the rice, the sesame sauce, and more sesame seeds and sambal oelek.

· Instead of broccoli, use another vegetable that's good both raw and crisp-tender, like snap peas, scallions, broccolini, or sweet mini peppers.

More with the sesame sauce

· **Cold noodles:** Coat fresh egg noodles with the sauce and eat with cucumbers, like Chinese sesame or peanut noodles.

· **Marinate:** Coat boneless chicken thighs or vegetables in the sesame sauce, then grill or roast. The sauce will toast and char.

· **Salad dressing:** For greens, grains, steamed vegetables, roasted sweet potatoes, chicken salad, and so on.

Skillet Thighs with Peas & Pickled Chiles

Spring for the chicken.

BONE-IN, SKIN-ON THIGHS

FRESH CHILES

RICE VINEGAR

SNAP PEAS

SOFT HERBS

FROZEN PEAS

CRUMBLY CHEESE

FOR 4

1. Pat **2 pounds bone-in, skin-on chicken thighs** dry and season with **1 teaspoon salt** and some pepper. Drizzle **1 tablespoon olive oil** in a large cast-iron skillet or Dutch oven. Add the thighs, skin side down, and set over medium. Cook, undisturbed, until the skin is deep golden brown and unstuck from the pan, about 15 minutes. If your stove is getting splattered, cover the skillet with a baking sheet. Flip the thighs over and cook until the meat is cooked through, 10 to 15 minutes.

2. Meanwhile, thinly slice **2 fresh chiles (red Fresno, Thai).** Add to a medium bowl with **1 tablespoon sugar, 3 tablespoons unseasoned rice vinegar,** and **2 teaspoons salt.** Pour **¼ cup boiling water** over the chiles and stir to dissolve the sugar. Trim **4 cups snap peas,** then thinly slice on a very sharp diagonal so they're almost shredded. Pluck **1 cup soft herb leaves (mint, dill).**

3. Transfer the chicken skin side up to a plate, leaving the fat behind. Still over medium, add **2 cups frozen peas (10 ounces)** and the pickled chile mixture to the pan. Cook, scraping the bottom of the pan for browned bits, until the peas are cooked through, 3 to 4 minutes. Off the heat, add the snap peas and herbs and crumble **½ cup crumbly cheese (feta, Cotija, ricotta salata)** over. Stir just once or twice to coat.

More veg for skillet chickens

· Asparagus + corn + turmeric + cumin seeds

· Escarole + white beans + honey + chile flakes

· Peppers + onions + za'atar

· Cauliflower + dates + dill

· Kimchi + boiled potatoes

· Broccoli + fish sauce + lime

· Shallots + red wine vinegar

· Cabbage + salami

· Parsley + croutons

Lemon-Pepper Chicken & Potatoes

Sorry about the dirty pan and longish cook time; not sorry about how undoubtedly delicious this is.

LEMONS

FENNEL SEEDS

BONE-IN, SKIN-ON THIGHS

CHICKEN STOCK

POTATOES

FOR 4

1. Heat the oven to 450°F. Zest **4 lemons** into a medium bowl. Crush **2 teaspoons fennel seeds** underneath a mug or skillet or in a spice grinder. Grind **1 whole tablespoon of pepper.** Stir the fennel seeds and pepper into the lemon zest, along with **1 tablespoon olive oil** and **1 teaspoon salt.** Pat **2 pounds bone-in, skin-on chicken thighs** dry, then transfer to the bowl and toss to coat.

2. On a sheet pan, combine ½ cup juice from the lemons, **½ cup chicken stock or water, ⅓ cup olive oil,** and **1 tablespoon salt.** Peel **3 pounds large Yukon Gold potatoes** (about 6). Cut each potato into 8 pieces by halving crosswise, then quartering each half. Toss the potatoes in the liquid on the sheet pan, then spread into an even layer. Add the chicken skin side up on top of the potatoes, along with any seeds and oil in the bowl.

3. Roast until the chicken's cooked through and the potatoes are golden and tender, 60 to 65 minutes. Season to taste with S&P.

· For an easier clean-up, line the sheet pan (including up the sides) with foil.

· Instead of or in addition to the chicken, you could warm slabs of feta or halloumi by adding in the last 15 minutes of the potatoes roasting. Or just make the potatoes (aka Greek lemon potatoes).

All the Time Chicken Thighs

Bright, flavorful chicken that can go anywhere dinner
(and leftovers) takes you.

BONELESS,
SKINLESS
THIGHS

GROUND
CUMIN

GROUND
CORIANDER

SMOKED
PAPRIKA

GARLIC

LEMON

FOR 4

1. Pat 1½ pounds boneless, skinless chicken thighs dry, then season all over with S&P. In a medium bowl, stir together ¼ cup olive oil, 1 teaspoon ground cumin, ½ teaspoon ground coriander, ½ teaspoon smoked paprika, and ½ teaspoon each S&P. Grate 3 garlic cloves and the zest of 1 lemon into the mix and stir to combine.

2. Add the chicken to the marinade. You can cook the chicken right away, or marinate up to 12 hours in the fridge. Bring to room temp before cooking.

3. To grill the chicken, heat a grill to medium-high. Oil the grates with olive oil. Wipe off excess marinade from the chicken, then grill over direct heat until juices run clear and the chicken is charred in spots, about 5 minutes per side. To cook on the stovetop, sear in a large skillet over medium-high for 5 minutes per side. Or roast at 425°F for 15 to 20 minutes.

4. Eat with a squeeze from the lemon, and in any way you eat chicken: in a taco, sandwich, soup, stew—with rice, mashed potatoes, grilled vegetables, black beans, hummus, green sauce, or hot sauce.

Chicken-Dill Patties with Zucchini

Chicken can't dry out with scandalously juicy zukes around.

ZUCCHINI

SHALLOT

RED WINE
VINEGAR

PANKO

FENNEL
SEEDS

DILL

GROUND
CHICKEN

GREEK
YOGURT

FOR 4

1. Cut **2 large zucchini** (about 1 pound) crosswise on the diagonal into ¼-inch-thick-slices. Spread into an even layer on a baking sheet and sprinkle with salt.

2. Thinly slice **1 large shallot** crosswise into rings. Transfer the shallot to a large bowl. Season with S&P. Stir in **3 tablespoons red wine vinegar** and **3 tablespoons olive oil.**

3. Position a box grater in a large bowl. Grate **another large zucchini** on the large holes. Add **½ cup panko bread-crumbs, 2 teaspoons fennel seeds, 1½ teaspoons red pepper flakes, 1½ teaspoons salt,** and **½ teaspoon pepper.** Stir to combine. Coarsely chop **½ cup dill fronds and stems** and add to the bowl. Stir in **1½ pounds ground chicken.** With wet hands, form into 12 patties about ½ inch thick (about ⅓ cup or 2½ ounces each). The patties will be soft, but if they can't hold their shape, refrigerate until you're ready to cook them.

4. In a large cast-iron skillet, heat **2 ta-blespoons olive oil** over medium-high. Pat the sliced zucchini dry. Working in batches as needed, add the zucchini and cook until golden and a little tender when pushed with your finger, 2 to 4 minutes per side. As they finish, transfer to the shallot mixture, stirring to combine.

5. Heat **another tablespoon olive oil** in the skillet. Working in batches and adjusting the heat as needed, add the chicken patties and cook until golden brown and cooked through, 3 to 5 minutes per side. If the splattering is wild, cover the skillet with a baking sheet. Eat the chicken and zucchini with a schmear of **full-fat Greek yogurt.**

· To make patties that are all the same size, weigh the meat, divide by 12, and then weigh each patty. Or you can guesstimate: Pat the meat down in the bowl, halve the meat with your hand or spatula, then keep halving until you get 12 portions.

Bacon Jalapeño Smashburgers

No need for ketchup or mustard when there's bacon fat.

RED ONION

JALAPEÑO

BACON

GROUND CHICKEN

BURGER BUNS

MAKES 4 burgers

1. Slice **1 small red onion** and **1 jalapeño** as thin as you can. Cut **8 regular (not thick-cut) bacon slices** in half crosswise. Working the meat as little as possible, roll **1 pound ground chicken** into 4 (4-ounce) meatballs, then press down slightly to give them flat tops.

2. Warm a little **neutral oil** in a large cast-iron skillet over medium-high, then toast the cut sides of **4 burger buns,** 1 to 2 minutes. Transfer to plates. Add half the bacon to the skillet and cook until crisp, 1 to 2 minutes per side. Transfer to 2 bottom buns.

3. Season 2 of the meatballs generously with S&P. Place them far apart in the skillet. Using a spatula, smash the meatballs down as thin as you can. Top each with a handful of the onion and jalapeño and press them into the meat. Cook, untouched, until browned, 1½ to 2 minutes.

4. Flip the patties and cook until the chicken's cooked through and the onions are golden, another 1 to 1½ minutes. Place the patties on the buns. Repeat with the remaining bacon, meat, onions, and jalapeño.

Really crispy oven fries: Heat the oven to 450°F. Place a sheet pan on the bottom rack of the oven. Cut 2 large russet potatoes into ¼-inch fries. Toss with 2 tablespoons olive oil and S&P. Place the potatoes on the heated sheet pan and roast on the bottom rack until tender and golden brown, 20 to 25 minutes.

Start with leftovers

Maybe you always have a baggie of chicken kicking around, or were tempted, again, by the well-lit rotisserie chicken at the store. These options may not carry the charisma of a fresh roast, but with a cooked bird in hand, you're halfway to dinner. The recipes in this section will stretch anywhere from 2 to 4 cups of already-cooked chicken into a meal (or poach breasts or thighs for the occasion; see page 284).

Don't cook for long, or at all. Day-old chicken can be dry (and the breasts on a rotisserie chicken are kind of always dry, don't you think?). Searing or braising might squeeze out more of its juices. Instead, futz as little as possible and eat it cold or just warmed through.

How to resurrect parched chicken. The mustard and mayo on your chicken sandwich make it taste good but also prevent it from eating dry. The same goes for anything made with leftover chicken: Moisture and fat prevent and remedy thirsty chicken. Add room-temp chicken to a well-dressed salad, make a really flavorful soup and add the chicken at the end, or warm chicken gently in sauce—maybe one with tomatillos (p. 374), tomato (p. 282), or hot sauce (p. 369). When reheating alone on the stove or in the microwave, add a little water.

The oil or butter in your dressing or sauce may be enough fat to keep the chicken feeling juicy, but if not, add another soft source of fat like mayo, ricotta, goat cheese, avocado, or sour cream.

Flavor. Leftover chicken is your proverbial blank canvas, so incorporate bright, big ingredients. Surprise with sweetness: dried fruit in dressing (p. 277), tomatoes in stew, or brown sugar in barbecue sauce. Tickle with spice: chili powder, fresh peppers, kimchi, or a splash of red pepper flakes. Or consider something acidic, like the tang of feta, pucker of lemon, or brine of pickles.

No skin in this game. The opportunity for crackly skin was yesterday (and over on page 256). Strip off the slacking skin before going for the meat.

Marbella Chicken Salad

Fowl play with chicken salad and Chicken Marbella, two classics from *The Silver Palate Cookbook*.

OLIVES
GARLIC
DRIED FRUIT
NUTS
CAPERS
OREGANO
RED WINE VINEGAR
HONEY
COOKED CHICKEN

FOR 4

1. Add these things to a medium saucepan as you prep them: Pit and halve **¼ cup green or Kalamata olives.** Thinly slice **6 garlic cloves.** Pit and coarsely chop **¼ cup dried fruit (dates, figs, apricots).** Coarsely chop **¼ cup roasted nuts (almonds, pecans).**

2. Add **½ cup olive oil, 3 tablespoons capers,** and **2 oregano sprigs** to the pot and place over medium-low. Cook, stirring occasionally, until the garlic is golden around the edges, 3 to 5 minutes. Off the heat, season with S&P.

3. Stir **¼ cup red wine vinegar** and **1 teaspoon honey** into the oil. Dunk a piece of chicken in there and try it, then adjust the seasonings until you find a good balance of sweet and salty. Shred **2 to 4 cups cooked chicken** into the dressing and stir to combine. If the chicken still has a chill from the fridge, return the pot to medium-low heat to warm slightly. (Keeps for 2 days in the fridge.)

· Good with bitter or crisp greens, like radicchio or Little Gem; boiled grains, lentils, or potatoes; or walnuts, tarragon, and celery like *The Silver Palate*'s chicken salad.

More chicken salads

· Roasted peppers + smoked paprika + almonds + Sherry vinegar + olive oil

· Smashed green beans (p. 214) + tahini-orange dressing (p. 217)

· Cabbage + peanut-mint dressing (p. 237)

· Yogurt + asparagus + crushed pita chips

· Romaine + corn + tomatillo salsa (p. 242)

· Lentils + celery + horseradish + crème fraîche

Chicken & Rice with Smoked Paprika

For those swayed by the singe and smoke of paella.

SCALLIONS

GARLIC

COOKED
CHICKEN

TOMATO
PASTE

SMOKED
PAPRIKA

SUSHI RICE

CHICKEN
STOCK

LEMON

FOR 4

1. Thinly slice **4 scallions,** keeping the white and green parts separate. Thinly slice **5 garlic cloves.** Shred **2 to 3 cups cooked chicken.**

2. Heat **3 tablespoons olive oil** in a large nonstick skillet over medium. Add the scallion whites, the garlic, **3 tablespoons tomato paste,** and **1 teaspoon smoked paprika.** Season with S&P and cook, stirring, until a shade darker, 3 to 4 minutes. Stir in **1 cup sushi rice** until well coated.

3. Add **2 cups chicken stock,** the chicken, and **1 teaspoon salt** and bring to a boil over medium-high. Reduce the heat to low, cover with a lid, baking sheet, or foil, and cook until the rice is tender and most of the liquid is absorbed, 15 to 20 minutes.

4. Uncover the skillet and poke five or six holes in the rice to help steam escape. Increase the heat to medium and cook undisturbed until you start to see browned rice at the edges, 5 to 7 minutes. If you don't see oil bubbling around the edges or in the holes, drizzle in another tablespoon or two of oil.

5. To eat, loosen the edges and flip the rice onto a big plate, or scoop spoonfuls from the pan, making sure to get some of the crispy rice on the bottom. Top with scallion greens, S&P, and a squeeze of **1 lemon.**

· Instead of chicken, use drained chickpeas, thinly sliced summer squash or asparagus, cherry tomatoes, peas, or cauliflower.

· Use 2 cups already-cooked rice instead of the sushi rice and stock.

· Also nice to toss the scallion greens with a soft herb (cilantro, parsley).

Kids' Menu Enchiladas

It's all (chili) gravy.

FLOUR

CHILI
POWDER

TOMATO
PASTE

CHICKEN
STOCK

SOUR CREAM

COOKED
CHICKEN

CHEDDAR

SCALLIONS

TORTILLAS

HOT CHEESE
for 4

1. Heat the oven to 425°F. Melt **3 tablespoons butter** in a medium saucepan over medium. When foaming, add **3 tablespoons all-purpose flour** and cook, stirring, until golden, 2 to 3 minutes. Add **2 tablespoons chili powder** and **2 tablespoons tomato paste**, season with S&P, and stir until dark brown, 1 to 2 minutes. Switch to a whisk and slowly pour in **2½ cups chicken stock**, whisking as you go. Bring the mixture to a simmer, then cook, whisking occasionally, until thick enough to coat the back of a spoon, 10 to 15 minutes. Turn off the heat, season generously with S&P, then whisk in **2 tablespoons sour cream** until smooth. Taste; if it's too spicy, add more sour cream.

2. Meanwhile, shred **2 to 3 cups cooked chicken** into a medium bowl. Coarsely grate **2 cups sharp Cheddar cheese** (about 8 ounces) and add half to the bowl. Thinly slice **6 scallions** and add half to the bowl. Season the chicken with S&P and stir to combine.

3. Pour ½ cup of the enchilada sauce into a 9 by 13-inch or other 3-quart baking dish. Spread to cover the bottom of the dish. Put **8 (6-inch) corn or flour tortillas** in a single layer on a sheet pan and heat in the oven until warmed and pliable, 1 to 2 minutes.

4. Line up the filling, sheet pan of tortillas, and baking dish. Divide the chicken mixture among the tortillas (¼ cup to ⅓ cup each). Roll up each tortilla and place in the baking dish, seam side down, as you go. Pour the remaining sauce over the enchiladas, then sprinkle with the remaining cheese. Bake until the cheese has melted, 8 to 10 minutes. Top with the remaining scallions and more sour cream if you want.

· This sauce is inspired by the Tex-Mex mash-up chili gravy, which is made by toasting flour with fat (oil, lard, bacon drippings, butter), then toasting spices, adding water or stock, and simmering until gravy-like. This recipe adds tomato paste for savoriness and sour cream for creaminess, and adds chicken where there's cheese and onion.

· You could also fill the tortillas with scrambled eggs, beans, peppers and onions, or pulled pork or turkey.

Cheesy Bread Potpie

A red sauce spectacle.

BROCCOLI
RABE

PICKLED
PEPPERS

BACON

GARLIC

CANNED
TOMATOES

MOZZARELLA

COOKED
CHICKEN

BAGUETTE

FOR 4 to 6

1. Heat the oven to 450°F. Remove the tough ends from **1 bunch broccoli rabe,** then slice crosswise ½ inch thick. Stem and coarsely chop **6 pickled cherry or Peppadew peppers** (hold on to the jar).

2. Over a large, ovenproof skillet, cut **4 thick-cut bacon slices** into ½-inch-thick pieces with scissors. Set the pan over medium and cook, stirring sometimes, until golden brown, 5 to 7 minutes. Add the broccoli rabe and peppers, finely grate in **2 garlic cloves,** season with S&P, and stir until wilted. Add **1 (28-ounce) can tomato puree or crushed tomatoes,** season with S&P, and bring to a gentle simmer. Reduce the heat to medium-low, cover, and let simmer.

3. Meanwhile, coarsely grate **1 cup low-moisture mozzarella** (about 4 ounces) into a bowl. Finely grate **2 garlic cloves** into the cheese. Season with black pepper and stir to combine. Shred **2 to 4 cups cooked chicken.** Slice **1 baguette** crosswise ½ inch thick and coat one side with **olive oil.**

4. Stir the chicken and ¼ **cup pickled pepper brine** into the tomato sauce. Season with S&P and add water if the skillet seems dry—you want it just thinner than stew. Taste and reseason with S&P as needed. Transfer the skillet to a sheet pan, then top with the baguette slices, oil sides up (they can overlap). Press the bread down slightly, then sprinkle the cheese over the bread. Bake until the mixture is bubbling and the cheese is melted, 10 to 15 minutes. Broil for a golden top.

· The broccoli rabe could be another hearty vegetable that cooks in 10 to 15 minutes, like cauliflower, carrots, or kale.

· Trade the shredded chicken for chicken or pork sausage (brown it with the bacon in step 2).

· The baguette could be one or two hoagie rolls or big torn pieces of any aging crusty bread.

Simmer softly

Cure-alls go by the names Tylenol and aspirin—as well as adobo, arroz caldo, avgolemono, cacciatore, chicken noodle, matzo ball soup, pho, pozole, and tagine. There's universal comfort in a bird simmering away until the broth gets fortified and chickeny, the meat melts, and your house smells wonderful.

Simmer for straight-up juicy meat.

For unembellished meat that's (bad word incoming) moist, simmer—or poach it, I think, if we're being technical. Start by covering the breasts, thighs, or ground meat in cold, salted water. (If you want to use the simmering liquid as a light broth for your meal, use chicken stock and/or add veg scraps or aromatics.) Bring to a simmer. If you see bubbles as big as a bubble bath, reduce the heat until you see Champagne bubbles, so the chicken doesn't tighten. Cook until the chicken's done, 10 to 20 minutes, then remove, let cool slightly, and slice or shred. Use it in salads, as a dipper (p. 365), or wherever you'd use leftover chicken (p. 274).

Brown first.

Brown food is flavorful food, so before the chicken meets liquid, use your still-empty pot to brown the meat. Not only will the chicken take on new layers of flavor, but it will beget drippings, which will mix into the broth and make it taste more richly of chicken. Synergy!

Pat the meat dry (otherwise it will steam) and season with S&P. Warm a little oil in the pot, then brown the chicken, only flipping or stirring after the underside has taken on color.

To avoid drying out the chicken, use thighs or ground meat instead of breasts and only sear until browned, not necessarily until cooked through. The simmering will take care of that part.

A covered pot always boils.

Most recipes don't specify to bring liquids to a boil with a lid on—the thinking being the liquid could bubble over and you'll have a mess to clean up. But a covered pot will get you to a boil a little quicker, so even if a recipe doesn't instruct to cover the pot, know that you can. Just keep one ear on it: When you hear bubbling, you're boiling.

Find your house chicken stock.

Cooking chicken in stock jump-starts the whole endeavor since your base is already meaty, seasoned, craveable. Problem is a lot of store-bought brands are weak or strangely sweet, or taste mostly of vegetables, so try a bunch and find one you like (at my house, it's Swanson).

Add starch to soak up juices.

As chicken cooks, it so generously shares its juices with the surrounding ingredients. Instead of eating your chicken *over* pasta or grains, add them *to* the liquid while the chicken is cooking. It's a reciprocal relationship: The starches plump with the flavorful liquid while thickening said liquid. As a result, orzo can be suspended in a lemon-garlic sauce (p. 289) and rice will turn broth into stew (p. 293).

One exception: If you're betting on leftovers, it's better to cook the starch separately because it will keep drinking as it sits (which is why reheated leftover pasta is always kinda mushy).

Shortcut Chicken Chili

Mom's world-famous recipe, with tweaks because that's what kids do.

ONION

GROUND CUMIN

GROUND CHICKEN

KETCHUP

HOT SAUCE

TOMATO PUREE

SALSA

BEANS

CILANTRO

FOR 4, or for the freezer

1. Coarsely chop **1 medium yellow onion.** In a large Dutch oven or pot, heat **2 tablespoons olive oil** over medium-high. Add the onions and **2 tablespoons ground cumin,** season with S&P, and cook until softened but not browned, 3 to 5 minutes. Push to one side of the pot and plop in **2 pounds ground chicken.** Season generously with S&P and cook, without stirring, until browned, 3 to 5 minutes. Break the chicken up into big pieces, stirring in the onions, and cook until opaque, a minute or two. Stir in ¼ **cup ketchup** and **2 teaspoons any hot sauce** until mostly absorbed.

2. Add **24 to 28 ounces tomato puree** and **12 to 16 ounces medium-hot jarred salsa** (Mom likes Pace). Season with S&P, bring to a simmer, then reduce the heat to medium-low and cook, stirring occasionally, until thickened and flavorful, 10 to 15 minutes. If it gets too thick, add some water. Taste every so often and adjust the amount of heat, salt, and spices to taste (if it's too spicy, add more ketchup). Drain and rinse **2 (15-ounce) cans pinto, black, or any beans you like in chili** (sorry Texas). Stir in the beans and cook until warmed.

3. Coarsely chop ½ **cup cilantro leaves and stems** and stir it in.

Chicken Larb

You're simply the best.

GROUND CHICKEN

FISH SAUCE

SHALLOT

SCALLIONS

SOFT HERBS

LIMES

TOASTED RICE POWDER

FOR 4

1. Cover **2 pounds ground chicken** with water in a medium saucepan. Bring to a simmer over medium-high, then cook, breaking up the chicken with a spoon into small pieces, until totally white and cooked through, 8 to 10 minutes. Drain the chicken and put it back in the saucepan. Season with **6 tablespoons fish sauce** and **2 teaspoons sugar** and set aside to cool slightly.

2. While the chicken cools, thinly slice **1 large shallot** and **4 scallions**. Coarsely chop or tear **2 cups cilantro and/or mint leaves**.

3. Stir the shallot and **2 teaspoons red pepper flakes** into the chicken, followed by the scallions and herbs. Squeeze the juice of **3 limes** (about 6 tablespoons) over and stir gently. Sprinkle with **¼ cup toasted rice powder** and season to taste with more sweetness (sugar), heat (red pepper flakes), salt (fish sauce), and acid (lime juice) as needed.

· Good with rice, sliced cucumber or radish, string beans, lettuce, solo.

· Nothing really compares to the nutty crunch of toasted rice powder. It's good here and in slaws, sauces, and anywhere you'd use breadcrumbs.

A lifetime of larbs: In Lao/Isan-style larb, chunks of a simple protein are seasoned with umami (fish sauce), sweetness (sugar), freshness (alliums, herbs), heat (red pepper flakes), acid (limes), and texture (toasted rice powder). Chicken larb is probably my favorite and most eaten food—at least once a week growing up. When I've desperately craved the jolt and hum of its flavors and lacked the chicken to get there, I've substituted 4 or so cups of peas or edamame, mushrooms or cauliflower, tofu or tempeh crumbles, fresh fish or canned tuna, hard-boiled eggs, or ground pork or sausage.

One-Pan Chicken Piccata & Orzo

Slumped, spoonable, sunshiny (reminds me of a snoozing cat).

BONELESS,
SKINLESS
THIGHS

GARLIC

LEMON

SHALLOT

ORZO

CAPERS

CHICKEN
STOCK

PARSLEY

FOR 4

1. Pat **1 pound boneless, skinless chicken thighs** dry and cut into 1-inch cubes (scissors makes this easy). Transfer to a medium bowl. Add **1 tablespoon olive oil** and **½ teaspoon each S&P.** Finely grate **2 garlic cloves** and the zest of **1 lemon** into the bowl and stir to combine. Coarsely chop **1 shallot.**

2. Heat **1 tablespoon olive oil** in a medium skillet over medium. Add the chicken in a single layer and cook, without touching, until browned on one side but not necessarily cooked through, 5 to 7 minutes. Transfer to a plate.

3. Add **2 tablespoons butter** and the shallot to the skillet. When melted, stir in **1 cup orzo, 1 tablespoon capers,** and **½ teaspoon salt.** Add **2 cups chicken stock** and bring to a simmer, scraping up browned bits. Add the chicken and any juices, then reduce the heat to low, cover, and cook until the orzo is al dente, 12 to 14 minutes (the liquid won't be completely absorbed).

4. Meanwhile, finely chop **¼ cup parsley leaves.** Turn off the heat, then add the juice from half the lemon (about 1½ tablespoons). Cover and let sit for a couple minutes. Stir in the parsley and the juice from the other lemon half, then season to taste with S&P.

· If you have a bottle of dry white wine open, or need an excuse to open one, add ⅓ cup before the stock and cook until mostly evaporated.

· To make this with shrimp instead of chicken, marinate 1 pound large peeled and deveined shrimp as described, skip step 2, then add the shrimp to the top of the orzo during the last 2 minutes of cooking.

· Sneak in a green by stirring in spinach or arugula in step 4.

Green Curry Meatball Soup

Meatball as life buoy, reviving and reassuring.

GINGER

TENDER SOUP GREENS

SCALLIONS

LIMES

GROUND CHICKEN

GREEN CURRY PASTE

FISH SAUCE

CHICKEN STOCK

RICE NOODLES

FOR 4

1. Bring a medium saucepan of salted water to a boil. Meanwhile, finely grate **4 inches ginger.** Finely chop ¼ cup tender soup greens (watercress, mizuna, spinach). Thinly slice **4 scallions,** keeping white and green parts separate. Using a vegetable peeler, peel the rind of **1 lime** into wide strips.

2. In a medium bowl, stir together **1½ pounds ground chicken, 3 tablespoons green curry paste, 2 tablespoons fish sauce,** half the ginger, the chopped greens, and **1 teaspoon sugar.** Using wet hands, form into 12 meatballs (about 3 tablespoons or 2 ounces each) and refrigerate.

3. Heat **2 tablespoons neutral or coconut oil** in a large Dutch oven over medium. Add the remaining ginger and the scallion whites and cook until fragrant, 1 minute. Add **8 cups chicken stock** and the lime peel, cover, and bring to a simmer over medium-high. Once simmering, carefully add the meatballs. Reduce the heat to medium-low to maintain a gentle simmer until the meatballs are cooked through (165°F), 8 to 10 minutes.

4. When the water's boiling, cook **8 ounces thin rice vermicelli noodles** according to the package directions. Drain, rinse under cold water, and transfer to serving bowls. Coarsely chop **4 more cups tender soup greens.**

5. Off the heat, season the soup with the juice from **2 limes** (about ¼ cup) and **2 tablespoons fish sauce.** Top the noodles with meatballs, broth, scallion greens, and greens.

More with the green curry meatballs

· **Brown them:** Pan-fry or broil for a rice noodle salad, lettuce cups, or a sandwich with herbs.

· **Sheet-pan them:** Broil with broccoli (p. 263) or roast with sweet potato (p. 312).

· **Coconut them:** Add coconut milk for a creamier soup.

· **Break them up:** Skip making meatballs and instead brown the seasoned chicken, breaking it up for fried rice or a stir-fry.

My Forever Chicken & Rice Soup

Soup so likeable, Maurice Sendak wrote a kid's book about it.

CHICKEN
STOCK

BONELESS,
SKINLESS
THIGHS

WHITE RICE

BAY LEAVES

LEMONS

FOR 4

1. In a large Dutch oven or pot, combine **8 cups chicken stock, 1 pound boneless, skinless chicken thighs, 1 cup long-grain white rice, and 3 bay leaves.** Salt lightly (some stocks have more salt than others, so start easy). Bring to a simmer over medium-high, then reduce the heat to medium-low and simmer until the chicken is cooked through and the rice starts to lose its shape, 20 to 25 minutes.

2. Meanwhile, think about what else you want to add to the soup, if anything (ideas below).

3. When the soup's ready, use two forks to shred the chicken into pieces (directly in the pot). Season the soup to taste with salt. Add **1 tablespoon butter.** Grate the zest of **1 lemon** into the pot and stir to combine. Squeeze in lemon juice a little at a time until the soup is bright but still chickeny (somewhere about ½ cup, from **2 to 3 lemons**).

Ideas for add-ins

· Grated garlic + parsley

· Grated ginger + celery

· Pinto beans + lime

· Horseradish + sour cream

· Grated zucchini + goat cheese

· Dried mint + chickpeas sizzled in olive oil

· Kale + cumin seeds sizzled in oil

The anti-marinade

After you've delayed dinner by thirty minutes for marinating, then discarded that liquid and struggled to get the chicken browned because it's so wet, you're left with something that faintly tastes of the ingredients you started with. If you know the feeling, you know that marinating over-promises and under-delivers. Something doesn't add up, and there are other options.

Option 1: Flip the script.
A marinade adds moisture and sugars that can steam or burn. Instead, cook the chicken naked with just oil and S&P, then let it rest in the marinade-sauce. You get all the flavors of the marinade full-force and made even more savory as it mingles with the chicken's resting juices. This also works for other meats (p. 317 and 324), seafood (p. 346), and vegetables, which means you could combine ingredients in the marinade for a full meal, like in the Low-Maintenance Grilled Chicken (p. 301).

Option 2: Schmear.
Chicken has nooks and crannies where a glaze can cling and caramelize when it's hit by heat. Instead of hoping your marinade will penetrate your meat, make it thick and flavorful enough to stick to just the exterior (no waiting time required). That glaze could simply be a slick of harissa or gochujang, or maybe a honey-soy mixture that you boil into a sauce (p. 297). Another idea: Use a sauce or dressing you're already using for dinner to coat the chicken, like Caesar (p. 298). Also, have you met mayo?

Mayo for haters and lovers.
Even if you don't like mayo (yep, me too), it will claim a spot on your fridge door as a coating for meat. When slathered on meat and vegetables (and grilled cheese), the condiment carries flavor, doesn't fall off in the pan, encourages browning, and insulates from burning. Your finished chicken will not taste like mayo: It will taste like whatever you added to the mayo (grated ginger or citrus zest, grated Parmesan, herbs, ground spices). Because mayo has so much fat in it, you don't need to grease your pan or grill before cooking.

Sticky Chicken with Pickled Vegetables

For members of the teriyaki chicken fan club.

SUSHI RICE

BONELESS, SKINLESS THIGHS

GINGER

GARLIC

SOY SAUCE

HONEY

RICE VINEGAR

CRUNCHY VEGETABLES

FOR 4

1. Make rice: In a medium saucepan, bring **1¼ cups water, 1 cup sushi rice,** and **½ teaspoon salt** to a boil. Cover, reduce the heat to the lowest setting, and cook until the rice is tender, 12 to 15 minutes. Remove from the heat and keep covered.

2. Meanwhile, pat **1½ pounds boneless, skinless chicken thighs** dry and cut into 1-inch pieces (scissors makes this easy). Toss with **1 teaspoon each S&P.** Peel and finely grate **2 inches ginger** and **3 garlic cloves** into a medium bowl. Add **½ cup low-sodium soy sauce, ⅓ cup honey,** and **2 tablespoons unseasoned rice vinegar.** Stir with a fork to combine. Add the chicken and stir to combine.

3. Make the pickles: In a measuring cup, stir together **½ cup unseasoned rice vinegar, 1 tablespoon sugar,** and **2 teaspoons salt** until the sugar and salt dissolve. Cut **1 cup matchsticks or thin slices crunchy vegetables (carrot, celery, raw sweet potatoes, or—my favorite—chard stems).** Stir into the vinegar (transfer to a bowl if you need to).

4. Heat **1 tablespoon neutral oil** in a large nonstick skillet over medium-high. Using a slotted spoon or tongs and shaking off excess glaze, add the chicken to the skillet. Cook, stirring once, until browned, 4 to 6 minutes. Add the marinade and bring to a boil (this is how you kill the chicken stuff). Cook, stirring the chicken in the sauce, until the sauce is dark and syrupy and the chicken is cooked through, 4 to 6 minutes. Remove from the heat and stir in **1 tablespoon butter** until it's melted. Season to taste with S&P.

5. Back to the rice: Hold the vegetables back with your hand and pour a tablespoon or two of the pickling liquid into the rice. Stir to combine. Eat the chicken and pickled vegetables on top of a mound of seasoned rice.

· Instead of chicken, use cubed tofu, tempeh, or salmon.

· After you sear the chicken and before you add the sauce, add any vegetables that cook in just a few minutes, like thinly sliced green beans or asparagus.

· Rice in sushi tastes like so much more because it was probably mixed with rice vinegar, salt, and sugar. Once you start seasoning your rice similarly, whatever's alongside becomes less important.

Not Just Another Chicken Caesar

It's hard to resist a good Caesar salad, so step right up.

GARLIC

ANCHOVIES

PARMESAN

LEMON

MAYO

SOY SAUCE

DIJON
MUSTARD

BONELESS,
SKINLESS
THIGHS

CRISP
LETTUCES

FOR 4

1. Finely chop and smash together **3 garlic cloves** and **4 anchovies** until a coarse paste forms. Transfer to a medium bowl. Finely grate **¾ cup Parmesan** (about 1½ ounces) and add ½ cup to the bowl. Zest half of **1 lemon** into the bowl. Stir in **1 cup mayo, 1 teaspoon low-sodium soy sauce,** and **2 teaspoons Dijon mustard.**

2. Transfer half the dressing to a shallow dish. Pat **1 pound boneless, skinless chicken thighs** dry, season with S&P, then add to the dish and turn to coat.

3. Heat a large nonstick skillet over medium. Add the chicken and cook until golden brown and juices run clear, about 5 minutes per side. Transfer the chicken to a cutting board.

4. Separate the leaves of **a few heads of crisp lettuces (Little Gem, romaine, chicories)** and toss into a big bowl. Squeeze half the lemon (about 1½ tablespoons) over the greens, sprinkle with salt, then toss to combine. Add the remaining dressing and remaining ¼ cup Parm and toss to combine. Thinly slice the chicken. Add to the salad and season to taste with S&P, lemon, and Parm.

· For croutons, after step 2, heat 2 tablespoons olive oil in the skillet over medium-high. Add 2 thick slices crusty bread and toast until golden brown, 2 to 3 minutes per side. Transfer to a cutting board and season with salt. Cut into croutons.

Low-Maintenance Grilled Chicken

Guaranteed razzle-dazzle no matter what's grilling.

BONELESS, SKINLESS THIGHS

GRILLING VEGETABLES

LEMON

OLIVES

FENNEL SEEDS

DRIED CHILES

BAY LEAVES

FOR 4

1. Heat the grill to medium-high. Pat **1 pound boneless, skinless chicken thighs** dry, then season all over with S&P. Cut **2 pounds grilling vegetables** into large pieces. Cut cauliflower and broccoli heads into 6 wedges through the root. Quarter peppers, onions, radicchio, and fennel. Halve corn, radishes, mushrooms, and shallots. Cut zucchini and eggplant into rounds. Leave green beans, asparagus, baby carrots, shishito peppers, and scallions whole. Toss the vegetables on a sheet pan with enough **olive oil** to coat, then season with S&P.

2. Using a vegetable peeler, peel the rind of **1 lemon** into wide strips. Pit and halve **1 cup Castelvetrano olives.** In a medium saucepan, combine the lemon peel and olives with **6 tablespoons olive oil, 1 teaspoon fennel seeds, 2 dried chiles,** and **3 bay leaves.** Season generously with S&P, then warm the mixture over medium-low. Once the mixture starts to sizzle, 4 or 5 minutes, remove from the heat.

3. Grease the grill grates with **olive oil.** Grill the chicken and vegetables over direct heat until the chicken is cooked through and charred in spots and the vegetables are just tender and charred, 10 to 12 minutes for chicken, 8 to 15 minutes for dense vegetables, 2 to 3 minutes for little things. Move ingredients around the grill as needed to char and avoid flare-ups. Transfer the ingredients to the sheet pan as they finish.

4. Pour the olives and infused oil over everything. Squeeze the lemon over, season with S&P, then let sit for 10 minutes or up to 1 hour (also keeps in the fridge for up to 2 days). Eat with more lemon as desired.

More options for the infused oil in step 2

· Smoked almonds + chili powder + garlic

· Marinated artichokes + anchovy + rosemary

· Honey + jalapeño

· Harissa + halloumi

· Capers + cornichons + mustard seeds

· Blanched hazelnuts + orange peel

BEEF, PORK & LAMB

Fast track with sausage

Sausages are weeknight superheroes. Because they're packaged with fat, flavorings, and salt, they don't require additional ingredients to cook up moist and juicy (like pork chops wish they could). They brown as well as bacon and give off umami-laced drippings—a hotspot to cook a side. And there are so many kinds at any kind of market. Sausages look good in capes, don't you think?

Use the insides like ground meat. Stripped of its casings, fresh sausage looks and cooks like ground meat, so why not use it as a burger patty (p. 311), taco filling (p. 309), or meatball? In stir-fries, soups, dumplings, or nachos? The texture will be slightly different—sausage is springy, ground meat is crumbly—but no one's ever been mad at a juicy sausage for snapping back.

Hot or not. Swap sausages based on heat levels instead of sausage type (fresh, fully cooked, smoked, cured, partially cooked). Use spicy fresh sausages (hot Italian, fresh chorizo, lamb merguez) interchangeably with already-cooked sausages with a kick, like Spanish chorizo (cured), andouille (smoked), or 'nduja (cured). They will play similarly in the dish. For instance, crisp cubes of Spanish chorizo for the radicchio salad on page 175 as you would the lamb merguez. Or make the corn pasta on page 149 with andouille instead of hot Italian. Mild fresh sausages (sweet Italian, bratwurst, breakfast sausage) can swap places with other delicate options, like mortadella (cured).

When swapping, adjust cooking time as needed: Fresh sausages (the ones that look like ground meat stuffed in a see-through sock) need to be cooked through, whereas cured and smoked sausages may not require cooking but always can be browned.

When in doubt, or just over it, sheet-pan it. A sausage sheet-pan meal feels like a trick: How can something so good take so little skill and attention? All you do is rub some links with oil and score in a few places. As they roast on a lined or greased sheet pan, they offer up their fat to your side dish, which is right there browning on the pan. Most fresh sausages will be cooked through when broiled for 10 to 15 minutes or roasted at 425°F for 20 to 30 minutes.

Every Batman needs a Robin. To turn sausage into dinner, you need just one sidekick that's cooked in the meat's rendered drippings. Cook the side alongside the links on a sheet pan, or remove the sausage from a skillet, leaving the fat behind, then sizzle your side in the drippings. Even humble root vegetables, brussels sprouts and other brassicas, canned beans, bread, or store-bought gnocchi (p. 308) will go from fine to "how'd you make this?"

Cut the fat. Sausages are delicious because they contain a good amount of fat. To counter the richness, add something bright or acidic at the end, like a squeeze of lemon, drizzle of vinegar, schmear of mustard, salty cheese, pickled pepper, or fresh herb.

Freeze for sausage on demand. Sausages will keep in the freezer for three to six months. So that all your sausages aren't frozen together, put raw, fresh sausages spaced apart on a sheet pan, freeze, then transfer to a freezer bag. Defrost only the quantity you need on a half or quarter sheet pan in the fridge (to catch any juices, and because aluminum helps food defrost quicker). The sausage will defrost in a few hours.

One-Pan Sausage & Lentils

A throw-it-in-the-oven deal where lentils plump with sausage juices.

CELERY

SHALLOTS

CHICKEN STOCK

BROWN LENTILS

FRESH SAUSAGE

SHERRY VINEGAR

DIJON MUSTARD

FOR 4

1. Heat the oven to 450°F. Thinly slice **4 celery stalks** and reserve any celery leaves. Finely chop **2 shallots.** Put half the shallots in a small bowl, season with S&P, and stir to combine. In a 9 by 13-inch or other 3-quart baking dish, stir together **4 cups chicken stock, 2 cups brown or green lentils,** the remaining shallots, the celery, and ½ **teaspoon salt.**

2. Score **1 pound fresh sausage (hot Italian, Bratwurst)** in a few places on both sides, making sure not to cut all the way through. Place on top of the lentils, then drizzle lightly with **olive oil.** Roast until the sausages and lentils are cooked, 25 to 30 minutes.

3. To the bowl of shallots, add ¼ **cup olive oil, 2 tablespoons Sherry or red wine vinegar,** and **1 tablespoon Dijon mustard.** Stir well and season to taste with S&P. Eat the lentils and sausages with plenty of vinaigrette tossed through, and celery leaves if you've got any. (Keeps for 4 days in the fridge.)

· Add a couple thyme sprigs to the lentils and/or thyme leaves to the vinaigrette. Or add dill to the vinaigrette. Instead of celery, use carrots, bok choy, or fennel.

Sausage & Gnocchi

Meat and potatoes for the spontaneous and unprepared.

PICKLED PEPPERS

ITALIAN SAUSAGE

GNOCCHI

ARUGULA

FOR 4

1. Thinly slice **8 jarred peperoncini or other pickled pepper,** like cherry or Peppadew. Transfer to a medium bowl, along with ¼ **cup olive oil** and **2 tablespoons pickled pepper brine.** Season with S&P.

2. Heat **2 tablespoons olive oil** in a large skillet over medium-high. Remove the casings from **1 pound hot or sweet Italian sausage.** Add the meat to the skillet and cook, breaking pieces up with your spoon, until browned, 5 to 8 minutes. Using a slotted spoon, remove the sausage, leaving the fat behind.

3. Break up stuck-together gnocchi from **1 (18-ounce) package shelf-stable or refrigerated gnocchi.** Add to the skillet, still over medium-high, in an even layer. Cover and cook, undisturbed, until golden brown on one side, 2 to 4 minutes. Cook, stirring, until crisp on both sides, another 2 to 3 minutes. Off the heat, stir in the sausage.

4. Stir the dressing once more, then add **4 cups arugula** and toss to combine. Taste and adjust seasonings accordingly (some peppers aren't as acidic as others). Eat the gnocchi and sausage with a pile of arugula and peperoncini on top or alongside.

More sauces for crispy gnocchi

· Brown butter + red pepper flakes

· Sour cream + dill

· Ricotta + lemon + spring veg

· Caramelized onion + cabbage

· Ketchup for dipping into like a French fry

BEEF, PORK & LAMB

Chorizo & Brussels Sprouts Tacos

Pork and brassicas have always been friends (smoked ham + collard greens, griot + pikliz, pork belly + Chinese broccoli).

BRUSSELS SPROUTS

GROUND CUMIN

FRESH CHORIZO

RED ONION

LIMES

TORTILLAS

SOMETHING CREAMY

FOR 4

1. Heat the oven to 450°F and stick a sheet pan inside. Trim and halve **1½ pounds brussels sprouts.** Toss in a large bowl with S&P, **3 tablespoons olive oil,** and **1½ teaspoons ground cumin.**

2. Place the brussels sprouts on the hot sheet pan cut sides down (reserve the bowl), then squeeze 1-inch pieces of **1 pound fresh chorizo** out of their casings onto and around the sprouts. Roast for 15 minutes, then flip the sprouts and cook until tender, another 5 to 10 minutes.

3. Meanwhile, halve and thinly slice **1 small red onion** and transfer to the reserved large bowl. Zest and juice **1 lime** over the red onions (about 2 tablespoons juice). Season heavily with S&P and toss with your fingers.

4. When the sprouts and chorizo are out of the oven, toast **8 corn or flour tortillas** directly on an oven rack or over your flame, 1 to 2 minutes per side. Add the red onions and the liquid in the bowl to the sheet pan and toss to coat, scraping up any browned bits from the pan. Scoop the chorizo and sprouts into tortillas and eat with juice from more **limes** and a dollop of **something creamy** (sour cream, yogurt, the guacamole on page 28).

· Instead of brussels sprouts, use broccoli or sweet potatoes.

· You're looking for fresh chorizo in the refrigerated section, not the cured one that resembles salami. In its place, use another fresh sausage and sprinkle chili powder over after roasting.

· For heat, add chopped chipotle in adobo or hot sauce to the onions.

Pork Sausage Burgers

Like a Philly roast pork sandwich between burger buns.

BROCCOLI RABE

GARLIC

HOT ITALIAN SAUSAGE

BURGER BUNS

SLICED PROVOLONE

FOR 4

1. Bring a medium saucepan of salted water to a boil. Cut **1 bunch broccoli rabe** crosswise into 1-inch pieces. Thinly slice **4 garlic cloves.** Add the rabe to the boiling water and cook until bright green, just a minute. Drain, rinse under cold water to cool, then squeeze the liquid from the rabe.

2. Remove the casings from **1 pound hot Italian sausage** and form into four patties ½ inch wider than your **4 burger buns (or English muffins).**

3. In a large cast-iron skillet, heat **2 tablespoons olive oil** and the garlic over medium. Cook, stirring, until the garlic starts to brown around the edges, 3 to 4 minutes. Add the rabe and cook until dark green and tender, 4 to 5 minutes. Season with S&P. Transfer to a bowl or cutting board.

4. Increase the heat to medium-high, add **1 tablespoon olive oil,** and toast the cut sides of the buns until golden, 1 to 2 minutes. Transfer to plates. Season the patties with S&P. Heat **another tablespoon olive oil,** then add the burgers and cook until well browned underneath, 3 to 4 minutes. Flip the burgers, pile the rabe on top, then place **provolone cheese (1 or 2 slices per burger)** over the rabe. Cover the skillet and cook until the pork is cooked through and the cheese has melted, another 2 to 3 minutes. Transfer to the bottom buns. Swipe the top buns through the sausage fat in the skillet (just do it), then top the burgers.

Building a burger patty: Use a gentle touch when forming the meat. Form patties slightly wider than your buns (they'll shrink as they cook). Season only the outsides with S&P and only right before cooking. The rest—grilled or griddled, cheesed or plain, smashed (p. 272) or chubby—is up to you.

Merguez with Sweet Potatoes & Dates

Sweet and spicy, opposites attract.

SWEET POTATOES

LEMON

DATES

LAMB MERGUEZ

MILD SOFT HERBS

GARLIC

FOR 4

1. Heat the oven to 425°F. Halve **2 pounds sweet potatoes** (about 2 medium) lengthwise, then cut crosswise into ½-inch-thick half-moons (no need to peel). Thinly slice half of **1 lemon** crosswise and pluck out the seeds. Pit **8 dates** and coarsely chop into ½-inch pieces (outsides up so the sticky middles don't gunk up your knife). Score **1 pound lamb merguez or another spicy sausage** in a few places.

2. On a sheet pan, toss the sausages, sweet potatoes, lemon slices, and dates with **3 tablespoons olive oil** (divide among 2 pans if things are cramped). Season with S&P. Roast until the sweet potatoes are tender and the sausages are crisp and cooked through, 25 to 30 minutes (no need to flip).

3. Meanwhile, grab **1 small bunch mild soft herbs (parsley, cilantro)** and coarsely chop ¾ cup leaves and stems. Add **1 garlic clove** and a pinch of salt to the pile. Chop until a wet, coarse paste forms. Transfer to a small bowl, then add **½ cup olive oil, ½ teaspoon red pepper flakes,** and the juice from the remaining lemon half (about 1½ tablespoons). Stir to combine and season with S&P.

4. When the sausages and sweet potatoes are done, coarsely chop the roasted lemon slices and add to the sauce. Taste and adjust seasonings as you wish. Eat the sausages, sweet potatoes, and dates with the sauce.

More sheet-pan sausage parties

· Hot Italian sausage + sweet mini peppers + little tomatoes + mozzarella

· Cured chorizo + shrimp + feta + watercress

· Kielbasa + brussels sprouts + horseradish cream (p. 197)

· Salami + radicchio + mushrooms + balsamic + Parmesan

· Chicken-apple sausage + winter squash + sage

· Hot dogs + tater tots + ketchup + mustard—?!

BEEF, PORK & LAMB

Brown, bother, repeat

This section is devoted to full-throttle cooking, where meat is cooked over high, direct heat quickly so that nothing has a chance to toughen. Whether sautéing, searing, grilling, or broiling ground or whole cuts of beef, pork, or lamb, all follow a similar setup for success. Know the basics, then mix and match cuts and seasonings for endless options.

Hot and dry, no matter what.

Wok whisperers, grill masters, steakhouse chefs, and short-order line cooks all cook meat essentially the same way: on a hot, dry, lightly greased surface. The same is true at home: Pat the meat dry (even ground meat if there are juices in the package) and work over highish heat. Heat a heavy skillet, grill, or broiler to medium-high or high. For cuts, oil the meat itself to prevent smoking. For ground meat, heat the oil on the cooking surface.

Twiddle thumbs, not meat.

If meat is tough and gray, you're smothering it with too much attention. Instead, spread the meat out as much as possible in the pan, then back away and let the direct heat do its thing. Only when pieces are browned at both the edge and in the middle can you stir, toss, or flip the meat, breaking it up into smaller pieces if it's ground. Repeat until the meat is as browned and cooked as you want it.

Pick steaks with less guesswork.

If hitting the right internal temperature is too much sometimes—you're right. Skip it. Instead, pick cuts that are so slim that when cooked over high heat, the inside will be medium-rare by the time the outside is browned. That includes skirt and hanger, called "butcher's cuts" because smart butchers used to save these once-undesirable and therefore more affordable cuts for themselves. They have big beefy flavor and good chew. Buttery-tender, kinda-bland filet mignon they are not.

(P.S. This is also true of cooking burgers: Whoppers require an instant thermometer, while crispy smashburgers reduce guesswork. See page 272.)

(P.P.S. Even if you don't need it for steaks, a meat thermometer is a very good thing to have for chicken, fish, meatballs, and sausage, which can be tricky to break into to check doneness.)

Pork shoulder isn't just for stewing. When cooked hot and fast, pork shoulder has everything you crave in a pork chop, but with more character, interesting textures, and a kinder price tag. So that it doesn't toughen, cut into pieces that cook to medium-rare in under 10 minutes. For steaks (like on page 324), purchase a boneless butt or shoulder, freeze for 15 to 20 minutes, then slice against the grain into ½-inch to 1-inch steaks (you might also see "pork shoulder steaks" sold at your grocery store). For a stir-fry, freeze and slice as thin as you can (like on page 325). Or cut into ½-inch cubes for crispy-chewy nubbins (p. 326).

Reverse your marinade. Marinating usually isn't worth it (there's a spiel about it on page 294). Instead, brown the meat naked, then let it rest in a sauce, just like the one you would've marinated the meat in and then poured down the drain. The meat's resting juices are captured in the sauce, so nothing is lost to the cutting board. Slice the meat, then pour the sauce over. You can do this with just about any marinade, sauce, or salad dressing and cut of beef, pork, or lamb (or chicken or fish).

Fail-safe dry rubs. Though they don't introduce moisture like marinades, dry rubs do risk burning and falling off the meat. To make your dry rub tacky and scorch-proof, stir it into mayo before coating your meat. There's more about mayo magic on page 294.

Steak & Potatoes with Herb Sauce

A feast in few moves.

POTATOES

STEAK

GARLIC

ANCHOVIES

DRIED
OREGANO

LEMON

SALAD
GREENS

FOR 4

1. In a medium saucepan, cover **1½ pounds little potatoes (baby Yukon Gold, fingerling)** with 1 inch of water. Salt, then bring to a simmer over medium-high. Cook until tender when pierced with a fork, 15 to 20 minutes. Drain and set aside to cool.

2. Meanwhile, cut **1½ to 2 pounds hanger, flank, or thick skirt steak** into pieces that will fit in a large skillet. Pat dry and season all over with salt. Set aside while you make the herb sauce: On a cutting board, smash and coarsely chop **3 garlic cloves** and **4 anchovies** until a coarse paste forms. Transfer to a medium bowl or shallow dish, then stir in **6 tablespoons olive oil, 1 tablespoon dried oregano,** and **1 teaspoon red pepper flakes.** Season to taste with S&P.

3. Set a large cast-iron skillet over high. When it's just smoking, lightly coat the steak with **olive oil** and cook until well browned and medium-rare (130°F), 3 to 5 minutes per side. Transfer to the herb sauce. Turn off the heat and reserve the skillet.

4. Smash the potatoes with the palm of your hand just until you feel the skin break (you can do this on the side of the colander or on a cutting board). Pour out the fat in the skillet (or soak it up with a paper towel). Heat **¼ cup olive oil** over medium-high, then add the potatoes and cook until browned and crispy, 3 to 5 minutes per side. Season with S&P and turn off the heat.

5. Transfer the steak to a cutting board. Squeeze the juice of **1 lemon** (about 3 tablespoons) into the herb sauce, then stir in **2 tablespoons hot water.** Slice the steak across the grain. Dress **4 cups full-flavored salad greens (arugula, radicchio)** lightly with S&P and **olive oil.** Pile the steak on top of the greens, with herb sauce and potatoes nearby.

· This sauce, which is a spin on salmoriglio and chimichurri, can also take soft- and hard-stem herbs. Finely chop and add to taste, adjusting the salt (salt and anchovies), fat (oil), and acid (lemon) until bright and rich. If it's too pungent, add more hot water.

· Also very good with the steak and potatoes grilled.

Skirt Steak with Corn & Feta

Produced by and starring paprika-lime mayo.

SKIRT STEAK

MAYO

SMOKED PAPRIKA

GARLIC

LIME

CORN

FETA

CRISP LETTUCES

FOR 4

1. Pat **1½ to 2 pounds skirt steak** dry, then cut into pieces along the grain that will fit in a large cast-iron skillet. Season with S&P.

2. In a medium bowl, stir together **6 tablespoons mayo** and **1 teaspoon smoked paprika.** Grate **2 garlic cloves** and the zest from **1 lime** into the bowl, season with **1 teaspoon each S&P,** and stir to combine. Spread half of the mayo onto both sides of the steak.

3. Cut the kernels off **4 ears of corn.** Add to the bowl with the remaining mayo and stir to combine. Crumble **4 ounces feta** into the bowl. Tear or thinly slice **a few heads crisp lettuces (romaine, Little Gem)** and add to the bowl. Don't stir just yet.

4. Set a large cast-iron skillet over high (no need to oil the pan). When it's just smoking, add the steak and cook until well browned, 2 to 4 minutes per side (if there are any particularly thick parts, use a thermometer to see that they reach 130°F for medium-rare). Transfer to a cutting board to rest.

5. Season the lettuces with S&P, then stir in the juice from the lime (about 2 tablespoons). Adjust S&P and the balance of smokiness (paprika), brightness (lime), and creaminess (mayo). Thinly slice the steak across the grain, season with S&P, and eat with the salad.

- If your corn isn't juicy-sweet, char kernels by cooking over high, undisturbed, until starting to pop, 3 to 4 minutes.

- Grill the steak over direct, medium-high heat for 3 to 5 minutes per side.

Other double-duty mayos for coating steak & dressing veg

- Mustard–black pepper mayo (with roasted potatoes)

- Pesto mayo (with asparagus)

- Gochujang mayo (with kale salad)

- Anchovy-lemon mayo (with grilled mushrooms)

- Dry rub–spiked mayo (with fries, p. 272)

Oregano Lamb Pita

A craggy jumble of juicy bites.

GOAT CHEESE

LEMON

CUCUMBERS

RED ONION

GROUND LAMB

DRIED OREGANO

PITA

FOR 4

1. Heat the broiler with a rack 5 or fewer inches from the heat source. Put **8 ounces goat cheese** in a small bowl to soften. Grate the zest of **1 lemon** over the top.

2. Smash **3 Persian or mini seedless cucumbers** with your palm, side of a knife, meat pounder, or rolling pin until they split. Tear them into bite-size pieces, then transfer to a medium bowl, season with salt, and stir.

3. Coarsely chop **1 red onion.** Transfer to a sheet pan with **1½ pounds ground lamb.** Add **1 teaspoon red pepper flakes** and **1 teaspoon dried oregano** and gently mix to combine. Smush the meat down into one giant patty around ½ inch thick, then sprinkle with **1 teaspoon salt** and a few grinds of pepper. Drizzle with **olive oil.**

4. Broil the lamb until cooked through and singed in spots, 7 to 10 minutes. Rotate the pan as needed for coverage under the broiler. Remove from the oven, then broil **4 pita or flatbreads** until toasted, just a few seconds on each side (if this seems risky, warm on the lower rack).

5. Stir the goat cheese with the lemon zest and season with S&P. Break the lamb up into 1- to 2-inch pieces (this prevents the pieces from escaping your pita). Add to the cucumbers, along with any straggling onions and a little of the lamb fat from the pan. Stir to combine.

6. To eat, schmear some goat cheese on a piece of pita. Add some lamb and cucumbers. Squeeze with the lemon. Fold/wrap/sandwich/eat.

Sizzled Pork & Pineapple **PAGE 324**

Sizzled Pork & Pineapple

For fans of Cuban mojo and al pastor.

PORK SHOULDER

PINEAPPLE

ORANGE

LIMES

GARLIC

FRESH CHILE

CORN TORTILLAS

AVOCADO

FOR 4

1. Heat a grill to medium-high. Slice **1½ pounds boneless pork shoulder** into ½-inch-thick steaks against the grain. Pat dry, drizzle with **olive oil,** and season with **1½ teaspoons salt** and lots of pepper. Peel **1 pineapple,** then cut into 1-inch-thick spears. Transfer to a sheet pan. Zest **1 orange** onto a cutting board, then halve the orange and add to the sheet pan. Coat the pineapple and orange halves with **olive oil** and S&P.

2. On the cutting board with the zest, zest **2 limes.** Coarsely chop **4 garlic cloves** and **1 fresh chile (jalapeño, serrano).** Bring the zest, garlic, and chile together, sprinkle with **1 teaspoon salt,** then chop until a coarse, juicy paste forms. Transfer to a medium bowl or shallow dish, then add the juice from the limes (about ¼ cup) and **¼ cup olive oil.** Go to your grill with your pork, fruit, sauce, and **8 to 12 corn tortillas.**

3. Grease the grill grates with **olive oil.** Add the pork, pineapple, and orange over direct heat. Grill the pork until cooked through and charred in spots, 5 to 8 minutes per side. Grill the pineapple and orange until charred, 3 to 5 minutes per side. Move ingredients around as needed to char and avoid flare-ups. As things finish, add them to the sauce and toss to coat. (Everything can sit in this sauce for up to an hour.)

4. Grill the tortillas until lightly charred, less than a minute. Keep warm in a kitchen towel. Cut the pork and pineapple into bite-size pieces, then return to the sauce. Squeeze the orange halves into the sauce. Chunk **1 avocado** and season with S&P. Eat the pork, pineapple, and avocado swaddled in a warm tortilla. Repeat.

- For easier slicing, freeze the pork for 10 to 15 minutes.
- To cook on the stovetop, in a large cast-iron skillet, heat olive oil over medium-high until just smoking. Working in batches as necessary, cook the pork until deeply browned, 5 to 8 minutes per side, then char the fruit.
- Instead of pork, use boneless chicken thighs, skirt steak, tempeh, or tofu.

Other friends for pork shoulder steaks

- Grilled scallions + grilled shishito peppers + lime + sesame oil
- Grilled tomatillos + red onions + lime
- Pickled peppers + brine + garlic
- Smoked paprika + grilled mini peppers
- Green sauce (p. 147)
- Mustard + horseradish + honey

Beef & Brussels Stir-Fry

Surf and turf.

1. Cook **1 cup long-grain white rice** for serving (p. 170 if you need a method).

2. Pat **1 pound flank steak** dry, then thinly slice against the grain. Cut pieces crosswise into 3- or 4-inch lengths. Add to a medium bowl with **2 teaspoons cornstarch, 1 teaspoon salt,** and a few grinds of pepper. Toss to coat. Trim and halve **1 pound brussels sprouts.** Pluck **½ cup cilantro leaves** and thinly slice the stems.

3. Heat **2 tablespoons neutral oil** in a large cast-iron skillet over medium-high. Add the steak in an even layer and cook, stirring just once or twice, until browned, 3 to 5 minutes. Stir in **1 tablespoon dark brown sugar** and **1 tablespoon fish sauce,** then transfer to a plate.

4. Add **another tablespoon neutral oil** and the brussels sprouts, cut sides down. Season with S&P and cook, without touching, until well browned underneath, 3 to 5 minutes. Add more oil if the pan looks dry. Cook, stirring, until crisp-tender, 3 to 5 minutes.

5. Off the heat, add **4 tablespoons butter** (½ stick), **1 tablespoon fish sauce,** the steak and any juices, the cilantro stems, and **½ teaspoon red pepper flakes.** Stir, scraping up browned bits, until the butter's melted. Eat the stir-fry on top of rice, with cilantro leaves and a squeeze of **1 lime.**

· For easier slicing, freeze the steak for 10 to 15 minutes to firm.

Red Curry Pork with Little Leaves

Each morsel chewy, crispy, and smoky (not unlike a burnt end).

WHITE RICE

PORK
SHOULDER

RED CURRY
PASTE

BROWN SUGAR

TURMERIC

SOFT HERBS
AND/OR CRISP
LETTUCES

FISH SAUCE

LIME

FOR 4

1. Cook **1 cup long-grain white rice** for serving (p. 170 if you need a method).

2. Cut **1½ pounds boneless pork shoulder** into ½-inch pieces. Transfer to a medium bowl and season with **1½ teaspoons each S&P**. Add **3 tablespoons red curry paste, 1 tablespoon neutral oil, 1½ teaspoons dark brown sugar, 1½ teaspoons ground turmeric,** and **½ teaspoon red pepper flakes.** Stir to combine. The pork can marinate up to 30 minutes at room temp or overnight in the fridge. Let it come to room temp before cooking.

3. Pluck the leaves and tender stems from some **soft herbs (basil, cilantro, mint)** and/or separate heads of **crisp lettuces (romaine, Little Gem).**

4. Heat a large cast-iron skillet over medium-high. Add the pork in a single layer and cook, without touching, until charred in spots, 1½ to 2 minutes. Stir and repeat until cooked through and golden all over, 4 to 6 minutes. Turn off the heat and add **1 teaspoon fish sauce.** Stir to combine, scraping up any browned bits. Zest **1 lime** over the pork and stir to combine.

5. Eat the pork with rice, crisp lettuces, herbs, and a squeeze of the lime for making rice bowls or lettuce cups.

· This can also be made with ground pork or beef or thinly sliced well-marbled steak.

· This recipe nods to the flavors in kua kling, a Southern Thai dry curry that involves slowly toasting a fresh red curry paste with ground pork ("kua" means toast). The pork fat renders, the curry paste deepens, and the pork ends up tender, juicy, and fragrant. Here, curry paste is used to crust pork shoulder, which, when cooked hot and fast, goes crispy-chewy instead of tender.

BEEF, PORK & LAMB

326

Other seasonings to toss with charred pork nubbins

· Flaky salt + coarsely ground pepper

· Sesame seeds + grated ginger + grated lime zest

· Za'atar or everything bagel mix

· Chili powder or taco seasoning

· Pastrami-spiced like on page 89

· Gochujang-glazed like on page 349

Green Chile Pork with Crispy Rice

Smoky and fresh like chorizo verde.

GARLIC

MILD GREEN
CHILES

HOT GREEN
CHILES

WHITE RICE

GROUND
CUMIN

GROUND
PORK

SPINACH

LIMES

FOR 4

1. Bring a medium pot of salted water to a boil. Thinly slice **5 garlic cloves.** Remove the seeds from **4 mild green chiles (poblano, Anaheim),** then cut into ½-inch pieces. Coarsely chop **2 hot green chiles (serrano, jalapeño),** removing the seeds if you fear heat.

2. Add **1 cup long-grain white rice** to the boiling water and cook until al dente, 10 to 12 minutes. Drain, rinse under cold water until cool to the touch, then shake dry.

3. While the rice is cooking, heat **2 tablespoons neutral oil** in a large nonstick skillet over medium-high. Add the mild chiles, season with S&P, and cook until softened and charred in spots, 5 to 7 minutes. Reduce the heat to medium. Add **1½ teaspoons ground cumin,** the hot chiles, and the garlic and stir until fragrant. Add **1 pound ground pork,** season with S&P, and cook, breaking up the pork into pieces, until cooked through, 3 to 5 minutes. Transfer to a medium bowl.

4. Heat **3 tablespoons neutral oil** in the same skillet over medium-high. Add the rice and press it down along the sides and bottom of the pan. Poke five or six holes in the rice to help steam escape. Cook undisturbed until you start to see golden rice at the edges, 5 to 7 minutes. If you don't see oil bubbling around the edges or in the holes, drizzle in another tablespoon or two of oil.

5. Off the heat, break up the rice, then stir in the pork and any juices and **2 packed cups baby spinach** (half a 5-ounce box). Add the juice from **2 limes** (about ¼ cup). Stir to combine and season to taste with S&P.

For something different

· **Hash:** Switch the rice for boiled, cubed potatoes.

· **Tortillas:** Skip the rice and make tacos, or enchiladas with a green sauce and sour cream.

· **Soup:** Just add chicken stock!

· **Vegetables:** Think of this like fried rice. What vegetable can't you add?

Simmer softly

For tender meat and deep flavors, take the pedal off the metal and cook over moderate heat in a wet environment. Think soups, stews, braises, and other spoonable numbers, but nothing that takes all day.

Use ground meat for a head start.

A wobbly, fork-shredded pork shoulder is a special thing, but it takes hours to get there. Instead, consider ground meat for your braises: Because its fibers are already broken down, it won't take as long to slump and soften.

Find the extrovert in the room.

Pick a party animal like ground lamb, sausage, or cured meat to start your dish—they have so much umami, you can't miss them in your bowl. As they brown, their drippings collect in the pot, which will dissolve into the liquid and travel through the whole dish (what social butterflies).

In comparison, ground beef and pork are wallflowers and need help from savory ingredients to carry the dish, such as deeply roasted vegetables, soy sauce, fish sauce, gochujang, anchovies, mushrooms, tomato paste, aged cheese, or cured meats. Ground beef also risks drying out and benefits from additional fat, whether cheese, eggs, yogurt, coconut milk, or pork. (Or use ground chuck, which at 20% fat clocks a high fat percentage.)

One stock fits all.

Store-bought beef broths and stocks sometimes have more vegetables and filler than beefy flavor, so chicken stock is a safer start to developing richness (and that means you only need to stock one type of stock). If you have a beef broth that fills you with deep savoriness, though, use that.

Skip browning sometimes.

For really tender meat, skip browning the meat first. Because none of the juices evaporate during browning, they are all either still in the meat, keeping it juicy—or they've released into and fortified the soup. This is especially nice with meatballs. Squeeze "meatballs" of sausage out of their casings or plop homemade, uncooked meatballs into a gently simmering liquid. Avoid a hard boil because the meatballs could fall apart, which then makes meat sauce, which—okay!

Mighty Meatballs

When ricotta stands in for eggs and breadcrumbs, meatballs lighten up—like they got a haircut.

GROUND BEEF

GROUND PORK

RICOTTA

PARMESAN

GARLIC

BASIL

CANNED TOMATOES

CRUSTY BREAD

FOR 4 (or more with pasta or polenta)

1. In a medium bowl, combine **1 pound ground beef, 1 pound ground pork, 1 cup whole-milk ricotta, 2½ teaspoons salt,** and **½ teaspoon pepper.** Finely grate in **1 cup Parmesan** (about 2 ounces) and **1 garlic clove.** Rip **2 tablespoons basil leaves** into the bowl; hold on to the stems. Stir with your hands to combine. Using wet hands, form into 8 balls (about ½ cup or 150 grams each).

2. Working in batches as needed, heat **2 tablespoons olive oil** in a large Dutch oven over medium-high. Add the meatballs and cook until browned on two sides, 5 to 8 minutes. Transfer to a plate and turn off the heat.

3. Still off the heat, finely grate **3 garlic cloves** into the pot. Add **½ teaspoon red pepper flakes.** Stir until you smell the garlic, then add **2 (28-ounce) cans crushed tomatoes, 4 basil sprigs,** and the reserved basil stems. Season with S&P. Partially cover, bring to a simmer over medium-high, then reduce to medium-low and add the meatballs back. Add water until the sauce is halfway up the sides of the meatballs. Gently simmer partially covered, flipping the meatballs halfway through, until the sauce is flavorful and the meatballs are cooked through (160°F), 15 to 20 minutes. Season the sauce with S&P to taste. If the sauce is really thick, oops—just add more water.

4. When the meatballs are about done, slice and toast some **crusty bread.** Rub one side with **1 garlic clove,** then smear some **ricotta** on each. Season with S&P. Eat the meatballs in sauce with more Parm, and ricotta toasts alongside for dunking.

· Before rolling the meatballs, fry off a spoonful of the meat to taste and adjust seasonings.

· If you're worried about the meatballs falling apart, refrigerate for 10 to 20 minutes before browning.

Pork & Beans Alla Gricia

Roman pasta alla gricia—porky, peppery, starchy, salty—without the pasta. I can hear the traditionalists now: *tsk tsk.*

WHITE BEANS

CURED PORK

PARMESAN

AMORÉ FOR 4

1. Drain **2 (15-ounce) cans white beans (Great Northern, cannellini);** no need to rinse. Cut **4 ounces cured pork (guanciale, pancetta, bacon)** into ¼-inch pieces.

2. Add the pork to a medium saucepan over medium and cook, stirring sometimes, until golden brown, 5 to 7 minutes. Stir in **1½ teaspoons black pepper** until you smell pepper (really do measure; it's more than you think). Add the beans, season lightly with salt, stir to coat, and cook until soft enough to smash, 2 to 3 minutes. Smash about half the beans with your spoon or a potato masher, then add **1½ cups water.** Scrape up any browned bits, then cover and cook, stirring sometimes, until creamy and slightly thickened, 5 to 7 minutes.

3. Off the heat, grate in some **Parmesan or pecorino** until it tastes like you could eat the whole pot (around ¼ cup or ½ ounce). Top bowlfuls with more Parm and pepper. (Keeps for 3 days in the fridge.)

· Good with sautéed greens, crusty bread, polenta (p. 203), ditalini, or orzo.

Gochujang Gravy

Because gochujang tastes long-cooked straight from the container, your ragù doesn't need all of Sunday.

ONION
GARLIC
GINGER
GROUND
BEEF
BROWN
SUGAR
GOCHUJANG
TOMATO
PASTE
SOY SAUCE
STARCHY
SIDE

FOR 4

1. Coarsely chop **1 large yellow onion, 6 garlic cloves,** and **2 inches ginger** (no need to peel the ginger).

2. Heat **2 tablespoons neutral oil** in a large Dutch oven over medium-high. Add **1 pound ground beef** in an even layer, season with S&P, and cook, without touching, until browned, 3 to 5 minutes. Add **2 tablespoons dark brown sugar, 2 tablespoons gochujang, 2 tablespoons tomato paste,** and the onion, garlic, and ginger. Cook, breaking up the meat, until the meat is cooked through and the onions are tender, 2 to 3 minutes. Add ¾ **cup water** and ¼ **cup low-sodium soy sauce,** bring to a simmer, then reduce the heat to medium-low and cook until thickened and flavorful, 20 to 25 minutes. (Keeps for 4 days in the fridge and also freezes well.)

3. Now pick **a starch** and cook it simply. Boil udon, ramyun, rigatoni, rice, or farro. Toast a slice of bread or potato buns. Bake a sweet or russet potato. (Also good with tofu, like mapo tofu.) When the gravy's good, season to taste with S&P and ladle it into or onto your starch.

· To counter the rich sauce, add hearty greens (mustard greens, Swiss chard) with the water in step 2. Or eat with vinegared cucumbers (p. 379), kimchi, or radishes.

· If your sauce has a lot of fat on top, skim it off with a spoon.

Lamb Meatball Soup

Tangy and sinus-clearing like sopa de lima, consomé de barbacoa, and Tex-Mex tortilla soup.

CARROTS

RED ONION

GROUND LAMB

CHICKEN STOCK

CILANTRO

BAY LEAVES

CHICKPEAS

TORTILLA CHIPS

LIMES

FOR 4

1. Cut **2 large carrots** into ¼-inch pieces. Finely chop **1 large red onion.** In a medium bowl, season **1 pound ground lamb** with **1 teaspoon salt** and some pepper.

2. In a large Dutch oven or pot, heat **¼ cup olive oil** over medium-high. Add the carrots and all but a handful of the red onion, season with S&P, and cook until softened and browned in spots, 3 to 5 minutes.

3. Add **4 cups chicken stock, 2 cups water, 6 or so cilantro sprigs,** and **4 bay leaves.** Season with S&P, bring to a boil, then reduce the heat to medium and simmer until the broth is flavorful, 5 to 7 minutes.

4. Add **2 (15-ounce) cans chickpeas,** including their liquid. Use a tablespoon measuring spoon to plop lamb meatballs into the broth. Simmer, stirring gently and occasionally, until the lamb is cooked through (160°F), 5 to 7 minutes. (Keeps for 4 days in the fridge.)

5. Finely chop **½ cup cilantro,** stems and all. Remove the soup from the heat and discard the bay leaves and cilantro sprigs. Season to taste with S&P. Crumble some **salty tortilla chips** into serving bowls, then spoon the soup on top. Add the remaining red onion, chopped cilantro, and a lot of fresh **lime** juice.

· Like the consommé made from barbacoa drippings, the lamb here fortifies the broth into something fatty and savory yet mellow and light. If you want to use another ground meat, consider adding warm spices like cinnamon or coriander to enhance the broth.

· Good with Chipotle-Tomato Baked Rice (p. 181), spinach, or pickled or fresh jalapeños.

SEA CREATURES

Cook fast & hot

That seafood takes well to high heat opens up a, ahem, sea of weeknight dinners. A flash in the pan, a blast from a hot oven, or a trip under the broiler can produce snappy shrimp, knife-and-forkable swordfish, crispy-skinned salmon, and more.

Buy fish like you buy produce.

Like strawberries and watermelons, seafood is too seasonal and regional to be consistent all year in all parts of the country. Defer to Seafood Watch to see what's in season, then shop with an open mind. Use thickness and weight to guide your shopping because regardless of the type of fish, fillets of similar size can be cooked in the same manner. Of course, the fish will vary in taste and texture depending on what you choose, but with the right thickness, you don't need to worry about over- or under-cooking—and you might even discover you like a fish just as much as salmon.

Thin fillets around ½ inch thick can cook in a few minutes under the broiler (p. 361) or basted in a pan (p. 353), but anything more substantial might cook unevenly. For fillets between ½ inch and 1 inch, consider roasting or flipping them in a pan (p. 354). Roast fillets thicker than an inch; the indirect heat gently cooks the fish all the way through without it drying out (p. 357).

Freshness can be frozen.

Fishes at the seafood counter are often previously frozen and thawed, their freshness ticking away as they've been sitting. Unless you know your fish was caught within a day or two (like at a local shop you trust), control the quality by purchasing frozen fish. Seafood is usually flash-frozen right on the boat when it's caught, as fresh as can be. Depending on where you're shopping, you might also have a greater selection among the frozen fish, including more sustainably caught options.

Precious shrimp deserve a few minutes of prep.

You may have a source for beautiful, nicely cleaned shrimp. More often than not, though, they come too mangled and mushy to cook up juicy and plump. Instead, purchase peel-on shrimp fresh or frozen and peel and devein them yourself. It's a few minutes of prep you can handle early in the day, and the reward is all you ever wanted: juicy, plump shrimp.

Eat the tails. Yes, leaving the tails on shrimp is one way to shirk some prep work from the cook to eaters, but they offer more texture than denuded shrimp. I have always eaten shrimp tails, for no reason other than I copied the grown-ups as a kid and have eaten them ever since. They're crispy-crunchy when cooked at high enough heat, like the too-often-discarded tip of a chicken wing. But even if they're not for you, they make you slow down, consider each bite, and get your hands dirty as you unpeel. Shrimp are worthy of that attention.

How to tell when shrimp's done. Shrimp that are pink and opaque on the sides are not necessarily cooked through (especially on large shrimp). Instead, zero in on the deveined canal: When the thickest part turns opaque and the edges of that canal start to curl, the shrimp's done.

Grill fish without grilling fish. A broiler is like an indoor, upside-down grill. It will kiss your fish with fire in a matter of minutes without the danger of sticking or flaring up. For an added buffer against the high heat, coat the meat with something fatty, like mayo or butter, or broil skin side up (p. 361).

Speed-demon, pan-seared fish. Perhaps the fastest way to cook fish with the crispiest skin is to sear it in a pan. But it's not always as easy as that. Fish can stick when it isn't dry enough or the pan isn't hot enough, so pat the fish dry with paper towel and/or do like Thomas Keller and squeegee the skin with the back of your knife to remove moisture. Then heat a nonstick or stainless-steel pan to medium-high. Right before you add the fish, reduce the heat to medium (so the skin quickly adheres to the fish rather than the pan but the skin doesn't burn). Lay the fish down away from you to avoid splatters, then press the fish down with your hand or a fish spatula so it doesn't curl. Cook the fish most of the way on the skin side (the skin acts as a buffer between the heat and the flesh). When the side of the fish is halfway opaque and the fish releases from the pan, flip and finish cooking for just a few beats until medium-rare—the sides of the fish will be mostly opaque, with a thin sliver of translucency in the middle.

A fish spatula is certainly not a unitasker. The most versatile and agile of the spatulas, a fish spatula's thin profile easily slips under delicate foods like fish, yes, but also pancakes and fried eggs. Because of its wide slats, it also can be a makeshift slotted spoon.

Turmeric Shrimp with Citrus & Avocado

California dreamin'.

SHRIMP

TURMERIC

CUCUMBERS

GRAPEFRUIT

FRESH CHILE

AVOCADO

LIME

FOR 4

1. Peel and devein **1 pound large or very large shrimp.** Pat very dry. Toss on the cutting board with **1 teaspoon salt** and **1 teaspoon ground turmeric.**

2. Cut **2 Persian or mini seedless cucumbers** into bite-size pieces (peel if desired) and transfer to a serving plate. Salt them. Cut the top and bottom off **1 grapefruit** and place the grapefruit on a cut side. Follow the curve of the fruit to cut away the peel and white pith. Halve the fruit through the top, then slice into ¼-inch-thick half-moons. If your pieces are especially large, halve again. Add to the cukes and season with salt. Cut **1 fresh chile (jalapeño, serrano)** in half lengthwise.

3. Heat a large cast-iron skillet over medium-high until smoking, about 3 minutes. Add **2 tablespoons olive oil,** then add the chile, skin side down, and the shrimp. Cook the shrimp and chile untouched until golden and charred in spots, about 2 minutes. Flip and cook until the shrimp is opaque on all sides, about a minute longer. Transfer the shrimp to the cucumbers and grapefruit and season with S&P.

4. Finely chop the chile, then add to the shrimp. Halve and pit **1 avocado.** Use a spoon to scoop thin slivers of the avocado and plop them right onto the plate. Season everything with S&P. Squeeze half of **1 lime** (about 1 table-spoon) over everything, and cut the remaining half into wedges for serving. Drizzle with olive oil and season with flaky salt and more pepper as you wish.

· Instead of grapefruit, use tangerines, mango, pineapple, or a mix.

· Grill the shrimp and chile over high heat for 2 to 3 minutes per side.

· Good with tortilla chips, tostadas, rice, quinoa, rice noodles, soba, mint, cilantro, or corn nuts.

Sweet & Salty Shrimp with Charred Cabbage

Sizzling cabbage and shrimp take a dive into nướ'c chấm.

SHRIMP

FISH SAUCE

GARLIC

LIME

CABBAGE

PEANUTS

SOFT HERBS

FOR 4

1. Peel and devein **1 pound large shrimp.** In a medium bowl, toss the shrimp with **1 teaspoon salt** and **1 teaspoon sugar.**

2. In a large bowl, stir together **3 tablespoons fish sauce, 2 tablespoons sugar,** and **½ teaspoon red pepper flakes.** Finely grate **1 garlic clove** and the zest from **1 lime** into the bowl, then squeeze in the juice from the lime (about 2 tablespoons).

3. Cut **½ medium green cabbage** (about 1 pound) into 1-inch pieces. Separate the leaves from one another. Coarsely chop **¼ cup roasted, salted peanuts** and pick **1 cup soft herbs (basil, mint).**

4. In a large skillet, heat **1 tablespoon neutral oil** over medium-high. Add the cabbage and cook, undisturbed, until charred in spots, 2 minutes. Salt, toss, and cook until all the leaves are crisp-tender and charred in spots, another 2 minutes. Transfer the cabbage to the nướ'c chấm and give it a toss.

5. Add **another tablespoon oil** to the skillet, still over medium-high. Add the shrimp and cook until cooked through and charred in spots, 1 to 2 minutes per side. Add to the cabbage, along with the peanuts and herbs. Give it a toss and serve right now.

Gochujang Shrimp & Shishitos

For five-minute shrimp and veg, douse in a fiery sauce and char under the broiler.

GOCHUJANG

SESAME OIL

SOY SAUCE

HONEY

SHRIMP

SHISHITO PEPPERS

CHEWY NOODLES

FROZEN EDAMAME

FOR 4

1. Heat the broiler with a rack 5 or fewer inches from the heat source. Bring a medium saucepan of water to a boil. In a large bowl, stir together **2 tablespoons plus 2 teaspoons gochujang, 1 tablespoon toasted sesame oil, 1 tablespoon low-sodium soy sauce,** and **2 teaspoons honey.** Peel and devein **1 pound large shrimp.** Stir the shrimp and **8 ounces shishito peppers** into the marinade.

2. When the water's boiling, cook **8 ounces Korean glass noodles (or udon or fresh ramen noodles)** according to the package directions (that might mean soaking instead of boiling). Reserve **½ cup noodle water,** then drain the noodles, rinse with cold water, and toss with a bit of **toasted sesame oil** to keep from sticking.

3. Spread the shrimp and peppers out on a sheet pan in a single layer, leaving behind excess marinade. Sprinkle over **1 cup frozen, shelled edamame.** Broil until the peppers are charred in spots and the shrimp are cooked through, 5 to 7 minutes. (Depending on your broiler, you may need to rotate the pan after 2 or 3 minutes so all the food gets exposure under the heat source.)

4. Add the noodles and 2 tablespoons of the reserved water to the sheet pan and toss until the noodles are saucy (add more water as needed). Eat right away, though leftovers are good cold or at room temp.

· Use any veg that cooks in 5 or 10 minutes: corn kernels, green beans, asparagus, sugar snap or snow peas, sliced garlic, or sweet mini peppers.

· Glass noodles are sometimes also called cellophane noodles or dangmyeon. You'll find them near the rice noodles. They have a great mix of heft, chew, and slipperiness. Also use them to make japchae, a stir-fry of meat, vegetables, sesame oil, soy sauce, and sugar.

· Instead of noodles, eat the shrimp and veg with rice, Korean rice cakes, scrambled or fried eggs, kimchi, or crisp lettuces.

White Bean Scampi Stew

Garlicky shrimp swaddled in a blanket of beans.

SHRIMP
GARLIC
LEMON
WHITE BEANS
BUTTER
WHITE WINE
CHICKEN STOCK
PARSLEY

FOR 4

1. Peel and devein **1 pound large shrimp.** Finely chop **6 garlic cloves.** In a medium bowl, stir together the shrimp, the zest of **1 lemon, ¾ teaspoon each S&P, ½ teaspoon red pepper flakes,** and half the garlic. Crack open **2 (15-ounce) cans white beans (cannellini, Great Northern).** Drain just one of the cans.

2. In a large pot, melt **4 tablespoons butter** (½ stick) over medium-high. Add the shrimp and cook, stirring occasionally, until pink on both sides, 2 to 3 minutes. Use a slotted spoon or tongs to transfer the shrimp to a plate.

3. Add the remaining garlic and stir until fragrant, 1 to 2 minutes. Add ⅓ **cup dry white wine** and stir, scraping browned bits, until nearly all evaporated, just a minute. Add **3 cups chicken stock** and the beans and bring to a boil. Reduce the heat to medium-low and simmer until thickened and flavorful, 15 to 20 minutes. Smash some beans against the side of the pot every so often to thicken the stew. Meanwhile, finely chop ½ **cup parsley leaves.**

4. Stir in the shrimp and any juices, the parsley, and the juice from the lemon (about 3 tablespoons). Season to taste with S&P, more lemon, and more red pepper flakes.

· Good just like this, or with crusty bread, little pastas, or sautéed greens.

Caramelized Black Pepper Trout

With a hot and sweet sauce that's good on more than fish.

WHITE RICE

BROWN SUGAR

SOY SAUCE

RICE VINEGAR

GARLIC

THIN FISH FILLETS

BROCCOLINI

CILANTRO

FOR 4

1. Cook **1 cup long-grain white rice** for serving (p. 170 if you need a method).

2. In a measuring cup, stir together **⅓ cup dark brown sugar, ¼ cup water, 3 tablespoons low-sodium soy sauce, 3 tablespoons unseasoned rice vinegar,** and **1 teaspoon black pepper.** Coarsely chop **4 garlic cloves** and add to the cup. Pat **4 (5- to 6-ounce) trout fillets (or mackerel or bluefish)** dry and season with S&P; skin can be on or off. Trim the tough ends from **2 bunches broccolini.** Halve any big pieces lengthwise so all the broccolini is about the same thickness. Chop **1 small bunch cilantro,** including the stems (about ¾ cup).

3. In a large nonstick skillet, heat **1 tablespoon neutral oil** over medium-high. Add the broccolini, season with S&P, and cook, tossing occasionally, until bright green and lightly charred, 3 to 5 minutes. Reduce the heat to medium, add **2 tablespoons water,** cover, and cook until crisp-tender, 1 to 2 minutes. Transfer to a plate.

4. Add the sauce to the skillet. When it's boiling, add the fish, skin side down (if there's skin), and simmer, basting the fish with the sauce, until the fish flakes with a fork and the sauce is syrupy, 3 to 5 minutes. If the sauce is syrupy before the fish is done, add a little water; if the fish is done before the sauce, remove the fish and keep cooking the sauce.

5. Add the cilantro to the rice and fluff until combined. Eat the fish and broccolini over the rice, with plenty of sauce.

More caramel: Like nước màu, agrodolce, or gastrique, this sauce simmers sugar with salt (soy sauce) and acid (vinegar) long enough to turn syrupy like caramel. Swap the elements any number of ways.

· Winter squash + brown sugar + apple cider vinegar

· Bratwurst + honey + mustard + chicken stock

· Chicken thighs + maple syrup + rice vinegar + turmeric (like on page 93)

· Instead of fish, use tofu, cubed chicken thighs, winter squash, or a brassica (cabbage, cauliflower, brussels sprouts). If the ingredient takes more than 4 minutes to cook, give it a head start by searing before adding the sauce.

Crispy-Skinned Fish with Creamy Cukes

Cheffy in only the good ways.

QUINOA

BULGUR

CUCUMBERS

LEMON

SOUR CREAM

DILL

SKIN-ON FISH

CLASSY FOR 4

1. In a medium saucepan, bring **3 cups water, 1 cup quinoa,** and **½ cup bulgur** to a boil. Reduce the heat to low, cover, and cook until tender and the water's been absorbed, 10 to 15 minutes. Remove from the heat and keep covered.

2. Place **4 Persian or mini seedless cucumbers** on a cutting board and smash with your palm, side of a knife, meat pounder, or rolling pin until craggy and split. Rip them into bite-size pieces. Transfer to a medium bowl and season with S&P. Halve **1 lemon.** Finely chop 2 tablespoons, skin, pith, fruit, and all— just pluck out the seeds. Transfer to the bowl, season with S&P, and stir to combine. Add **6 tablespoons sour cream** and stir once more. Finely chop **½ cup dill fronds and stems.**

3. Pat dry **4 (5- to 6-ounce) skin-on, firm fish fillets (salmon, arctic char, bass)** no thicker than 1 inch. Season both sides with S&P. Heat **2 tablespoons neutral oil** in a large nonstick or stainless-steel skillet over medium-high. Once shimmering, reduce the heat to medium and lay the fillets, skin side down, into the pan away from you to prevent splattering. Press the fillets down with your hands or a spatula for 30 seconds to prevent curling. Cook, pressing occasionally, until the skin is browned and releases easily from the pan and the fish is opaque halfway up the sides, 4 to 8 minutes. Flip the fish away from you, then turn off the heat. The fish will cook through from the lingering heat.

4. Add the dill to the quinoa and bulgur and fluff with a fork. Season to taste with S&P. Spoon the grains onto plates, then top with the fish, skin side up, and the cukes and their dressing. Eat with a squeeze of the lemon if there's any left.

Swordfish with Za'atar Tomatoes

Little tomatoes are like water balloons of ready-made sauce.

GARLIC

ISRAELI COUSCOUS

TOMATOES

CAPERS

ZA'ATAR

SWORDFISH

LEMON

FOR 4

1. Heat the oven to 425°F. Smash but don't peel **6 garlic cloves.** Heat **1 tablespoon olive oil** in a small saucepan over medium. Add **1½ cups Israeli couscous and ½ teaspoon red pepper flakes** and cook, stirring from time to time, until toasted, 3 to 5 minutes. Season with S&P, then add **2¼ cups water** and bring to a boil. Reduce the heat to low, cover, and cook until tender, 10 to 12 minutes. Remove from the heat and keep covered.

2. Meanwhile, on a sheet pan, toss together **2 pints (4 cups) cherry or Sungold tomatoes, ⅓ cup olive oil, ¼ cup capers, 1 tablespoon za'atar,** and the garlic. Season with S&P. Pat **4 (1-inch-thick, 6-ounce) swordfish steaks** dry and season all sides with S&P. Nestle the fish among the tomatoes and rub with **olive oil.** Roast until the swordfish is opaque and flakes with a fork, 15 to 18 minutes.

3. Zest **1 lemon** into the couscous and stir to combine. Transfer the couscous and fish to plates; if you want the tomatoes more blistered, broil them for a few minutes. Eat the fish and couscous with the tomato sauce and a squeeze of the lemon.

· Instead of Israeli couscous, use another grain or pasta (orzo, spaghetti).

· Instead of swordfish, use the fillets of another firm, white fish or a whole fish like red snapper, branzino, or black bass (stuff the cavity with lemon slices).

Sour Cream & Onion Fish

The fish *is* the chip.

SOUR CREAM

ONION POWDER

LEMON

CHIVES

PANKO

FISH FILLETS

CRISP LETTUCE

FOR 4

1. Heat the oven to 450°F. In a medium bowl, stir together **1½ cups sour cream** and **2 tablespoons onion powder.** Zest **1 lemon** into the bowl. Snip ¾ of **1 small bunch of chives** into the bowl with scissors (hold on to the rest). Stir to combine and season to taste with S&P. In a small bowl, stir together **½ cup panko breadcrumbs** and **2 tablespoons olive oil.** Season with S&P.

2. Pat dry **4 (6-ounce) fish fillets (cod, salmon, halibut, trout)** that are max 1½ inches thick. Transfer to a parchment-lined sheet pan, season with S&P, and cover the flesh with a thin layer of the sour cream mixture (reserve the rest). Press the panko mixture on top, then bake until the fish flakes easily and the panko is browned, 10 to 12 minutes per inch of thickness. (If your fish is cooked through before the panko's browned, broil for a minute or two.)

3. Meanwhile, squeeze the juice from half the lemon (about 1½ tablespoons) into the remaining sour cream mixture. Slice **1 big head crisp lettuce (romaine, iceberg).**

4. Divide the lettuce between plates and season with S&P. Drizzle with **olive oil** and the juice from the remaining lemon. Add the fish to the plates, then snip the remaining chives over. Eat with the sour cream and onion dip.

Sheet Pan Fish with Bitter Greens

A dreamscape of good textures.

**SKIN-ON FISH
FILLETS**

**BITTER
GREENS**

ORANGE

GARLIC

MAYO

FOR 4

1. Heat the broiler with a rack in the upper third of the oven. Pat dry **1 pound thin, skin-on fish fillets** no thicker than ½ inch. That could be mackerel, striped bass, black bass, snapper, arctic char, trout, or salmon. Using a sharp knife, score the skin a few times, avoiding cutting through the flesh (this keeps it from curling). Season all over with **1 teaspoon salt** and some pepper.

2. Trim the stem ends from **1 to 1½ pounds bitter greens (radicchio, broccoli rabe, escarole, mature watercress, dandelion).** Cut everything into 3- or 4-inch lengths. The quantity is not super important—you just want the sheet pan filled with greens so some wilt while others char. Toss on a sheet pan with S&P and enough **olive oil** to lightly coat. Quarter **1 orange** and nestle into the greens.

3. Place the fish on top of the greens, skin side up. Pat dry and coat with **olive oil.** Broil until the fish is just cooked through and the orange and greens are charred in spots, 6 to 10 minutes. Depending on your broiler, you may need to rotate the pan for even exposure under the heat source.

4. Grate **1 small garlic clove** into **½ cup mayo.** Season with S&P. Eat the fish and greens with a squeeze of orange, drizzle of olive oil, more S&P, and the mayo for dragging through.

· For more smoke, add small pieces of Spanish chorizo, pancetta, or bacon with the greens.

Cook fast & low

"Low and slow" is pretty hard with seafood: No matter how low, it's always fast. That's great news for your schedule, and your seafood: It's easier to dodge overcooking with gentle heat, even if (when) you lose track of time. If you're speeding over high heat (p. 342), you'd better be paying attention because your target can whizz right by you and oops hi dry fish.

Commit this one method to memory.

Heat the oven to 300°F. Pat fish dry and transfer to a sheet pan, baking dish, or skillet. Season with olive oil, S&P, and other seasonings if you want (p. 380). Bake until the fish flakes when prodded with a fork or when an instant-read thermometer inserted into the thickest part reaches 120°F.

This is called slow-roasting fish, which is actually more like fast-baking, but whatever it's called, it's a forgiving method that consistently produces such bewilderingly buttery fish, people always ask how on earth it's done. While you can use many types of fish and seafood, salmon works especially well because of its high fat content (p. 379 and 382). A two-pound piece will take 15 to 25 minutes.

Fall-back plan: Lemon and yogurt.

A good piece of fish doesn't need more than some salt, lemon, and *maybe* a puddle of something creamy like yogurt. If that's how the pros at the fish shacks serve up their fish, it's surely good enough for us too. Anything extra is just—extra.

Shrimp like the steam room.

Because steaming creates a very hot but moist environment, delicate shrimp won't toughen. Use a steamer basket, or steam the shrimp directly on nearly-cooked-through grains (p. 366), orzo (p. 289), or vegetables—a one-pot wonder if there ever was one. While the "bed ingredients" are cooking, marinate the shrimp with olive oil, S&P, and maybe something spicy, briny, or bright: garlic, citrus zest, ground spices, and so on. Once they're just about done, add the shrimp on top and cover the pan or pot. In 2 to 4 minutes, the hot steam will cook the shrimp. To tell whether a shrimp is done, see page 343.

Forget fillets sometimes. Instead, consider cutting firm fish like swordfish, tuna, or halibut into 1-inch pieces before simmering (p. 378) or sautéing (p. 373). Smaller pieces have a hard time breaking apart and an easy time cooking evenly and quickly. To cushion against toughening, cook over moderate heat, with plenty of liquid or fat in the pot or pan. You may not get a ton of browning, but you'll get nicely cooked fish very, very fast. Pop the morsels into tortillas, salad, on top of grains or pasta—or right in your mouth?

Slip seafood back into its natural habitat. Braising or simmering seafood in a stew, broth, or sauce captures their juices and minimizes the chances for dryness. Once the liquid is warm and simmering (but not boiling, as big bubbles could fracture fish), submerge fillets, smaller chunks, or shrimp into the liquid. In minutes they'll cook through.

The bacon of the sea. Hot-smoked fish is rich, smoky, flaky, meaty, minerally, and not at all fishy. Like bacon crossed with fish, it has so much flavor in a little package, keeps for at least a week in the fridge, and is wildly versatile. Flake into a salad, sandwich, dip, or grain bowl, or quickly warm through in a stir-fry, soup, chowder, pasta, or scrambled eggs (more ideas on page 249). Trout is a personal favorite, but you'll also find hot-smoked tuna, salmon, mackerel, and white fish.

Shrimp Cocktail for Dinner

Just give the people what they want.

BOILING
VEGETABLES

SHRIMP

EGGS

LEMONS

KETCHUP

HORSERADISH

CHILE SAUCE

ACCOUTREMENTS

FOR 4

1. Bring **6 cups water** to a boil in a big pot. Pick your **boiling vegetables (little potatoes, broccolini, artichokes, asparagus, cauliflower).** Cut them down to one- or two-bite pieces. Peel and devein **1 pound large shrimp,** keeping the tails on. Prepare a small bowl of ice water.

2. Add **4 large eggs** to the water and simmer for 7 minutes, then transfer to the ice bath. Add **¼ cup salt** to the water and return to a boil. Boil each vegetable in batches until al dente (taste to check). The longest vegetable (the potatoes) can take about 20 minutes, while snap peas take 3 minutes. Transfer with a slotted spoon or tongs to a sheet pan to cool, then repeat with the remaining vegetables.

3. Boil the shrimp until bright pink, 2 to 4 minutes. Transfer to the sheet pan. If you have room in your fridge, stick the sheet in there to cool everything down.

4. Cut **2 lemons** into wedges. To make the cocktail sauce, in a small bowl, stir together **1 cup ketchup, 2 tablespoons prepared horseradish, 1 teaspoon black pepper,** and **½ teaspoon chile sauce (sambal oelek, harissa).** Add 2 tablespoons juice from the lemons (save the rest for serving) and season with salt.

5. Peel and halve the eggs, then add to the sheet pan. Look around for **accoutrements** that bring crunch, brightness, or brininess and would be good dunked in cocktail sauce (ideas below). You could also add another sauce element, like salsa verde, mustard, or mayo. Then eat everything right from the sheet pan.

· Accoutrements: potato chips, Ritz crackers, radishes, celery, olives, pickles.

One-Pot Coconut Rice & Shrimp

Where shrimp and green beans conveniently cook on rice.

SHRIMP

LIME

GINGER

WHITE RICE

CUMIN SEEDS

COCONUT MILK

GREEN BEANS

FOR 4

1. Peel and devein **1 pound large shrimp** and transfer to a medium bowl. To the shrimp, add ¾ **teaspoon each S&P** and ½ **teaspoon red pepper flakes.** Zest **1 lime** and half a **3-inch piece ginger** into the bowl, then squeeze in the juice from half the lime (about 1 tablespoon). Stir to combine. Rinse **1½ cups long-grain white rice** until the water runs (nearly) clear.

2. Heat **2 tablespoons coconut or olive oil** and **2 teaspoons cumin seeds** in a large Dutch oven over medium. Grate in the remaining ginger and cook until sizzling and fragrant, 1 to 2 minutes.

3. Add the rice, **1 (14-ounce) can full-fat coconut milk,** and **1½ teaspoons salt.** Fill the empty can with water and pour into the pot. Stir to combine, then bring to a boil over medium-high. Cover, reduce the heat as low as it will go, and cook for 15 minutes.

4. While the rice is cooking, trim **10 ounces green beans** and slice crosswise into ½-inch pieces (line up a handful and slice them all at once).

5. When the 15 minutes are up, add the shrimp on top of the rice and the green beans on top of the shrimp. Season with S&P, cover, and cook until the green beans are crisp-tender and the shrimp is cooked through, 4 to 6 minutes. Remove from the heat and let sit for 5 minutes. Eat the shrimp, green beans, and rice with a sprinkle of red pepper flakes and a squeeze of the lime.

· Instead of green beans, use anything that steams in 10 minutes, like thinly sliced dark leafy greens, frozen peas or edamame, or sliced fennel.

· For more crunch, top with toasted coconut chips and/or peanuts.

Shrimp Boil with Cholula Butter

A many-napkin mess fest.

BUTTER

HOT SAUCE

GARLIC

LEMON

CORN

SHRIMP

POTATOES

CILANTRO

FOR 4

1. Bring **4 quarts water** (16 cups) to a boil in a big pot. Cut **4 tablespoons butter** (½ stick) into small pieces and add to a large bowl along with **6 tablespoons Cholula or another thick, tangy hot sauce (Valentina, Tapatío).** This will make a pretty spicy mix, so hold back if that scares you.

2. Grate **2 small garlic cloves** and the zest of **1 lemon** into the bowl, then add the juice of the lemon (3 tablespoons). Add the spent lemons to the pot.

3. Shuck **4 ears of corn** and snap them in half crosswise. Peel and devein **1½ pounds large shrimp.** Scrub **1 pound little potatoes (baby red, Yukon Gold)** if necessary.

4. Add **1 tablespoon salt** to the now-boiling water, then add the potatoes, reduce the heat to medium, and simmer for 15 minutes. While you're waiting, pluck ½ **cup cilantro leaves.** Add the corn to the potatoes and simmer for 8 minutes. Turn off the heat, add the shrimp, and let sit until the shrimp are just cooked through, 2 to 3 minutes.

5. Drain the shrimp and vegetables, shake dry, then add to the butter mixture. Toss vigorously until well coated in the spicy butter. Season to taste with S&P, then add the cilantro.

· This Cholula butter comes from my grilling mentor Paula Disbrowe, who uses it on wings. It'd also be good tossed with roasted vegetables, over steak or roast chicken, on hard-boiled eggs, or stirred through sautéed hearty greens.

· Step 4 would be a good time to toast some crusty bread. Swipe with a garlic clove.

More butters for boiled shrimp

· Charred lemon + charred scallions

· Orange + jalapeño

· Sage + jarred Calabrian chile

· Ginger + curry powder

· Frank's hot sauce + lemon + garlic (Buffalo)

· Red curry paste + fish sauce

Bloody Mary Tomatoes with Smoked Fish

Brunch for dinner—without vodka, yet somehow still a good time.

TOMATOES
LEMON
SOY SAUCE
HORSERADISH
HOT SAUCE
CELERY
OLIVES
HOT-SMOKED FISH
CRÈME FRAÎCHE

FOR 4

1. Halve **2 pints (4 cups) cherry or Sungold tomatoes.** Transfer to a serving plate and toss with **1 teaspoon each S&P.** Zest **1 lemon** over the tomatoes.

2. Squeeze the lemon into a medium bowl (about 3 tablespoons), then stir in **¼ cup olive oil, 4 teaspoons low-sodium soy sauce, 1 tablespoon prepared horseradish,** and **1 teaspoon hot sauce.** Season with S&P.

3. Add these things to the dressing as you chop: Thinly slice **4 celery stalks** (add leaves if you have them). Pit and halve **1 cup green olives (Castelvetrano, Picholine, Cerignola).** Break **5 or 6 ounces hot-smoked trout or salmon** into 1-inch pieces, removing the skin if necessary. Stir everything to combine. Taste and season, adjusting heat (with black pepper and hot sauce), brightness (with lemon), and salt (with salt or soy sauce) as needed.

4. Dollop spoonfuls of **crème fraîche** over the tomatoes (about ½ cup), then spoon the salad over. Don't stir: Instead, eat like nachos by angling for scoops with a little bit of everything.

· Little tomatoes are more reliable year-round, but if you have delicious big tomatoes, use a pound or so of those.

· Add anything else you like on your bagel or in your Bloody Mary: parsley, capers, cucumber, red onion, blue cheese, pickled jalapeños, bacon.

· Instead of smoked trout, sear steak and rest in the dressing (like on page 317).

Swordfish with Asparagus & Little Beans

Friendly reminder: Don't overthink it.

LEMONS

SWORDFISH

WHITE BEANS

ASPARAGUS

GARLIC

SOFT HERBS

SIMPLICITY
FOR 4

1. Pour **½ cup olive oil** into a liquid measuring cup. Zest and juice **2 lemons** into the cup (about 6 tablespoons juice). Add **1 teaspoon red pepper flakes** and season to taste with S&P.

2. Cut off and discard the skin from **1½ pounds (1-inch-thick) swordfish steaks (or mahi-mahi).** Pat dry, then cut into 1-inch pieces. Toss with S&P.

3. Drain and rinse **2 (15-ounce) cans little white beans (navy, Great Northern).** Trim and thinly slice **1 pound asparagus** and **1 garlic clove.** Pluck **½ cup soft herbs,** like mint, dill, basil, parsley, or a combination.

4. Heat **2 tablespoons olive oil** in a large skillet over medium. Add the beans, asparagus, garlic, and **¼ cup water.** Season with S&P and cook until the beans are warm and the asparagus is crisp-tender, 3 to 5 minutes. Transfer to a bowl and mix in a couple tablespoons of the lemon dressing. Season to taste with S&P.

5. Heat another **2 tablespoons olive oil** in the skillet over medium. Add the fish and cook, stirring from time to time, until the fish flakes easily, 5 to 7 minutes. Add the herbs and fish to the beans and stir once. Season with S&P and the lemon dressing. Good warm or at room temp.

· Good with orzo, Israeli couscous, bulgur, or toasted breadcrumbs.

· Thinly slicing your asparagus like this works for young, middle-aged, and chunky spears.

Tomatillo Poached Cod

Bright and cozy like the pozole verde that inspired it.

WHITE RICE

JALAPEÑO

ONION

TOMATILLOS

CILANTRO

COD

LIME

HOMINY

FOR 4

1. Cook **1 cup long-grain white rice** for serving (p. 170 if you need a method).

2. Meanwhile, halve and remove the seeds from **1 jalapeño.** Coarsely chop, along with **1 yellow onion.** Transfer to a medium bowl to make room on your cutting board. Remove the husks from **1½ pounds tomatillos** and coarsely chop. Pluck **½ cup cilantro leaves** and thinly slice their stems.

3. Heat **¼ cup neutral oil** in a large skillet over medium-high. Add the onion, jalapeño, and cilantro stems, season with S&P, and cook until the onion is soft and charred in spots, 5 to 7 minutes. Add the tomatillos and season with S&P. Cook, stirring, until the tomatillos are soft and blistered in spots, 3 to 5 minutes. Add **1½ cups water,** bring to a simmer, then reduce the heat to medium and cook, smashing with a spoon or potato masher occasionally, until the tomatillos have broken down, 10 to 15 minutes.

4. Meanwhile, pat **1½ pounds cod** dry. Cut into 4 (6-ounce) pieces and season all over with S&P. Zest **1 lime** over the fish. Drain and rinse **1 (15-ounce) can hominy.** When the tomatillo mixture is ready, stir in the hominy. Lay the fish on top, cover, and cook until the fish is opaque and easily flaked with a fork, 7 to 10 minutes. Taste the tomatillo mixture and season accordingly with S&P.

5. Eat the fish, hominy, and sauce over a bowlful of rice. Top with cilantro and a squeeze of the lime.

· Also good with sour cream, limey cabbage, beans (or cook beans with the rice like on page 183), sliced radishes, or tortilla chips.

Fish & Chips Tacos

With the—surprise!—crunch of tortilla chips.

CABBAGE
ONION
CILANTRO
LIMES
GREEN HOT SAUCE
WHITE FISH
GROUND CUMIN
TORTILLAS

FOR 4

1. Heat the oven to 350°F. Core and thinly slice ½ **medium green or Savoy cabbage** (about 1 pound). Transfer to a large bowl, season with salt, and squeeze with your hands until it looks wet. Finely chop **1 small white onion** and ½ **cup cilantro leaves and stems.** Add to the bowl. Squeeze **2 limes** (¼ cup juice) over and stir to combine. Add **green hot sauce** to taste.

2. Grease a sheet pan with **olive oil.** Pat dry **1 pound mild, white fish (halibut, mahi-mahi, cod)** that's max 1 inch thick. Transfer to half of the sheet pan and rub all over with **1½ teaspoons ground cumin** and S&P. Add **2 corn tortillas** to the other half of the pan. Coat the fish and tortillas lightly with **olive oil.** Bake until the tortillas are crisp like tostadas and the fish flakes easily and registers 120°F in the thickest part, 12 to 15 minutes. Season the baked tortillas with salt.

3. Warm **8 corn tortillas** directly on an oven rack or over your flame. Flake the fish into the soft tortillas, add a scoop of slaw, then crush the chips over top.

· Instead of ground cumin, use chili powder, chipotle in adobo, smoked paprika, and/or onion powder.

· Nix the soft tortillas for a taco salad.

Hot & Sour Fish Soup

Tom Yum and Cioppino walk into a bowl and . . .

LEEKS

FENNEL

RED CURRY PASTE

CANNED TOMATOES

FISH SAUCE

FIRM FISH

RICE NOODLES

LIME

FOR 4

1. Bring a medium saucepan of water to a boil. Remove the two outer layers of **2 leeks,** then cut into ½-inch rounds (rinse if gritty). Chop **1 medium fennel bulb** (about 1 pound) into ½-inch pieces, reserving the stalks and fronds.

2. Heat **2 tablespoons olive oil** in a large Dutch oven over medium-high. Add the leeks and fennel, season with S&P, and cook, stirring occasionally, until browned in spots, 3 to 5 minutes. Add **4 ounces red curry paste** (about ⅓ cup) and cook, stirring until it sticks to the bottom of the pot, 1 to 2 minutes. Add **1 (28-ounce) can whole, peeled tomatoes;** fill up the can with water and add that too, along with **3 tablespoons fish sauce.** Partially cover and bring to a boil, then uncover, reduce the heat to medium-low, and simmer until flavorful and reduced slightly, 8 to 10 minutes.

3. Thinly slice at most a cup of the reserved fennel stalks crosswise. Cut **1 pound skinless firm fish (cod, halibut, striped bass, swordfish)** into 1-inch pieces. Season with S&P. Add **10 ounces rice vermicelli noodles** to the boiling water and cook according to the package directions. Drain, rinse, and transfer to bowls.

4. Reduce the heat under the soup to low, add the fish and fennel stalks, cover, and cook until the fish is opaque, 2 to 4 minutes. Off the heat, stir in the juice of **1 lime** (about 2 tablespoons). Adjust to taste with more lime and S&P. Spoon the soup over the noodles, and top with some fennel fronds.

· Instead of fish, use shrimp, tofu, white beans, or chicken (add boneless thighs in step 2).

· Other vegetables to add: mushrooms, celery, potatoes (skip the noodles), peas, escarole. Basil!

Slow-Roasted Salmon with Chile Oil

This salmon's pampered and relaxed from a soak in chile oil.

SALMON

SHALLOT

GINGER

SESAME
SEEDS

CUCUMBERS

RICE
VINEGAR

CILANTRO

SOBA

FOR 4

1. Heat the oven to 300°F. Bring a large pot of salted water to a boil. Pat a **1½- to 2-pound skinless salmon fillet** dry and season with S&P. Set aside. Coarsely chop **1 shallot**. Peel **2 inches ginger** and coarsely chop. Transfer the shallot and ginger to a large ovenproof skillet that can fit the salmon, then add **¾ cup neutral oil, 2 tablespoons toasted sesame seeds, 1 teaspoon red pepper flakes,** and **½ teaspoon each S&P.** Cook over low heat, stirring occasionally, until the oil is warm, 2 to 3 minutes.

2. Place the salmon in the spiced oil. Spoon some of the oil over the salmon, then bake, basting occasionally with the oil, until cooked through, 15 to 25 minutes. (You'll know the salmon is done when it flakes easily or when an instant-read thermometer inserted into the thickest part reaches 120°F.)

3. Meanwhile, cut **4 Persian or mini seedless cucumbers** in thirds crosswise, then cut into matchsticks. Transfer to a medium bowl, then toss with salt and **4 teaspoons unseasoned rice vinegar.** Pluck **½ cup cilantro leaves,** then finely chop the stems. Add the stems to the cucumbers.

4. When the salmon's done, add **8 ounces dried soba** to the boiling water and cook according to the package directions. Drain, rinse until cool to the touch, then shake dry.

5. Add the soba to the cucumbers and toss to combine, then add chile oil from the skillet to taste, including seeds and bits (start with 2 tablespoons and go from there). Taste and adjust acid (vinegar), salt (salt), fat (oil), and heat (chile oil). Eat with a nice piece of salmon and some cilantro.

· You can also make this with individually portioned fillets; cook time will be similar.

· The flavors in this oil channel chile crisp, but yours can be infused with any number of aromatics (p. 126).

Slow-Roasted Salmon with Chile Oil   PAGE 379

More seasonings for slow-roasted salmons

- Citrusy like on page 382
- Just olive oil + S&P
- Pastrami spices (p. 89)
- Dates + olives + pistachios
- Grated ginger + dill

- Grated chile + honey + turmeric
- Fish sauce + brown butter + lime
- Mustard + chives
- Mayo + chipotle + lime zest

Citrus Salmon with Black Olive Breadcrumbs

Fancy but not fussy.

SALMON
ORANGES
LEMON
FENNEL
OLIVES
PANKO
YOGURT

FOR 4

1. Heat the oven to 300°F. Line a sheet pan or baking dish with parchment paper. Place a **1½- to 2-pound salmon fillet,** skin side down if there's skin, in the pan and season with S&P. In a medium bowl, zest **2 oranges** and **1 lemon.** Add **1 tablespoon olive oil** and **½ teaspoon red pepper flakes,** season with S&P, and stir to combine. Spoon over the flesh of the salmon (reserve the bowl). Roast until cooked through, 15 to 25 minutes. (You'll know the salmon is done when the fish flakes easily or when an instant-read thermometer inserted into the thickest part reaches 120°F.)

2. While the salmon roasts, cut the tops and bottoms off the oranges. Place an orange on one of the cut sides and follow the curve of the fruit to cut away the peel and white pith. Halve the fruit from top to bottom, then cut into ¼-inch-thick half-moons. If your pieces are especially large, halve them again. Repeat with the other orange, then transfer to the reserved bowl along with any juices on the cutting board. Add **3 tablespoons olive oil** and the juice from the lemon (about 3 tablespoons) and season with S&P. Cut **1 large or 2 medium fennel bulbs** (about 2 pounds) through the core. Discard any tough outer layers, then thinly slice the bulb and stalks crosswise. If you have fronds, rip a handful into smaller pieces. Add the fennel (including the fronds) to the bowl and stir to combine. Adjust to taste with S&P and lemon.

3. Pit and coarsely chop **¼ cup oil-cured black olives.** In a medium skillet, heat **3 tablespoons olive oil** and the olives over medium. Add **1 cup panko breadcrumbs** and cook, stirring often, until golden brown, 2 to 3 minutes. Transfer to a little bowl and season to taste with S&P and red pepper flakes.

4. Eat the salmon and salad with a spoonful of **full-fat Greek or regular yogurt** and a sprinkle of the breadcrumbs.

All the Staples

Here is every pantry and shelf-stable ingredient used in this book. With one or a few ingredients from each section on hand all the time, you'll have so many levers to pull to make dinner on the fly. Ingredients are organized by what they contribute to a dish so that you can improvise, substitute, and flourish with abandon.

Starches

GRAINS
Bulgur
Cornmeal
Long-grain white rice
Quinoa (technically a seed!)
Sushi rice
Whole grains (farro, brown rice, or chef's choice)

PASTA & NOODLES
Glass noodles
Lasagna noodles
Long noodles (fettuccine, linguine, spaghetti)
Shelf-stable gnocchi
Short, curly or ridged pastas (orecchiette, shells)
Small pastas (ditalini, orzo, Israeli couscous)
Soba
Thin rice vermicelli noodles
Tubular pastas (mezzi rigatoni, rigatoni)

THICKENERS
Cornstarch
Flour

Legumes

DRIED
Brown or green lentils
Red lentils

CANNED
Black beans
Chickpeas
Pinto beans
White beans (little beans, medium cannellini or Great Northern, big gigante or butter)

Crunchy Sprinkles

Blanched hazelnuts
Coconut chips
Fritos
Furikake
Panko breadcrumbs
Pepitas
Pistachios
Pita chips
Roasted, salted peanuts
Smoked almonds
Toasted rice powder
Toasted sesame seeds
Tortilla chips
Walnuts
Za'atar

Acids

CITRUS
Lemon
Lime
Orange

VINEGARS
Apple cider vinegar
Red wine vinegar
Sherry vinegar
Unseasoned rice vinegar

TOMATO PRODUCTS
Canned crushed tomatoes
Canned fire-roasted tomatoes
Canned whole tomatoes
Ketchup
Tomato paste
Tomato puree

BRINY, PICKLY, PUNCHY POPS
Black olives
Capers
Green olives (Castelvetrano, Picholine)
Horseradish
Kalamata olives
Mustard (Dijon and whole grain)
Peperoncini
Pickled cherry peppers

Fats

Butter
Coconut oil
Full-fat coconut milk
Mayo
Neutral oil
Olive oil
Tahini
Toasted sesame oil

Heat & Smoke

Black pepper
Chili powder
Chipotles in adobo
Cured chorizo
Gochujang
Harissa
Hot sauce (Cholula, Frank's, green)
Kimchi
Red pepper flakes
Salsa
Sambal oelek
Smoked paprika
Thai curry pastes (green, red)

Umami Oomphs

Anchovies
Chicken stock
Cocoa powder (unsweetened)
Dried porcini mushrooms
Fish sauce
Low-sodium soy sauce
Salt

Spices, Dried Herbs & Other Aromatics

HERBY
Bay leaves
Dried oregano

WARM & TOASTY
Cinnamon
Coriander (ground and whole)
Cumin (ground and whole)
Fennel seeds
Ginger
Turmeric

ONIONY & GARLICKY
Garlic
Onion powder
Red onion
Shallots
Yellow onion

Sweeteners

Dark brown sugar
Dates
Dried apricots
Granulated sugar
Honey
Maple syrup

Recipes by Cravings, Mood & Realities

Here's one recipe from every chapter that finishes the sentence "Tonight I need ..."

Dinner in 10 minutes

- Green Eggs & Ham Quesadilla (p. 28)
- Pan Con Tomate plus White Beans (p. 68)
- Tortellini with Mortadella & Peas (p. 125)
- Crispy Grains with Kielbasa & Cabbage (p. 197) with cooked grains
- Salad That Never Repeats (p. 222)
- Bacon Jalapeño Smashburgers (p. 272)
- Sausage & Gnocchi (p. 308)
- Sheet Pan Fish with Bitter Greens (p. 361)

Dinner when there's nothing fresh in the house

- Harissa Eggs with Pita & Dates (p. 24)
- Olive Oil–Braised Chickpeas (p. 104)
- One-Pot Puttanesca (p. 140)
- One-Pot Rice & Beans (p. 183)
- Creamy Tomato Soup (No Cream) (p. 247)
- All the Time Chicken Thighs (p. 268)
- Gochujang Gravy (p. 337)
- White Bean Scampi Stew (p. 350)

Max two dirty dishes

- Garlic Bread Egg in a Hole with Mushrooms (p. 53)
- Creamy Beans & Greens (p. 99)
- Skillet Broccoli Spaghetti (p. 154)
- Buttered Quinoa with Bok Choy (p. 172)
- Squash & Sage Skillet Lasagna (p. 228)
- Skillet Thighs with Peas & Pickled Chiles (p. 264)
- One-Pan Sausage & Lentils (p. 306)
- Shrimp Boil with Cholula Butter (p. 369)

To set it and forget it

- Bacon-Chile Frittata (p. 31)
- Black Bean Soup with Lots of Fritos (p. 100)
- Good Sauce of So-So Tomatoes (p. 139)
- Mixed Grain Porridge (p. 206)
- Green Beans & Grains with Gochujang Butter (p. 253)
- Lemon-Pepper Chicken & Potatoes (p. 267)
- Gochujang Gravy (p. 337)
- Slow-Roasted Salmon with Chile Oil (p. 379)

To also make lunch

- Godmother's Egg Salad (p. 38)
- Chickpeas, Yogurt & Za'atar Nuts (p. 69)
- Couscous & Lentil Greek Salad (p. 161)
- Whole Grains, Chorizo & Dates (p. 188)
- Broccoli Bits with Cheddar & Dates (p. 221)
- Marbella Chicken Salad (p. 277)
- Pork & Beans Alla Gricia (p. 334)
- Bloody Mary Tomatoes with Smoked Fish (p. 370)

To clear the veg drawer

- Stovetop Frittata Any Way (p. 29)
- Marinated Beans with Crunchy Vegetables (p. 64)
- Noodles with Juicy Fruits & Peanuts (p. 158)
- Green Rice with Singed Feta (p. 178)
- Charred Vegetables with Turmeric Peanuts (p. 226)
- Sticky Chicken with Pickled Vegetables (p. 297)
- Green Chile Pork with Crispy Rice (p. 329)
- Shrimp Cocktail for Dinner (p. 365)

To also stock the freezer

- Stovetop Frittata Any Way (p. 29)
- Sloppy Lennys (p. 111)
- Good Sauce of So-So Tomatoes (p. 139)
- Coconut-Ginger Rice & Lentils (p. 209)
- Creamy Tomato Soup (No Cream) (p. 247)
- Shortcut Chicken Chili (p. 286)
- Mighty Meatballs (p. 333)
- Hot & Sour Fish Soup (p. 378)

Gooey, creamy cheese

- Croque Monday (p. 58)
- French Onion White Bean Bake (p. 103)
- All-Corner-Pieces Baked Pasta (p. 143)
- Rice & Cheese (p. 200)
- Cheddar Broccoli with Mustard Crumbs (p. 238)
- Kids' Menu Enchiladas (p. 281)
- Oregano Lamb Pita (p. 321)
- Swordfish with Za'atar Tomatoes (p. 357) plus feta

To eat plant-based

- Egg & Charred Pepper Stew (p. 44) with chickpeas instead of eggs
- Chipotle Mushroom-Tempeh Tacos (p. 90)
- Spaghetti Aglio e Olio (p. 129)
- Chipotle-Tomato Baked Rice (p. 181)
- Asparagus, Scallion & Tofu Tangle (p. 237)
- Chicken & Rice with Smoked Paprika (p. 278) without chicken
- Chorizo & Brussels Sprouts Tacos (p. 309) with sweet potato instead of chorizo
- One-Pot Coconut Rice & Shrimp (p. 366) with fried tofu instead of shrimp

Dinner on a sick day

- Coconut Curry with Swirled Eggs (p. 34)
- Lentil Soup on Spring Break (p. 108)
- Mushroom Orzotto (p. 150)
- Coconut-Ginger Rice & Lentils (p. 209)
- Green Soup to the Rescue (p. 248)
- My Forever Chicken & Rice Soup (p. 293)
- Lamb Meatball Soup (p. 338)
- White Bean Scampi Stew (p. 350)

To just feed myself— freedom!

- Egg Sliders (p. 48)
- Kinda Refried Beans (p. 96)
- Salumi Butter Rigatoni (p. 120)
- Farro Carbonara with Brussels Sprouts (p. 207)
- Fennel & Radicchio with Macerated Apricots (p. 234)
- One-Pan Chicken Piccata & Orzo (p. 289)
- Pork Sausage Burgers (p. 311)
- Crispy-Skinned Fish with Creamy Cukes (p. 354)

So Many Thanks

Writing this book just so happened to coincide with a global pandemic! Flexibility, resourcefulness, and patience have never been more essential than as I write this in 2020. My hope is it made the book more adaptable for your life, but boy was it not without difficulties, none of which I could've handled without an incredible team and support system.

Without Jenn Sit and Kari Stuart, this book not only wouldn't have happened but wouldn't have been so enjoyable to make. Jenn, you championed this book before I did and are the kind of editor anyone would be lucky to have. Thank you for your patience, attentiveness, great memory, and cooking nearly every recipe in this book. Kari, you never laughed (to my face) at my silly questions, and I'm thankful for all the behind-the-scenes magicking I know you did.

Without Sarah Jampel, this book also would not have happened. SJ, thank you for improving this book in every single way, for answering constant questions and quelling endless fears, and for being so good at being a friend (not in that order).

To my photo dream team, Mark Weinberg, Sam Seneviratne, and Eliza Winograd: Shooting in my apartment, during a pandemic, doesn't sound like a recipe for full-body fun, but it so was: Thank you for those days, these images, and for being such generous people. Thanks to Matt Hallyburton, Alex Marshall, Jono and Nick Pandolfi, and Jen Bernstein at Meilen Ceramics for lending their ceramics to these pages. And to the Fort Greene Community Fridge for finding homes for shoot leftovers.

Thank you to the whole Potter and PRH team, including those who championed and improved this book without my knowing.

Special thanks to Marysarah Quinn, for your graceful design and calming smile; Bianca Cruz, the most stellar EA; and Allison Renzulli, for your infectious enthusiasm.

Thank goodness for the eagle eyes: Laura Arnold for expert recipe testing and CB Owens for fact checking and general nitpicking. You both taught me so much along the way, and for that I'm grateful.

I never doubt that I've cobbled together a career because of women who have self-nominated themselves as my mentors. Thanks to Yossy Arefi, Michele Crim, Kristen Miglore, and Christine Muhlke for simultaneously encouraging and challenging me. Thank you to the editors and readers who've supported my work, and the professional and home cooks who've taught me everything I know, including the recipe creators on page 390 and my colleagues past and present.

To my people, Caro, Sam, and Alex, for being constant sources of good eyes, good vibes, great props, long walks, and eucalyptus.

To my home team and quarantine crew: Ryan, thank you for finding my smile when I misplaced it. For your remarkable calm and patience and washing so many dishes. For accepting . . . all this. And Auggie Doodle, the best little cat who never left my side. Love you both.

And of course, to my mom, *for* my mom, without whom nothing would be possible. The kitchen is a safe, creative, and life-giving place because of you, and for that I can never thank you enough.

SO MANY THANKS

Resources

A recipe is a web: It doesn't stand alone, untethered, but rather is connected to so many recipes, ideas, and people. Below is a list of people whose work I turn to for guidance and whose recipes and wisdom can jump-start many, many meals.

Yossy Arefi
Molly Baz
Paul Bertolli
Nami Chen
Kay Chun
Felicity Cloake
Paula Disbrowe
Fuchsia Dunlop
Sohla El-Waylly
Renee Erickson
Sara Forte
Evan Funke
Suzanne Goin
Dorie Greenspan
Nancy Singleton Hachisu
Gabrielle Hamilton
Marcella Hazan
Mary-Frances Heck
Anissa Helou
Sarah Jampel
Eric Kim
Diane Kochilas
Leah Koenig
Yewande Komolafe
Francis Lam
Caroline Lange
Emma Laperruque
Lara Lee
J. Kenji López-Alt

Maangchi
Deborah Madison
Rick Martinez
Carla Lalli Music
Joan Nathan
Andrea Nguyen
Samin Nosrat
Yotam Ottolenghi
Josh Ozersky
Deb Perelman
Cal Peternell
Charles Phan
Carolyn Phillips
Leela Punyaratabandhu
Amelia Rampe

Tejal Rao
Andy Ricker
Judy Rodgers
Alison Roman
Roberto Santibañez
Nancy Silverton
Nigel Slater
Meera Sodha
Molly Stevens
Heidi Swanson
Lesley Téllez
Julia Turshen
Paula Wolfert
Kris Yenbamroong
Joe Yonan

Moreover, so many age-old food traditions have carried on dismembered from their creators and origin stories, including many that have influenced recipes in this book and are from cultures not my own. As an attempt to recognize these contributions and promote the food legacies being kept alive in home and professional kitchens, a portion of the royalties from this book will go to La Cocina, a nonprofit organization that cultivates food businesses run by low-income, female, and POC entrepreneurs.

Index